WE
BOUGHT
A

WE BOUGHT A ZOO

Benjamin Mee

WEINSTEIN
BOOKS

ISBN-13 978-1-60286-048-3
ISBN 1-60286-048-3

First Edition
10   9   8   7   6   5   4   3   2   1

Contents

WE
BOUGHT
A
ZOO

Prologue

Mum and I arrived as the new owners of Dartmoor Wildlife Park in Devon for the first time at around six o'clock on the evening of 20 October 2006, and stepped out of the car to the sound of wolves howling in the misty darkness. My brother Duncan had turned on every light in the house to welcome us, and each window beamed the message into the fog as he emerged from the front door to give me a bone-crushing bear hug. He was more gentle with Mum. We had been delayed for an extra day in Leicester with the lawyers, as some last-minute paperwork failed to arrive in time and had to be sent up the M1 on a motorbike. Duncan had masterminded the movement of all Mum's furniture from Surrey in three vans, with eight men who had another job to go to the next day. The delay had meant a fraught standoff in the entryway to the park, with the previous owner's lawyer eventually conceding that Duncan could unload the vans, but only into two rooms (one of them the fetid front kitchen) until the paperwork was completed.

So the three of us picked our way in wonderment between teetering towers of boxes and into the flagstoned kitchen, which was relatively uncluttered and, we thought, could make a good center of operations. A huge old trestle table I had been hoarding in my parents' garage for twenty years finally came into its own, and was erected in a room suited to its size. It's still there as our dining-room table, but on this first night its symbolic value was immense. Some boxes and carpets Duncan had managed to store in the back pantry had just been flooded, so while he unblocked the drain outside I drove to a Chinese takeout I'd spotted on the way from Route A38, and we sat down to our first meal together in our new home. Our spirits were slightly shaky but elated, and we laughed a lot in this cold, dark, chaotic house on that first night, and took inordinate comfort from the fact that at least we lived near a good Chinese place.

That night, with Mum safely in bed, Duncan and I stepped out into the misty park to try to get a grip on what we'd done. Everywhere the flashlight shone, eyes of different sizes blinked back at us, and without a clear idea of the layout of the park at this stage, the mystery of exactly what animals lurked behind them added greatly to the atmosphere. We knew where the tigers were, however, and made our way over to one of the enclosures that had been earmarked for replacement posts to get a close look at what sort of deterioration we were up against. With no tigers in sight, we climbed over the stand-off barrier and began peering by flashlight at the base of the structural wooden posts holding up the chain-link fence. We squatted down and became engrossed, prodding and scraping at the surface layers of rotted wood to find the harder core, in this instance reassuringly near the surface. We decided it wasn't so bad, but as we stood up we were startled to see that all three tigers in the enclosure were now only a couple of feet away from where we were standing, ready to spring, staring intently at us. Like we were dinner.

It was fantastic. All three beasts—and they were such glorious beasts—had maneuvered to within pawing distance of us without either of us noticing. Each animal was bigger than both of us put together, yet they'd moved silently. If this had been the jungle or, more accurately in this case, the Siberian tundra, the first thing we'd have known about it would have been a large mouth around our necks. Tigers have special sensors along the front of their two-inch canines that can detect the pulse in your aorta. The first bite is to grab, then they take your pulse with their teeth, reposition them, and sink them in.

As they held us in their icy glares, we were impressed. Eventually, one of these vast, muscular cats—acknowledging that due to circumstances beyond their control (i.e., the fence between us), this had been a mere dress rehearsal—yawned, flashed those curved dagger canines, and looked away. We remained impressed.

We started back toward the house. The wolves began their eery night chorus, accompanied by the sounds of owls—there were about fifteen on site—the odd screech of an eagle, and the nocturnal danger call of the vervet monkeys as we walked past their cage. This was what it was all about, we felt. All we had to do now was work out what to do next.

It had been an incredible journey to get there. A new beginning, it also marked the end of a long and tortuous road, involving our whole family. My own part of the story starts in France.

1

In the Beginning . . .

L'Ancienne Bergerie, June 2004, and life was good. My wife Katherine and I had just made the final commitment to our new life by selling our London flat and buying two gorgeous golden-stone barns in the heart of the South of France, where we were living on baguettes, cheese, and wine. The village we had settled into nestled between Nîmes and Avignon in Languedoc, the poor man's Provence, an area with the lowest rainfall in the whole of France. I was writing a column on do-it-yourself home improvement for the weekly newspaper the *Guardian*, and two others for *Grand Designs* magazine, and I was also writing a book on humor in animals, a long-cherished project which, I found, required a lot of time in a conducive environment. And this was it.

Our two children, Ella and Milo, bilingual and sun-burnished, frolicked with kittens in the safety of a large, walled garden, chasing enormous grasshoppers together, pouncing amongst the long parched grass and seams of wheat, probably seeded from kernels spilled from trailers when the barns were part of a working farm. Our huge dog, Leon, lay across the threshold of vast, rusty gates, watching over us with the benign vigilance of an animal bred specifically for the purpose, panting happily in his work.

It was really beginning to feel like home. Our meager sixty-five square meters of central London had translated into twelve hundred square meters of rural southern France, albeit slightly less well-appointed and not so handy for Marks and Spencer, the South Bank, or the British Museum. But it had a summer that lasted from March to November, and the locally made wine, which sold for £8 in Tesco, a British market, cost three and a half euros at source. Well, you had to take advantage of this—it was part of the local culture. Barbeques of fresh trout and salty sausages from the Cévennes to our north, glasses of chilled rosé with ice that quickly melted in the heavy southern European heat. It was idyllic.

This perfect environment was achieved after about ten years of wriggling into the position, professionally and financially, where I could just afford to live like a peasant in a derelict barn in a village full of other much more wholesome peasants earning a living through honest farming. I was the mad Englishman; they were the slightly bemused French country folk—tolerant, kind, courteous, and yet, inevitably, hugely judgmental.

Katherine, whom I'd married that April after nine years together (I waited until she'd completely given up hope), became the darling of the village. Beautiful and thoughtful, polite, kind, and gracious, she made a real effort to engage with and fit into village life. She actively learned the language, which she'd already studied at Advanced Level, to become proficient in local colloquial French, as well as her Parisian French, and the bureau-speak French of the "admin-heavy" state. She could josh with the art-gallery owner in the nearby town of Uzes about the exact tax form he had to fill out to acquire a sculpture by Elisabeth Frink—whom she also happened to have once met and interviewed—and complain with the best of the village mums about the complexities of the French medical system. My French, on the other hand, already at Ordinary Level grade D, probably made it to C while I was there, as I actively tried to block my mind from learning it in case it somehow further impeded the delivery of my already late book. I went to bed just as the farmers got up, and rarely interacted unless to trouble them for some badly expressed elementary questions about DIY. They preferred her.

But this idyll was not achieved without some cost. We had to sell our cherished shoebox-size flat in London in order to buy our two beautiful barns, totally derelict, with floors of mud trampled with sheep dung. Without water or electricity we couldn't move in straight away, so in the week we exchanged contracts internationally, we also moved locally within the village, from a rather lovely natural-stone summer sublet that was about to triple in price as the season began, to a far less desirable property on the main road through the village. This had no furniture and neither did we, having come to France nearly two years before with the intention of staying for six months. It would be fair to say that this was a stressful time.

So when Katherine started getting migraines and staring into the middle distance instead of being her usual tornado of office-keeping, packing, sorting, and labeling efficiency, I put it down to stress. "Go to the doctor's, or go to your parents if you're not going to be able to help," I said sympathetically. I should have known it was serious when she cut short a shopping trip (one of her favorite activities) to buy furniture for the children's room, and we both experienced a frisson of anxiety when she slurred her words in the car on the way back from that trip. But a few phone calls to migraine-suffering friends assured us that this was well within the normal range of symptoms for this often stress-related phenomenon.

Eventually she went to the doctor and I waited at home for her to return with some migraine-specific pain relief. Instead I got a phone call to say that the doctor wanted her to go for a brain scan, immediately, that night. At this stage I still wasn't particularly anxious, as the French are renowned hypochondriacs. If you go to the surgery with a runny nose the doctor will prescribe a carrier bag full of pharmaceuticals, usually involving suppositories. A brain scan seemed like a typical French overreaction; inconvenient, but it had to be done.

Katherine arranged for our friend Georgia to take her to the local hospital about twenty miles away, and I settled down again to wait for her to come back. And then I got the phone call no one ever expects. Georgia, sobbing, telling me it was serious. "They've found something," she kept saying. "You have to come down." At first I thought it must be a bad joke, but the emotion in her voice was real.

In a daze I organized a neighbor to look after the children while I borrowed her unbelievably dilapidated Honda Civic and set off on the unfamiliar journey along the dark country roads. With one headlight working, no third or reverse gear, and very poor brakes, I was conscious that it was possible to crash and injure myself badly if I wasn't careful. I overshot one turn and had to get out and push the car back down the road, but I made it safely to the hospital and abandoned the decrepit vehicle in the empty car park.

Inside I relieved a tearful Georgia and did my best to reassure a pale and shocked Katherine. I was still hoping that there was some mistake, that there was a simple explanation that had been overlooked and would account for everything. But when I asked to see the scan, there indeed was a golf-ball-size black lump nestling ominously in her left parietal lobe. A long time ago I did a degree in psychology, so the MRI images were not entirely alien to me, and my head reeled as I desperately tried to find some explanation that could account for this anomaly. But there wasn't one.

We spent the night at the hospital bucking up each other's morale. In the morning a helicopter took Katherine to Montpellier, our local (and probably the best) neuro unit in France. After our cozy night together, the reality of seeing her airlifted as an emergency patient to a distant neurological ward hit home, hard. As I chased the copter down the *autoroute*, the shock really began kicking in. I found my mind was ranging around, trying to get to grips with the situation, so that I could barely make myself concentrate properly on driving. I slowed right down, and arrived an hour later at the car park of the enormous Gui de Chaulliac hospital complex to find there were no spaces. I ended up parking creatively, French style, along a sliver of curb. A porter wagged a disapproving finger at me but I strode past him, by now in an unstoppable frame of mind, desperate to find Katherine. If he'd tried to stop me at that moment I think I would have broken his arm and directed him to X-ray. I was going to Neuro Urgence, fifth floor, and nothing was going to get in my way. It made me appreciate in that instant that you should never underestimate the emotional turmoil of people visiting hospitals. Normal rules did not apply, as my priorities were completely refocused on finding Katherine and understanding what was going to happen next. I found Katherine sitting up on a trolley bed, dressed in a yellow hospital gown, looking bewildered and confused. She looked so vulnerable but noble, stoically cooperating with whatever was asked of her. Eventually we were told that an operation was scheduled in a few days' time, during which high doses of steroids would reduce the inflammation around the tumor so that it could be taken out more easily.

Watching her being wheeled around the corridors, sitting up

in her backless gown, looking around with quiet, confused dignity, was probably the worst time. The logistics were over, we were in the right place, the children were being taken care of, and now we had to wait for three days and adjust to this new reality. I spent most of that time at the hospital with Katherine or on the phone in the lobby dropping the bombshell on friends and family. The phone calls all took a similar shape: breezy disbelief, followed by shock and often tears. After three days I was an old hand, and guided people through their stages as I broke the news.

Finally Friday arrived, and Katherine was prepared for the operation. I was allowed to accompany her to a waiting area outside the operating room. Typically French, it was beautiful, with sunlight streaming into a modern atrium planted with trees whose red and brown leaves picked up the light and shone like stained glass. There was not much we could say to each other, and I kissed her goodbye not really knowing whether I would see her again, or if I did, how badly she might be affected by the operation.

At the last minute I asked the surgeon if I could watch the procedure. As a former health writer I had been in operating rooms before, and I just wanted to understand exactly what was happening to her. Far from being perplexed, the doctor, one of the best neurosurgeons in France, was delighted. I am reasonably convinced that he had high-functioning Asperger's syndrome. For the first, and last, time in our conversation, he looked me in the eye and smiled, as if to say, "So you like tumors too?" and excitedly introduced me to his team. The anaesthetist was much less impressed with the idea and looked visibly alarmed, so I immediately backed out, as I didn't want anyone involved underperforming for any reason. The surgeon's shoulders slumped and he resumed his unsmiling efficiency.

In fact the operation was a complete success, and when I

found Katherine in the intensive care unit a few hours later, she was conscious and smiling. But the surgeon told me immediately afterward that he hadn't liked the look of the tissue he'd removed. "It will come back," he warned. By then I was so relieved that she'd simply survived the operation that I let this information sit at the back of my head while I dealt with the aftermath of family, chemotherapy, and radiotherapy for Katherine.

Katherine received visitors, including the children, on the immaculate lawns studded with palm and pine trees outside her ward building—at first in a wheelchair, but then perched on the grass in dappled sunshine, her head bandages wrapped in a muted silk scarf, looking as beautiful and relaxed as ever, like the hostess of a rolling picnic. Our good friends Phil and Karen were holidaying in Bergerac, a seven-hour drive to the north, but they made the trip down to see us and it was very emotional to see our children playing with theirs as if nothing was happening in these otherwise idyllic surroundings.

After we spent a few numbing days on the Internet, the inevitability of the tumor's return was clear. The British and the American Medical Associations, every global cancer research organization, and indeed every other organization I contacted, had the same message for someone with a diagnosis of a grade 4 glioblastoma: "I'm so sorry."

I trawled my health contacts for good news about Katherine's condition that hadn't yet made the literature, but there wasn't any. Median survival—the most statistically frequent survival time—was nine to ten months from diagnosis. The average was slightly different, but 50 percent survived one year, and 3 percent of people diagnosed with grade 4 tumors were alive after three years. It wasn't looking good. This was heavy information, particularly as Katherine was bouncing back so well from her craniotomy to remove the tumor (given a rare 100 percent excision rating), and the excellent French medical system was fast-forwarding her on to its state-of-the-art radiotherapy and chemotherapy programs. The people who survived the longest with this condition were young, healthy women with active minds—Katherine to a tee. And despite the doom and gloom, there were several promising avenues of research, which could possibly come online within the time frame of a recurrence.

When Katherine came out of the hospital, it was to a TARDIS-like, empty house in an incredibly supportive village. Her parents and brothers and sister were there, and on her first day back there was a knock at the window. It was Pascal, our neighbor, who unceremoniously passed through the window a dining-room table and six chairs, followed by a casserole dish with a hot meal in it. We tried to get back to normal, setting up an office in the dusty attic, working out the treatment regimens Katherine would have to follow, and working on the book of my DIY columns, which Katherine was determined to continue design-ing. Meanwhile, a hundred yards up the road were our barns, an open-ended dream renovation project that could easily occupy us for the next decade, if we chose. All we lacked was the small detail of the money to restore them, but frankly at that time I was more concerned with giving Katherine the best possible quality of life, to make use of what the medical profession assured me was likely to be a short time. I tried not to believe it, and we lived month by month between MRI scans and blood tests, our con-fidence growing gingerly with each negative result.

Katherine was happiest working, and knowing the children were happy. With her brisk efficiency she set up her own office and began designing and pasting up layouts, color samples, and illustrations around it, one floor down from mine. She also ran our French affairs, took the children to school, and kept in touch with the stream of well-wishers who contacted us and occasionally came to stay. I carried on with my columns and researching my animal book, which was often painfully slow over a rickety dial-up Internet connection held together with gaffer's tape and subject to the vagaries of France Telecom's "service," which, with the largest corporate debt in Europe, made British Telecom seem user-friendly and efficient.

The children loved the barns, and we resolved to inhabit them in whatever way possible as soon as we could, so we set about investing the last of our savings in building a small wooden chalet—still bigger than our former London flat—on the back of the capacious hangar. This was way beyond my meager knowledge of DIY, and difficult for the amiable lunch-addicted French locals to understand, so we called for special help in the form of Karsan, an Anglo-Indian builder friend from London. Karsan is a jack-of-all-trades and master of them all as well. As soon as he arrived, he began pacing out the ground and demanded to be taken to the lumber yard. Working for thirty solid days straight, Karsan erected a viable two-bedroom dwelling, complete with running water, a proper bathroom with a flushing toilet, and electricity, while I got in his way.

With some building-site experience and four years as a writer on DIY, I was sure Karsan would be impressed with my wide knowledge, work ethic, and broad selection of tools. But he wasn't. "All your tools are unused," he observed.

"Well, lightly used," I countered.

"If someone came to work for me with these tools I would send them away," he said. "I am working all alone. Is there anyone in the village who can help me?" he complained.

"Er, I'm helping you, Karsan," I said, and I was there every day lifting wood, cutting things to order, and doing my best to learn from this multiskilled whirlwind master builder. Admittedly, I sometimes had to take a few hours in the day to keep the plates in the air with my writing work—national newspapers are extremely unsympathetic to delays in sending copy, and excuses like "I had to borrow a cement mixer from Monsieur Roget and translate for Karsan at the builders' supply" just don't cut it, I found. "I'm all alone," Karsan continued to lament, and so just before the month was out, I finally managed to persuade a local French builder to help, and he, three-hour lunch breaks and other commitments permitting, did work hard in the final fortnight. Our glamorous friend Georgia, one of the circle of English mums we tapped into after we arrived, also helped a lot, and much impressed Karsan with her genuine knowledge of plumbing, high heels, and low-cut tops. They became best buddies, and Karsan began talking of setting up locally, "where you can drive like in India," with Georgia working as administrative assistant and translator. Somehow this idea was vetoed by Karsan's wife.

When the wooden house was finished, the locals could not believe it. One even said, "*Sacré bleu.*" Some had been working for years on their own houses on patches of land around the village, which the new generation was expanding into. Rarely were any actually finished, however, apart from holiday homes commissioned by the Dutch, German, and English expats, who often used outside labor or micromanaged the local masons to within an inch of their sanity until the job was actually done. This life/work balance with the emphasis firmly on life was one of the most enjoyable parts of living in the region, and perfectly suited my inner putterer, but it was also satisfying to show them a completed project built in the English way, in back-to-back fourteen-hour days with a quick cheese sandwich and a cup of tea for lunch. We bade a fond farewell to Karsan and moved into our new home, in the back of a big open barn looking out over another, in a walled garden where the children could play with their dog, Leon, and their cats in safety, and where the back wall was a full-grown adult's Frisbee throw away. It was our first proper home since before the children were born, and we relished the space and the chance to be working on our own house at last. Everywhere the eye fell, there was a pressing amount to be done, however, and over the next summer we clad the house with insulation and installed broadband Internet, and Katherine began her own vegetable garden, yielding succulent cherry tomatoes and raspberries. Figs dropped off our neighbor's tree into our garden, wild garlic grew in the hedgerows around the vineyards, and melons lay in the fields often uncollected, creating a seemingly endless supply of luscious local produce. Walking the sunbaked dusty paths with Leon every day, through the landscape ringing with cicadas, brought back childhood memories of Corfu, where our family spent several summers. Twisted olive trees appeared in planted rows, rather than the haphazard groves of Greece, but the lifestyle was the same, although now I was a grown-up with a family of my own. It was surreal, given the backdrop of Katherine's illness, that everything was so perfect just as it went so horribly wrong.

We threw ourselves into enjoying life, and for me this meant exploring the local wildlife with the children. Most obviously different from the UK were the birds, brightly colored and clearly used to spending more time in North Africa than their dowdy UK counterparts, whose plumage seems more adapted to perpetual autumn than to the vivid colors of Marrakesh.

Twenty minutes away was the Camargue, whose rice paddies and salt flats are warm enough to sustain a year-round population of flamingos, but I was determined not to get interested in birds. I once went on a "nature tour" of Mull that turned out to be a bird-watchers' tour. Frolicking otters were ignored in favor of surrounding a bush waiting for something called a redstart, an apparently unseasonal visiting reddish sparrow. That way madness lies.

Far more compelling, and often unavoidable, was the insect population, which hopped, crawled, and reproduced all over the place. Crickets the size of mice sprang through the long grass entertaining the cats and the children, who caught them for opposing reasons, the latter to try to feed, the former to eat. At night, exotic-looking and endangered rhinoceros beetles lumbered across my path like little prehistoric tanks, each one fiercely brandishing its utterly useless horns, resembling more a triceratops than the relatively svelte rhinoceros. These entertaining beasts would stay with us for a few days, rattling around in a glass bowl containing soil, wood chips, and usually dandelion leaves, to see if we could mimic their natural habitat. But they did not make good pets, and invariably I released them in the night to the safety of the vineyards. Other nighttime catches included big fat toads, always released onto a raft in the river in what became a formalized ceremony after school, and a hedgehog carried between two sticks and then housed in a tin bath and fed on worms, until his escape into the compound three days later. It was only then that I discovered these amiable but flea-ridden and stinking creatures can carry rabies. But perhaps the most dramatic catch was an unidentified snake, nearly a meter long, also transported using the stick method, and housed overnight in a suspended bowl in the sitting room, lidded, with holes for air. "What do you think of the snake?" I asked Katherine proudly the next morning. "What snake?" she replied. The bowl was empty. The snake had crawled out through a hole and dropped to the floor right next to where we were sleeping (on the sofa bed at that time) before sliding out under the door. I hoped. Katherine was not amused, and I resolved to be more careful about what I brought into the house.

Not all the local wildlife was harmless. Adders, or *les vipères*, are rife, and the protocol was to call the fire brigade, or *pompiers*, who come and "dance around like little girls waving at it with sticks until it escapes," according to Georgia, who has witnessed this procedure. I once saw a *vipère* under a stone in the garden, and wore thick gloves and gingerly tapped every stone I ever moved afterward. Killer hornets also occasionally buzzed into our lives like malevolent helicopter gunships, with the locals all agreeing that three stings would kill a man. My increasingly well-thumbed animal and insect encyclopedia revealed only that they were "potentially dangerous to humans." Either way, whenever I saw one, I adopted the full *pompier* procedure diligently.

But the creature that made the biggest impression early on was the scorpion. One appeared in my office on the wall one night, prompting levels of adrenaline and panic I thought only possible in the jungle. Was nowhere safe? How many of these things *were* there? Were they in the kids' room now? An Internet trawl revealed that fifty-seven people had been killed in Algeria by scorpions in the previous decade. Algeria is a former French colony. It was nearby. But luckily this scorpion—dark brown and the size of the end of a man's thumb—was not the culprit, and actually had a sting more like a bee. This jolt, that I was definitely not in London and had brought my family to a potentially dangerous situation, prompted my first (and last) poem for about twenty years, unfortunately too expletive-ridden to reproduce here.

And then there was the wild boar. Not to be outdone by mere insects, reptiles, and arthropods, the mammalian order laid on a special treat one night when I was walking the dog. Unusually, I was out for a run, a bit ahead of Leon, so I was surprised to see him up ahead about twenty-five meters into the vines. As I got closer, I was also surprised that he seemed jet-black in the moonlight, whereas when I'd last seen him he was his usual tawny self. Also, although Leon is a hefty eight stone, or 112 pounds, of shaggy mountain dog, this animal seemed heavier and more barrel-shaped. And it was grunting, like a great big pig. I began to realize that this was not Leon, but a *sanglier*, or wild boar, known to roam the vineyards at night and able to make a boar-shaped hole in a chain-link fence without slowing down. I was armed with a dog lead, a mechanical pencil (in case of inspiration), and a lighted helmet, turned off. As it faced me and started stamping the ground, I felt I had to decide quickly whether or not to turn on the headlamp. It would either definitely charge at it or it would find it aversive. As the light snapped on, the grunting monster slowly wheeled around and trotted into the vines, more in irritation than fear. And then Leon arrived, late and inadequate cavalry, and shot off into the vineyards after it. Normally Leon will chase imaginary rabbits relentlessly for many minutes at a time at the merest hint of a rustle in the undergrowth, but on this occasion he shot back immediately, professing total ignorance of anything amiss, and stayed very close by my side on the way back. Very wise.

The next day I took the children to track the boar, and they were wide-eyed as we found and photographed the trotter prints in the loose gray earth, and had them verified by the salty farmers in the Café of the Universe in the village. "*Il était gros,*" they concluded, belly laughing and filling the air with clouds of *pastis* when I mimicked my fear.

So, serpents included, this life was as much like Eden as I felt was possible. With the broadband finally installed, and bats flying around my makeshift office in the empty barn, the book

I had come to write was finally seriously under way, and Katherine's treatment and environment seemed as good as could reasonably be hoped for. What could possibly tempt us away from this hard-won, almost heavenly niche? My family decided to buy a zoo, of course.

2

The Adventure Begins

I t was in the spring of 2005 that it landed on our doorstep: the brochure that would change our lives forever. Like any other brochure from a real estate agent, at first we dismissed it. But, unlike any other brochure from a real estate agent, here we saw Dartmoor Wildlife Park advertised for the first time. My sister Melissa had sent me a copy in France, with a note attached: "Your dream scenario." I had to agree with her that although I thought I was already living in my dream scenario, this odd offer of a country house with zoo attached seemed even better—if we could get it, which seemed unlikely. And if there was nothing wrong with it, which also seemed unlikely. There must have been some serious structural problems in the house, or the grounds or enclosures, or some fundamental flaw with the business that was impossible to rectify.

Yet, even with this near certainty of eventual failure, the entire family was sufficiently intrigued to investigate further. A flight of fancy? Perhaps, but it was one for which, we decided, we could restructure our entire lives.

My father, Ben Harry Mee, had died a few months before,

and Mum was going to have to sell the family home where they had lived for the last twenty years, a five-bedroom house in Surrey set on two acres, which had just been valued at £1.2 million. This astonishing amount not only reflected the pleasant surroundings, but also, most important, its proximity to London, comfortably within the economic security cordon of Route M25. Twenty-five minutes by train from London Bridge, this was the stockbroker belt, an enviable position on the property ladder achieved by my father, who, as the son of an enlightened Doncaster miner, had worked hard and invested shrewdly on behalf of his offspring all his life.

Ben did in fact work at the stock exchange for the last fifteen years of his career, but not as a broker, a position he felt could be morally dubious. Dad was administration controller, overseeing the administrative duties for the London Stock Exchange, and for the exchanges in Manchester, Dublin, and Liverpool, plus a total of eleven regional and Irish amalgamated buildings. (At a similar stage in my life I was having trouble running my admin as a single self-employed journalist.) So, as a family, we were relatively well-off, though not actually rich, and with no liquid assets to support any whimsical ventures. In 2005, Halifax Bank, with one of the largest real estate agencies in Britain, estimated that there were 67,000 such properties valued at over £1 million in the UK, but we seemed to be the only family who decided to cash it all in and a have a crack at buying a zoo.

It seemed like a lost cause from the beginning, but one that we knew we'd regret if we didn't pursue. We had a plan of sorts. Mum had been going to sell the house and downsize to something smaller and more manageable, like a two- or three-bedroom cottage, then live in peace and security with a buffer of cash, but with space for only one or two offspring to visit with their various broods at any time. The problem, and what we all worried about, was that this isolation in old age could be the waiting room for a gradual deterioration (and, as she saw it, inevitable dementia) and death.

The new plan was to upsize the family assets and Mum's home to a twelve-bedroom house surrounded by a stagnated business about which we knew nothing. I would abandon France altogether and put my book on hold, Duncan would stop working in London, and we would then live together and run the zoo full-time. Mum would be spared the daily concerns of running the zoo, but would benefit from the stimulating environment and having her family around in an exciting new life looking after two hundred exotic animals. What could possibly go wrong? Come on, Mum . . . it'll be fine.

In fact, it was a surprisingly easy sell. Mum has always been adventurous, and she likes big cats. When she was seventy-three, I took her to a lion sanctuary where you could walk in the bush with lions and stroke them in their enclosures; many were captive bred, descended from lions rescued from being shot by farmers. I was awestruck by the lions' size and frankly terrified, never quite able to let go of the idea that I wasn't meant to be this close to these predators. Every whisker twitch triggered in me a jolt of adrenaline that was translated into an involuntary flinch. Mum just tickled them under the chin and said, "Ooh, aren't they lovely?" The next year this adventurous lady tried skiing for the first time. So the concept of buying a zoo was not dismissed out of hand.

None of us liked the idea of Mum being on her own, so we were already looking at her living with one of us, perhaps on a larger property with pooled resources. Which is how the details of Dartmoor Wildlife Park, courtesy of Knight Frank, a real estate agent in the South of England, happened to drop through Mum's letterbox. My sister Melissa was the most excited, ordering several copies of the details and sending them out to all her four brothers: the oldest, Vincent; Henry; Duncan; and me. I was in France, and received my copy with the "your dream scenario" note. I had to admit it looked good, but quickly tossed it onto my teetering, "soon to be sorted" pile. This was already carpeted in dust from the mistral, that magnificent southern French wind that periodically blasted down the channel in southwest France created by the mountains surrounding the rivers Rhône and Saône. And then it came right through the ancient lime mortar of my north-facing barn-office wall, redistributing the powdery mortar as a minor sandstorm of dust evenly scattered throughout the office over periods of about four days at a time. Small rippled dunes of mortar dust appeared on top of the brochure, then other documents appeared on top of the dunes, and then more small dunes.

But Melissa wouldn't let it lie. She wouldn't let it lie because she thought it was possible, and had her house valued, and kept dragging any conversation you had with her back to the zoo. Duncan was quickly enthused. Having spent a short stint as a reptile keeper at London Zoo, he was the closest thing we had to a zoo professional. Now an experienced business manager in London, he was also the prime candidate for overall manager of the project, if he, and almost certainly others, chose to trade their present lifestyles for an entirely different existence.

Melissa set up a viewing for the family, minus Henry and Vincent, who had other engagements but were in favor of exploration. So it was agreed, and "Grandma" Amelia and a good proportion of her brood spanning three generations arrived in a small country hotel in the South Hams district of Devon. There was a wedding going on, steeping the place in bonhomie, and the gardens, chilly in the early-spring night air, occasionally echoed with stilettos on gravel as underdressed young ladies hurried to their hatchbacks and back for some essential commodity missing from the revelry inside.

A full, or even reasonably comprehensive, family gathering outside Christmas or a wedding was unusual, and we were on a minor mission rather than a holiday, yet accompanied by a gaggle of children of assorted ages. Our party was definitely toward the comprehensive end of the spectrum, with all that that entails. Vomiting babies, pregnant people, toddlers at head-smash age, and children accidentally ripping curtains from the wall trying to impersonate Darth Vader. The night before the viewing, we were upbeat but realistic. We were serious contenders, but probably all convinced that we were giving it our best shot and that somebody with more money, or experience, or probably both, would come along and take it away.

We arrived at the park on a crisp April morning in 2005, and met Ellis Daw for the first time. An energetic man in his late seventies with a full white beard and a beanie hat that he never removed, Ellis took us around the park and the house like a pro on autopilot. He'd clearly done this tour a few times before. On our quick trip around the labyrinthine twelve-bedroom mansion, we took in that the sitting room was half full of parrot cages, the general decor had about three decades of catching up to do, and the plumbing and electrical systems looked like they could absorb a few tens of thousands of pounds to be put right.

Out in the park we were all blown away by the animals and Ellis's innovative enclosure designs. Tiger Mountain, so called because three Siberian tigers prowl around a manmade mountain at the center of the park, was particularly impressive. Instead of chain-link or wire-mesh fence, Ellis had adopted a "ha-ha" system, which basically entails a deep ditch around the perimeter that in turn is surrounded by a wall more than six feet high on the animal side but only three or four feet on the visitor side. This creates the impression of extreme proximity to these most spectacular cats, who pad about the enclosure like massive flame-clad versions of the domestic cats we all know and love, making you completely reappraise your relationship with the diminutive predators many of us shelter indoors.

There were lions behind wire, as stunning as the tigers, roaring in defiance of any other animal to challenge them for their territory, particularly other lions, apparently. And it has to be said that these bellowing outputs, projected by their hugely powerful diaphragms for a good three miles across the valley, have over the years proved 100 percent effective. Never once has this group of lions been challenged by any other group of lions, or anything else, for their turf. It's easy to argue that this is due to lack of predators of this magnitude in the vicinity, but one lioness did apparently catch a heron at a reputed fifteen feet off the ground a few years before, confirming that this territorial defensiveness was no bluff.

Peacocks strolled around the picnic area, from where you could see a pack of wolves prowling through the trees behind a wire fence. Three big European bears looked up at us from their woodland enclosure, and three jaguars, two pumas, a lynx, some flamingos, porcupines, raccoons, and a Brazilian tapir added to the eclectic mix of the collection.

We were awestruck by the animals, and surprisingly not daunted at all. Even to our untutored eyes there was clearly a lot of work to be done. Everything wooden, from picnic benches to enclosure posts and stand-off barriers, was covered in algae that had clearly been there for some time. Some of it, worryingly, at the base of many of the enclosure posts, was obviously having a corrosive influence.

We could see that the zoo needed work, but we could also see that it had until recently been a going concern, and one that would give us a unique opportunity to be near some of the most spectacular—and endangered—animals on the planet.

As part of our official viewing of the property, we were asked by a film crew from *Animal Planet* to participate in a documentary about the sale. The journalist in me began to wonder whether this eccentric English venture might be sustainable through another source. Writing and the media had been my career for fifteen years, and, while not providing a huge amount of money, had given me a tremendous quality of life. If I could write about the things I liked doing, I could generally do them as well, and I was sometimes able to boost the activity itself with the media light that shone on it. Perhaps here was a similar model. A once thriving project now on the edge of extinction, functioning perfectly well in its day, but now needing a little nudge from the outside world to survive . . .

Mum, Duncan, and I were asked to stand shoulder to shoulder amongst the parrots in the living room, to explain for the camera what we would do if we got the zoo. At the end of our burst of amateurish enthusiasm, the cameraman spontaneously said, "I want you guys to get it." The other offers were from leisure industry professionals with a lot of money, against whom we felt we had an outside chance, but nothing more. My skepticism was still enormous, but I began to see a clear way through, if, somehow, chance delivered it to us. Though it still felt far-fetched, like looking around all those houses my parents seemed to drag us to when we were moving as kids: *Don't get too interested, because you know you will almost certainly not end up living there.*

On our tour around the park itself, Ellis finally switched out of his professional spiel and looked at me, my brother Duncan, and my brother-in-law Jim, all relatively strapping lads in our early to mid-forties, and said, "Well, you're the right age for it anyway." This vote of confidence registered with us, as clearly, Ellis had seen something in us that he liked. Our ambitions for the place were modest, which he also liked. He said he'd actually turned away several offers because they involved spending too much on the redevelopment. "What do you want to spend a million pounds on here?" he asked us, somewhat rhetorically. "What's wrong with it? On your way, I said to them." I can imagine the color draining from his bankers' faces when they heard this good news. Luckily we didn't have a million pounds to spend on redevelopment—or, at this stage, even on the zoo itself—so our modest, family-based plans seemed to strike a chord with Ellis.

At about three thirty in the afternoon, our tour was over and we began to notice that the excited chattering of the adults in our group was interrupted increasingly frequently by minor, slightly overemotional outbursts from our children, who were milling around us like progressively more manic and fractious over-wound toys. In our enthusiasm for the park we had collectively made an elementary, rookie parenting mistake and missed lunch, leading to Parents' Dread: low blood sugar in under-tens. We had to find food fast. We walked into the enormous Jaguar Restaurant, built by Ellis in 1987 to seat three hundred people. Then we walked out again. Rarely have I been in a working restaurant less conducive to the consumption of food. A thin film of grease from the prolific fat fryers in the kitchen coated the tired Formica tabletops, arranged in canteen rows and illuminated by harsh fluorescent strips mounted in the swirling mess of the grease-yellowed Artex ceiling. The heavy scent of the oil used to cook french fries gave a fairly accurate indication of the menu and mingled with the smoke of hand-rolled cigarettes rising from the group of staff clad in gray kitchen whites sitting around the bar, eyeing their few customers with suspicion.

Even at the risk of total mass blood-sugar implosion, we were not eating there, and asked for directions to the nearest supermarket for emergency provisions. And then, for me, the final piece of the Dartmoor puzzle fell into place, for that was when we discovered the Tesco at Lee Mill. Seven minutes away by car was not just a supermarket, but an übermarket. In the climax of the film *Monty Python and the Holy Grail*, King Arthur finally reaches a rise that gives him a view of "Castle Aaargh," thought to be the resting place of the Holy Grail, the culmination of his quest. As Arthur and Sir Bedevere are drawn across the water toward the castle by the pilotless dragon-crested ship, music of Wagnerian epic proportions plays to indicate that they are arriving at a place of true significance. This music started spontaneously in my head as we rounded a corner at the top of a small hill, and looked down into a man-made basin filled with what looked almost like a giant spaceship, secretly landed in this lush green landscape. It seemed the size of Stansted Airport, its lights beaming out their message of industrial-scale consumerism into the rapidly descending twilight of the late-spring afternoon. Hot chickens, fresh bread, salad, hummus, batteries, children's clothes, newspapers, and many other provisions we were lacking were immediately provided. But more important, wandering around its cathedral-high aisles, I was hugely reassured that, if necessary, I could find here a television, a camera, an iron, a kettle, stationery, a DVD, or a child's toy. And it was open twenty-four hours a day. As I watched the thirty-seven checkouts humming their lines of customers through, my final fear about relocating to the area was laid to rest. A Londoner for twenty years, I had become accustomed to the availability of things like flat-screen TVs, birthday cards, or sprouts at any time of the day or night, and one of the biggest culture shocks of living in southern France for the last three years had been their totally different take on this. For them, global consumerism stopped at 8 PM, and if you needed something urgently after that, you had to *wait till the next day*. This Tesco, for me, meant that the whole thing was doable, and we took our picnic to watch the sunset on a nearby beach in high spirits.

Although my mum's house was not yet even on the market, it had been valued at the same as the asking price for the park; so, with some trepidation, we put in an offer at that price in a four-way sealed-bid auction and waited keenly for the outcome. But two days later we were told that we were not successful. Our bid was rejected by Ellis's advisors on the basis that we were inexperienced and had no real money. Which we had to admit were both fair points. We went back to our lives with the minimum of regrets, feeling that we had done what we could and had been prepared to follow through, but now it was out of our hands. Melissa went back to her family in Gloucestershire; Duncan was busy in London with his new business; Vincent, at fifty-four our eldest brother, had a new baby; Mum went back to the family home in Surrey, preparing to put it on the market. All relatively comfortable, successful, and rewarding. My life in particular, I felt, was compensation enough for missing out on this chance. Having spent nearly a decade maneuvering into a position of writing for a living with low overheads in a hot country, watching the children grow into this slightly strange niche, I was content with my lot and anxious to get back to it.

But after all the excitement, I couldn't help wondering about what might have been. Sitting in my makeshift Plexiglas office in the back of my beautiful derelict barn with the swallows dipping in and out during the day and the bats buzzing around my head at dusk, I couldn't stop thinking about the life we could have built around that zoo.

Katherine was getting stronger every day, wielding my French pickax/mattock in her vegetable garden with increasing vigor, and her muscle tone and body mass—wasted to its furthest extreme by the chemotherapy so that she went from looking like a catwalk model to an etiolated punk rocker, with her random tufts of hair—improved throughout the summer. Her neurologist, Madame Campello, a fiercely intelligent and slightly forbidding woman, was pleased with her progress and decided to shift her MRI scans from monthly to once every two months, which we saw as a good sign. It gave us longer between the inevitable anxiety of going into Nîmes to get the results, a process that both of us, particularly Katherine, found pretty daunting.

Mme Campello was obviously compassionate, and I'm sure I saw her actually gasp when she first saw Katherine, the children, and myself for Katherine's initial postoperative consultation. From that moment she fast-forwarded almost every part of the treatment, and I could see that this lady was going to do everything she could to make sure that Katherine survived. In her normal clinical consultations, however, Mme Campello was rather like a strict headmistress, which made Katherine, always the good girl, feel unable to question her too closely about treatment options. However, with one or two school expulsions under my belt, I have never been overly intimidated by school heads, and felt quite entitled to probe. Mme Campello turned out to be extremely receptive to this, and several times I called her after speaking with Katherine once we had got home, and we decided on an adjustment to her medication.

My nighttime excursions with Leon continued to yield interesting creatures, like fireflies from impenetrable thickets that never produced the goods in daylight in front of the children, scorpions toward whom I was beginning to habituate but was still jittery, and probably the most surprising for me, a long-horn beetle. Never before or since have I seen such a beetle in the wild, and I was convinced he was on the wrong continent. Long—perhaps three inches—with iridescent wing casings, a small head, and enormous antennae, from which, I assume, he got his name. I took great pleasure in identifying him with the children in our voluptuously illustrated French encyclopedia bought from a book fair in Avignon, and photographing him standing on the page next to his template self, though he was inordinately more impressive and colorful.

Katherine was well and in capable hands, the children were blooming, and I was writing about home improvement for the *Guardian* and even occasionally doing some, and gradually making contact with professors around the world on topics like chimpanzee predation of monkeys for sexual rewards, elephant intelligence, and the dolphin's capacity for syntax. It was close to heaven, with local friends popping in for mandatory glasses of chilled rosé from the vines on our doorstep, and me able to adjust my working hours around the demands of the village and family life relatively easily. Apart from all that rosé.

But still I kept thinking about the zoo. The park sat on the edge of Dartmoor, surrounded by the lush woodland and beautiful beaches of South Hams. The two days I had spent in this region of Devon would not go away. Our family had enjoyed their stay, but it was more than that—somehow enchanting, something I could only very reluctantly let go of, even though I knew it was already lost.

Standing in my French hayloft door, free of Health and Safety Commission interference, the barn's ancient portals bleached like driftwood by the sun and sandblasted by the mistral, with its interior and exterior dripping rusted door furniture, some of it reputedly dating back to the Napoleonic era, it was the zoo that kept coming back to me.

When Napoleon passed through our village of Arpaillargues in 1815, he famously killed two local dissenters, known (admittedly among a relatively select few local French historians) as the Arpaillargues Two. In 2005 the Tour de France passed through the village, causing no deaths but quite a lot of excitement (though not enough for the local shopkeeper, Sandrine, to forgo her three-hour lunch break to sell cold drinks to the hundreds of sweltering tourists lining the route). So, in two centuries, two quite big things had happened in the village. In between, it settled back into being baked by the sun and blasted by the mistral. And, only slightly wistfully, I settled back into that, too.

A year passed, with the zoo as a mournful but ebbing distraction. Those big trees, so unlike the parched scrub of southern Europe, the nearby rivers and sea, and the ridiculously magnificent animals, so close to the house, so foolishly endangered by mankind and yet right there in a ready-made opportunity for keeping them alive for future generations.

Partly because the whole family was in a bit of a daze about my father's death, Mum's house was still not on the market, so we were unprepared for what happened next. As an expat without satellite TV (that's cheating), I nevertheless craved English news and probably visited the BBC News online two or three times a day. Suddenly, on 12 April 2006, there it was again. Ellis had released a statement saying that the sale had fallen through yet again, and that many of the animals would have to be shot if a buyer wasn't found within the next eleven days.

It didn't give us long, but I knew exactly what I had to do. I called Melissa and Duncan, who had been the main drivers of the previous attempt, and told them that we had to try again. I was not entirely surprised, however, when neither of them seemed quite as excited as I was. Both had delved deeply into the machinations required for the purchase, and Duncan in particular had been alarmed at the time by a demand for a "non-refundable deposit" of £25,000 to secure a place at the head of the line. "If you can get it in writing that he will definitely sell it to us, and we can sell the house in time, I'll back you up," he said. He felt it was just an endless time-sink, but gladly gave me all the information he had. Brother-in-law Jim too had a list of contacts and offered his help preparing spreadsheets for a business plan should it get that far.

Peter Wearden was the first call. As environmental health officer for the South Hams district, Peter was directly responsible for issuing the zoo license. "Can a bunch of amateurs like us really buy a zoo and run it?" I asked him. "Yes," he said unequivocally, "providing you have the appropriate management structure in place." This structure consists primarily of hiring a curator of animals, an experienced and qualified zoo professional with detailed knowledge of managing exotic animals who is responsible for looking after the animals on a day-to-day basis. Peter sent me a flowchart that showed the position of the curator beneath the zoo directors, which would be us, but still in a position to allocate funds for animal management at his/her discretion. "You can't just decide to buy a new ice-cream kiosk if the curator thinks there is a need for, say, new fence posts in the lion enclosure," said Peter. "If you haven't got money for both, you have to listen to the curator." That seemed fair enough. "There is, by the way," he added, "a need for new fence posts in the lion enclosure." And how much are those? "No idea," said Peter. "That's where you'll have to get professional advice. But that's just one of many, many things you'll need to do before you can get your zoo license." Peter explained a bit about the Zoo Licensing Act, and that Ellis was due to hand in his license to operate a zoo within a couple of weeks, hence the eleven-day deadline for the sale.

In fact, the animals would not have to be dispersed by then, as they would be held under the Dangerous Wild Animals Act (DWA) as a private collection. It just meant that visitors were not allowed, so the park's already seriously faltering finances would reach a crunch point. But not absolutely necessarily an eleven-day crunch point, it seemed. If we could mount a credible bid, there was every chance that we could carry on negotiating for a few weeks after the park closed. Already, there was reason to hope that this apparently hopeless task was not necessarily impossible.

"Is it viable?" I asked Peter. This time he took longer to respond. "Erm, I'm sure it is," he said. "With the right management, a lot of money invested in the infrastructure, and a hell of a lot—and I mean a hell of a lot—of hard work, it should be viable, yes. For a long time it was one of the area's most popular attractions. It's declined over the last few years due to lack of investment and not keeping up with the times. But until quite recently it was a thriving business."

I was deeply suspicious that there must be more to it than this, and that there was some sort of black hole in the whole fabric of the place that meant that it couldn't work. Why had the other sales fallen through? So many industry professionals had cruised up to this project and somehow not taken the bait. Were we going to be the suckers who bought it and then discovered the truth?

Clearly, I needed professional help, which came in the form of a text message from a friend whose sister-in-law Suzy happened to be a fairly senior zoo professional, easily equivalent in fact to the rank of curator, currently working in Australia. I had met Suzy once at a wedding a long time ago and liked her instantly. I was impressed with the way that even in a cocktail dress, with her wild mane of blonde hair, she managed to give the impression that she was wearing work boots, leggings, and a heavy fleece. Her job at the time had involved educating Queensland cattle farmers about the need for conservation of local wildlife, a tough-enough sounding proposition for a bare-knuckle prize-fighter, I would have thought. But not for Suzy, who was now working as head of animal procurement for the three zoos in the State of Victoria, including the flagship Melbourne Zoo where she was based. Suzy offered any help she could give, and said she would even consider taking a sabbatical for a year in order to act as curator. "I can't guarantee it," she said. "But you can put me down as a candidate until we see how things develop. In the meantime, before you go any further, you need to get a survey done by a zoo professional who can tell you whether it works or not." Suzy shared my concerns about the possibility of a black hole, having read about Dartmoor's decline through the zoo-community literature. Did she have anyone in mind for this inspection? "There's someone I used to work with at Jersey who could give you a pretty definitive opinion," said Suzy. "He's a bit too senior to do that sort of thing now I think, but I'll see what he thinks."

And that's how we came to meet Nick Lindsay, head of International Zoo Programs for the Zoological Society of London (ZSL), in the car park of Dartmoor Wildlife Park a few days later. This tall, slightly avuncular man shook hands with me and Melissa, who was now about eight months pregnant, and agreed that we should walk up the drive along the normal visitor access route to get a feel for how the park works. We had commissioned a report from ZSL and Nick kindly agreed to carry out the inspection himself, as he too had been following the plight of the zoo, and as a local boy had an interest in it. He even stayed with his mum down the road so that we didn't have to pay a hotel bill.

On the way up the drive we were as candid as we could be. "We know nothing about zoos, but if this really is a viable zoo, do you think it's possible for us to do it?"

"Oh, there's no reason for you to know about zoos in order to buy one." said Nick, laughing. "You'd have to be a bit mad, but I assume you've got that part covered. Let's just see if it really is a viable zoo first."

Our first stop was Ronnie the tapir, whose enclosure ran parallel to the drive. Nick bent down and called him over, and to my surprise he came. I had never seen a tapir this close before, and was impressed that this large, strange-looking animal was so biddable and friendly. Resembling a large pig with a hump on its back and a miniature elephant's trunk for a nose, the tapir was made, the Indonesians say, from the parts left over when God had finished making all the other animals.

Nick held his fingers through the mesh, and Ronnie wibbled his extended proboscis onto it, and then onto our hands, happy to make our acquaintance. With this charming encounter, however, came the first of the things that would need addressing. "This fence should have a stand-off barrier," said Nick. "We have to be sure his house is heated in the winter, and it looks a bit muddy in there for him. He's an ungulate, so his feet are quite delicate." I'd been determined to take notes all day to keep track of the kind of expenditure we would be looking at, but already I'd run into an unforeseen problem: tapir snot, all over my hand and notepad. "Don't worry," said Nick. "I'll put everything in the report."

The day went well, and we were halfway around the park when we were intercepted by Robin, a strained-looking man with a long gray ponytail, who introduced himself as a member of the staff, clearly prepared to undergo the unpleasantness of seeing us around the park, though not relishing it. Though we had made an appointment to view, we should be escorted at all times, for legal and security reasons, he told us. He was our guide for the rest of the outside tour. It soon became clear that there was no question about the park that Robin could not answer. History, attendance figures, animal diets, names of plants—he knew it all. And then something happened that gave him a tricky one. A huge shot boomed out, echoing across the valley. It could only have been a gunshot, and from something big, the kind of sound you generally only hear in films. We stopped in our tracks. "Er, bit of trouble with the tigers?" I asked. Robin paused, looked a bit more strained but now tinged with sadness, and said, "No, it's one of the lionesses, actually. She had lung cancer." He turned to lead us on and I looked at Nick, utterly agog. I had never been anywhere where they had shot a lion within fifty meters of where I was standing. Was this okay? Are they allowed to do that? Does it sound justified? Is this somehow connected with the black hole? Nick looked slightly taken aback, but seemed to take it in his stride. "If she had lung cancer and the vet says it's time, it's completely justified," he said. And the use of a gun rather than an injection was also quite normal, if the animal was difficult or dangerous to dart. So it was all okay, everything normal, just that a lion had been shot. If the head of the International Zoo Program at ZSL said it was all right, it must be, but I confess I found it slightly unsettling.

So did Rob, the man who had pulled the trigger. We met him later in the Jaguar Restaurant, along with Ellis, and Ellis's sister Maureen. Ellis was also unsettled, by a toothache, he said, which was why he was holding a glass of whiskey. There was a difficult, tense atmosphere as the edifice of a once successful family business lay in ruins, creditors circled, and emotions were near the surface. But there were questions we and Nick needed to ask Ellis, and he also had questions for us. Rob seemed almost close to tears after his ordeal of shooting the lioness, Peggy, an animal he had known for thirteen years, and was reluctant to come to the table at first, but Maureen persuaded him that it might be necessary, as he now held the license to keep the collection on site under the DWA. Ellis paced the room, cursing, not quite under his breath.

Eventually we all sat down and Nick said hello to Ellis as a teacher might greet a former student, expelled but at the reunion, as was only right. They knew each other from various Zoo Federation meetings over the years, and Ellis nodded, acknowledging that here was a man with whom he needed to cooperate. Nick began his line of questions for his report, and everything went well until he mentioned the name of Peter Wearden, the South Hams environmental health officer. "Peter Wearden? Peter Wearden? I'll kill him, I will. I'll cut his head off with a sword and stick it on a spike at the top of the drive. That'll show them what I think of him." He went on for a while, explaining how he had killed men before, in the war—"I'm good at killing men"—as well as every kind of animal on the planet. He wouldn't make a fuss about shooting a lion, like Rob.

At this point I interjected, and said I personally didn't think it was unreasonable for Rob to be upset, but we needed to talk about Peter Wearden. "I'd kill him without a thought, just like the lion," he said, looking me in the eye. Not sure what to say, I thought I'd try to claw back toward some references to reality. "Well, that would at least sort out your accommodation problems for the next few years," I said. He weighed this remark, looked at me again and said, "I've got his coffin ready for him up here before." And it was true. A coffin with a picture of Peter Wearden in it had been in the restaurant for a period of about six months, even while the park was open to the public. "Now then, Ellis," said Nick, moving seamlessly on, "what about those stand-off barriers?"

Ellis was polite but perceptibly preoccupied as he took us on the tour of the house again, even more briskly than last time, and I was surprised to see that it seemed in significantly worse condition than I remembered it. Whether this was cosmetic, due to an increase in mess, or me misremembering the fabric of the place was hard to tell, but the impression was strong enough to cause a new entry in my mental spreadsheet of expenditures.

The first warning was the increase in the strength of the odor in the kitchen, at the front of the house. This was Ellis's entry point, and obviously one of the key rooms he used, but it stank. Last time it stank badly, but this time the stench was like a fog that you felt was clinging to your clothes. Women in Melissa's condition are particularly sensitive to smells, and she nearly gagged as she passed through, pressing her hand to her mouth in case she had to forcibly suppress some vomit—it is impolite after all, when someone is proudly showing you around their home, to throw up in it.

The main source of the smell seemed to be a bucket in the corner containing raw mackerel and dead day-old chicks to be fed in the mornings to the heron and jackdaw population. It was an ancient, yellowed plastic vessel, and there had to be some doubt about its structural integrity, as a large, ancient, multicolored stain rippled outward from its base like a sulphur bog, but more virulent. Even Ellis was moved to comment, "Bit whiffy in here. But you don't have to keep that there," he added, gesturing toward the bucket. "You'll be moving things around, I suppose." Somehow I didn't think that simply repositioning the bucket would expunge this odor. I vowed on that threshold that, if we got the park, no food would ever be prepared in this room again.

The rest of the house seemed more dishevelled than we remembered, and we still didn't have time to get a full picture of how the floor plan worked. Half the house had been used for students, and this section was coated in plastic signs declaring, NO SMOKING, TURN OFF THE LIGHTS, and oddly, BEING SICK ON THE STAIRS IS FORBIDDEN. But it mostly seemed like a standard rewiring, replumbing, and plastering job would make it good. The other half of the house, with a grand galleried staircase and stone-flagged kitchen, was marred by decades of clashing wallpapers and patchwork surface rewiring that snaked wildly like the tendrils of an aggressive giant creeper gradually taking over the house. And of course the all-pervading smell coming from the front kitchen.

The stone-flagged kitchen had not been used as such for decades, and in the fireplace, behind a ragged, dusty sheet hanging on a string nailed to the high mantel above it, lay a rusted hulk of an ancient range, a door hanging off, clogged inside with what appeared to be bird droppings from the chimney above. "My grandma used to cook on that," said Ellis. "Bit of work would get it going again. Worth a few bob, that." I wasn't so sure. But this room looked out over an old cobbled courtyard, now overgrown with weeds, which looked across to the cottage opposite, above the stables (read "junk depository"). Melissa, who is good at spotting potential and visualizing a finished house, lit up. "This is the best bit of the house," she said. Really? "I can imagine doing the breakfast in here, looking across the courtyard, waving to Katherine or Mum in their kitchen in the cottage." At that time Melissa was still seriously considering selling up and moving in too, five kids and Jim included. It sounded good. But in the time allowed, and with enough clutter to fill a hundred rummage sales strewn about, it was hard to gauge what it might be like to live in this house. Except that it, like the park, would require a lot of (expensive) work.

We came back out of the house and met Nick in the restaurant again, thanked our hosts, and strolled down the drive. By now our objective and impartial advisor had become a little partisan. "I think it's a great place," enthused Nick. "Much better than I thought it would be from all the stories. You'll need a proper site survey, to be sure, but as far as I can see, this could be a working zoo again without too much trouble." As an advisor on zoo design, Nick also had a few ideas to throw in at this stage. "Get the customers off the drive"—which ran up the center of the lower half of the park for a fifth of a mile—"and into the paddock next to it. You could put a wooden walkway through it—meandering, so that they don't notice the climb—and get something striking in there, like zebras, and maybe some interesting antelopes, so that as soon as they pass through the kiosk they enter a different world." Could we get zebras? I asked. "Oh, I can get you zebras," said Nick casually, as if they were something he might pick up for us at Tesco. This I liked. Spoken almost like a wheeler-dealer: video recorders, leather jackets, zebras, roll up, roll up. But there was more about this glimpse into the workings of the zoo world that appealed. Nick was painting with the animals, as well as designing a serious commercial layout in his head. "You need more flamingos," he said. "Flamingos look good against the trees. The lake up there with the island has trees behind it, so if you put a few more in it they'll look marvelous when the punters reach the top of the path. Then, having climbed that hill, they'll be hot. So that's where you sell them their first ice cream." Wow. Unfortunately, flamingos are one of the few animals that don't usually come free from other zoos, costing anything from £800 to £1,500 each. Which is a lot of ice cream. And with the prospect of bird flu migrating over the horizon there was the possibility of a mass culling order from DEFRA (Department for Environments, Food, and Rural Affairs) shortly after we took delivery of these beautiful, expensive birds. Our flamingo archipelago might have to wait.

I went back to France, Melissa went to her children in Gloucester, and Nick went back to Whipsnade, where he prepared the report that was to dictate the direction of our lives. If it was negative, it would be definitively so, and there would be no point chasing this dream any further. In many ways, as before, I was half hoping that this would be the case and I could finally lay the idea to rest knowing categorically that it would be a mistake to proceed. If it was positive, however, we knew we had to continue, and the report itself would become instrumental in finding the backing to make it happen.

Meanwhile, I was learning more about the zoo every day. Ellis had once been seen as a visionary, designing innovative enclosures, putting in disabled access on a difficult sloping site long before legislation required him to do so, and developing an aggressive outreach education program, one of the first of its kind in the country and now copied by almost every other zoo. But he had absolute, total control. There was no one to tell him when to stop. And with overinvestment in expensive infrastructure like the enormous restaurant (against advice, which he overruled), an expensive divorce, and other zoos learning, copying, and developing his techniques and continually changing their game while he began to grind to a halt, visitor numbers declined.

My life became a series of long phone calls to lawyers, real estate agents, bankers, family members, and Ellis. Every time I spoke to Ellis, I noticed, he inexorably steered the conversation toward conflict. We were frank with him. We didn't have the money to buy it yet, but we had assets of equal value, which we could borrow against or sell, if he could only hold on. "You'd think when someone offered to buy a place they'd at least have the money to do it," he said once, the type of observation that gave me an indication of why so many other sales had fallen through. Apart from anything else, Ellis was in the terrible position of having to sell his much-loved park, built largely with his own hands, the expression of his life's vision over the last forty years, so it was no wonder he was irascible. The only other bidder left was a developer wanting to turn it into a nursing home, and Ellis didn't want that. So, to his enormous credit, he agreed to wait for us.

In this tense situation, I was genuinely concerned for Peter Wearden, who had become the focus of Ellis's vexation, crystallized as the deliberate, Machiavellian architect of his downfall. It had all started with a routine inspection several years ago, which had concluded that the hand-painted signs on the animal enclosures were illegible and needed replacing. Ellis escorted the inspector from the park (some say at the end of a shotgun), and refused to carry out the directive. This activated a one-way process of head-on confrontation with the authorities, which escalated into many other areas over the years, and ultimately led to him handing in his zoo license in April 2006. When we'd visited that last time, after so many years of gradual decline, it felt like we'd been to the Heart of Darkness, to a place where a charismatic visionary had created an empire once teeming with life and promise, but where human frailties had ultimately been exposed by the environment, with terrible consequences. I telephoned Peter and told him of my concerns. It was not uncommon for council officials to be attacked in the course of their work, even occasionally killed, and Ellis was, in my opinion, a man with his back to the wall. The word *amok*, in Malay, describes a syndrome whereby someone feels they have received an intolerable insult that has ruined their life, and that the only way to redeem their status is to kill the perpetrator, or perpetrators. The amok syndrome is a universal phenomenon, just as likely to present itself in South Hams as in Malaysia or Southern California. And Ellis owned an elephant gun with a range of about three miles. "Oh, I'm not bothered about that." Peter laughed, with a bravery I doubt I would have shown in his position.

"He does seem very difficult to deal with," I said. "Is there anyone else it might be possible to talk to there?" His lawyer? Rob?

"Try Maureen, his sister," advised Peter. "She talks sense."

And so another vital piece fell into place for the acquisition of the park. Maureen was devoted to her brother, and on both tours of the house we had been shown a picture of her as a teenager falling out of the back of a stock car during a jump Ellis was performing (among other things he had been a stunt-car driver). She had worked outside the park in a hotel all her life, and understood the pressures of the outside world perhaps better than he did. I spoke to Maureen two or three times a day as we tried to piece together a plan that would save the park.

Another key person, without whom we would never have succeeded, was Mike Thomas. To get backing we needed a site survey, which would cost about three thousand pounds. But I knew that several (nine, in fact) such surveys had been commissioned recently, and was reluctant to pay for another. I asked Maureen if she knew of anyone of the recent potential buyers who might be prepared to sell us their survey. "Try Mike Thomas," she said. So I ended up pitching on the phone to a complete stranger that we were trying to buy the park and had heard he had commissioned a full site survey recently. "Go on," said a gravelly voice. I told him everything about our inexperience and lack of funds, surprised as I continued that he didn't put the phone down. "You can have the survey," he said at the end. "Where shall I send it?" This was the first of many generosities from Mike, whose reassuring voice often saw me through difficult times in the months ahead.

Mike was the former owner of Newquay Zoo, which he had turned from a run-down operation with 40,000 visitors a year to a thriving center of excellence with about 250,000 visitors, in the space of nine years. He knew what he was doing. His bid had foundered on the twin rocks of Ellis and Mike's business partner, but he wished the park well. More important, he had been appointed by Peter Wearden to oversee the dispersal of the animal collection to other zoos, should it be necessary. He was in daily contact with Rob, the holder of the DWA license, and Peter, and as a man on the inside could not have been better placed. His unswerving support and sound advice were absolutely pivotal for us in securing the park.

Weeks dragged on, and the main positive development— apart from the arrival of Nick Lindsay's report from ZSL, which gave a ringing endorsement to the park as a future enterprise— was that a cash buyer was found for my mum's house. But he was a cautious man, in no hurry, and any inclination that we desperately needed the money *right now* would have almost certainly reduced his bid. Bridging loans—those expensive, dangerous arrangements offered by commercial banks in the hope of snaffling all your assets in a year—were arranged, and fell through. Commercial mortgages, likewise, were offered and withdrawn. Several high-end banks let us down badly. Lloyds three times extended the hand of friendship and then, just as we were shaking it, pulled it away, put their thumb up to their nose, and gave it the full hand waggle. Very funny, guys. Private banks were similarly fickle. Perhaps eight banks altogether promised support in protracted negotiations on which we relied, and then we passed the good news on to the naturally keenly interested other side, and committed more funds on the basis of that. Then the offer would be withdrawn. Corporate managers were generally persuadable and good at giving you a 100 percent verbal agreement and a physical shake of the hand. But the backroom boys with the calculators and gray suits who constituted what were known as risk teams, invariably balked. Lawyers were also busy. At one point a six-acre paddock disappeared from the map of what was included in the price, which I made clear to Maureen was a deal breaker, and it reemerged.

For light relief at the end of a twelve-hour day of circular phone calls, we would watch the series *24*, boxed sets of which were making the rounds of the English mums in France. Kiefer Sutherland plays Jack Bauer, a maverick CTU (counterterrorism unit) agent who, over several episodes, always has to save the world in twenty-four hours, shown in real time an hour at a time. The ground shifts under his feet as he pursues, with total commitment, leads that turn out to be blind alleys. He is betrayed by his superiors, double agents, and miscellaneous villains, and faces new disasters with every tick of the clock. Allies become enemies, enemies become friends but then get killed; yet he somehow adapts and finds a new line to go for. I knew exactly how he felt. Every day there were impossible obstacles, which by the afternoon had been resolved and forgotten, in preparation for the next.

But the situation at the other end seemed far more desperate. Running costs—seven tigers, three lions, and six keepers to feed—continued without ticket sales to cover them, interest on debts stacked up, and creditors brushed up close with increasing frequency. Then, just as the buyer for my mum's house agreed to sign sooner rather than later, Maureen told me we had to begin paying running costs for the zoo in order to stop it going to the nursing-home developer. By now we were pretty committed, so Duncan and I melted credit cards to pay, by whatever means possible, £3,000 a week to keep our bid open. This was way beyond our means and could not last long, particularly for something that might not pay off. Luckily, Duncan conjured a donor—who wants to remain anonymous—who lent us £50,000, to use as a "semi-refundable deposit." This was good news, but obviously it needed to be paid back, win or lose, and the "lose" scenario didn't really have that contingency.

By agreeing to pay the semi-refundable deposit (we got half back if the sale fell through), we were now one of Ellis's creditors. We were going upriver to see Kurtz. We'd done the reconnaissance. Now we had to see if we could go all the way. All we had to remember was not to get out of the boat. Then, just as the sale of my mum's house was finally agreed, we had our worst moment. My brother Henry, who had been supportive of the venture at the beginning, suddenly lost his nerve and mounted a costly legal battle against the rest of the family. Henry was executor for my dad's half of the estate, so could delay the release of funds as he saw fit. He refused to be contacted except by letter sent through the post, which in a situation changing hourly was simply untenable for such a key player. Mum, Duncan, and I tried to go around and discuss it with him several times, but he wouldn't answer the door or phone. It was looking bad. We felt for Henry with whatever it was he was going through, but there was a bigger picture that every single other member of the family was in agreement on.

Finally, the whole family ended up on the doorstep of his expensive lawyers (paid for out of the estate), and after being kept waiting for three hours, persuaded them that this was Mum's wish and the wish of all the beneficiaries of my dad's will. We all wanted to buy the zoo.

Eventually Henry agreed, as long as we all signed a clause that we wouldn't sue him when it all went wrong, and each sibling took the full £50,000 they were entitled to under the Nil Rate Band legislation (the value of an estate that is not subject to inheritance tax). This meant that there wouldn't be enough to buy the zoo unless at least four of us gave the money straight back, which everyone but Henry instantly agreed to, though in order to do so we each had to seek independent legal advice first. This meant each of us finding another lawyer and paying for written evidence to show that we had been made aware of the risks, which was fun.

Also, instead of the zoo being bought in the name of a limited company, a business- and tax-efficient vehicle and the basis of all our months of negotiations, it had to be bought in Mum's name. And no one lends a seventy-six-year-old lady half a million pounds, however spry and adventurous she may be. Back of the envelope calculations revealed that if everything went according to plan, there would be enough money to buy the zoo, pay all the legal fees, and have £4,000 left over, equivalent to about ten days' running costs.

We leaped at it. Well, my two brothers, sister, and Mum did. Katherine had remained slightly bemused by the idea throughout the negotiations, partly because of the inherent uncertainty about whether we would get the zoo, but also because running a zoo had never featured very high on her to-do list. However, she thought about how much the children would enjoy it, she observed my enthusiasm, and investigated a role for herself doing graphics and money management. These were both well-honed skills from her days as an art director on glossy magazines, and once she was able to equate the whole thing to organizing a large, complicated ongoing photo shoot, she gave her cautious support. Now that it was becoming a reality, she knew what she had to do, and she was ready. The children, as you can imagine, were very enthusiastic, jumping up and down, clapping and squealing. I'm not sure they really believed it—but it was true.

3

The First Days

From the outset, we knew that it was going to be tough. Employ twenty staff members, when we had never employed staff before? Take care of two hundred wild and exotic animals? The house we had moved into was as run-down as the zoo over which it looked. Though once a grand, twelve-bedroom mansion, now its plumbing groaned, its paper peeled, its floorboards creaked—but it was home. Most people, especially at Mum's age, are looking to downsize their lives, but we were upsizing dramatically, into an utterly unfamiliar avenue of work, and the stakes were high. Everything, frankly, that my mum and dad had worked for over fifty years together was on the table. And still we needed more—half a million more—just to be able to take the chance that the zoo might be able to reopen, and that when it did, it would work. Normally this level of uncertainty over something so important would seem impossibly crazy, but the late legal challenge from our own side had forced our hand, leaving us uncertain, penniless, and paddling like mad to find some money. Yet, in the context of the last six months of negotiations, it simply seemed like just another bad but probably weatherable development.

We were also comforted by the fact that although we hadn't done anything like this before—and we didn't have a license to trade nor even a particular curator in mind (Suzy in Australia was having health problems, which put her out of the picture)—at least we owned the entire place outright. This, surely, stood us in good stead with creditors. Plus we had a whole £4,000 left over.

The meticulously researched business plan I had evolved with Jim—or, more accurately, Jim had put into spreadsheets based on his business knowledge and rumors I'd picked up from the twenty or so leading attractions in Devon—was now very much hypothetical. The urgent spending that was due to commence as we arrived was now delayed as we searched for new lenders, who circled again, sniffing with renewed interest, since, as holders of actual assets, we had lurched to a new status with their backroom boys.

As it turned out, the backroom boys remained less than impressed. We could hear their collective eyebrows creak up, releasing small puffs of dust, but the calculators were quickly deployed, and though some offers were tentatively made, all were swiftly withdrawn. This problem was going to catch up with us fast, so with phones glued to our ears, we set about trying to solve immediate crises on the ground without actually spending any money. In those first few days we walked in wonder around the park, meeting the animals, gathering information, marveling at the bears, wolves, lions, and tigers, getting to know the keepers, and grinning wildly over our new life.

The first time I met Kelly I got a surprise. As with Hannah, she was one of the two dedicated cat keepers who had stayed on against the odds to look after the animals, sometimes not being paid, and having to pay for vitamin supplements for the animals (and rudimentary sundries—like flashlight batteries and toilet paper) out of their own pockets. "Are you the new owner?" she asked, wide-eyed and intense, to which I replied I was one of them. "Can you please do something about the situation with these tigers?" I had no idea what situation Kelly was talking about, but she soon filled me in.

The top tiger enclosure is a moated range of 2,100 square meters called Tiger Rock, after the enormous Stonehenge-like boulder construction that is its centerpiece. It contained three tigers: Spar, at nineteen the elderly patriarch of the park; and two sisters, Tammy and Tasmin, ten and eleven. But only two tigers were ever out in the enclosure at any one time. This was because Spar, though old, was still a red-blooded male, and occasionally tried to mate with the two girls, even though his back legs were arthritic and wobbly and they were his granddaughters. Five years earlier, Tammy and Tasmin were given contraceptive injections to prevent inbreeding (and because Ellis was not allowed to breed tigers anymore, having recently been prosecuted for thirty-two counts of illegal tiger breeding). The unfortunate result of this hormonal change in the two sisters was that they suddenly hated each other and began to fight, and fighting tigers are very difficult to separate; it could only end in death. So, one of the sisters was always locked in the tiger house for twenty-four hours at a time while the other played fondly with her granddad. Then the other tiger would be locked away for twenty-four hours, allowing her sister a daylong taste of freedom. As Kelly explained this to me, she drew my attention to the arrhythmic banging coming from the tiger house, which I had assumed was some maintenance work. In fact it was Tammy, frustrated by her confinement in a two-by-three-meter (six-by-twelve-foot) cell, banging on the metal door to get out. Kelly was on the brink of tears as she told me that this had been going on for five years, causing enormous suffering to the tigers (and keepers), and making them much more dangerous to handle. "It's unacceptable in a modern zoo," Kelly ended, somewhat unnecessarily, as even an amateur like me could appreciate this. I immediately promised her that we would do whatever was necessary to rectify the situation, which turned out to be finding one of the warring sisters a new home. A new tiger enclosure was expensive and unfeasible (we already had two), and would have meant permanent isolation for one of the girls. I asked Kelly to research new homes for whichever tiger was most suitable to pass on, and walked away from the encounter amazed that such an ongoing systemic problem had not arisen in the negotiations to buy the zoo. On the bright side, it was a big improvement we could make for almost no cost, but it was one we hadn't been expecting, and it was worrying that we hadn't known about it before we bought the zoo. Why had Peter Wearden or Mike Thomas not told me about this? What else would emerge?

It was all the more surprising given that Peter and Mike had not been shy about throwing me in at the deep end with difficult animal-management decisions already. On the phone from France, probably about three months before we bought the park, Peter sprang something on me as the last bidder planning to run the place as a zoo. "What are you going to do about the two female jaguars?" he asked. Er, they're lovely. What's the problem? "The house fails to meet with industry standards and there is a serious concern about the possibility of an escape." Can't it be rebuilt, or refurbished? "It's been patched up too many times already, and rebuilding it with the animals in the enclosure is unfeasible. They have to be moved. If you're going to be the new owner, you have to decide now what you are going to do."

Standing barefoot in my hot, dusty, French barn office, looking out over sun-drenched vineyards throbbing with cicada song seven hundred miles away from this unfamiliar problem, I was taken aback. I wriggled for a bit, suggesting we rehouse them in the puma enclosure and move the less dangerous pumas else-where, desperately searching for a way of keeping these two gor-geous big cats on the site. Hand-reared from cubs, they were particularly responsive to humans, answered to their names and rubbed up against the wire like epic versions of domestic house cats. Sovereign, the male jaguar housed separately, only got on with one of the females, who could be tried with him, but the sis-ter cats were inseparable from birth and would pine for each other. As a keeper of cats (albeit domestic ones) since childhood, I understood the very real suffering this would cause, and instinc-tively shied away from that option.

In the end I realized that this was a test, and the correct re-sponse was to roll with it, however uncomfortable it felt. For the good of the animals, and in the interests of demonstrating a break from the past to the council, I asked Peter what he recom-mended. "Donate them permanently to another zoo as soon as you take over," he said. "Mike Thomas will organize it for you." I canvassed Mike and Rob, the head keeper currently responsi-ble for the jags, and they both said the same thing: To prevent the very real risk of an escape, we should donate them as soon as possible. With a very deep sigh, I eventually agreed. "That's the right answer," said Mike. "For that, you can probably get a cou-ple of those zebras you've been on about, some way down the line, when you're ready to receive them. And probably a breed-ing female for Sovereign later on." This I liked—spots for stripes—and it made me feel a little closer to the zoo world, knowing I had made a tough decision everyone approved of and was building credibility.

But with two prime big cats going, the Tammy/Tasmin ques-tion loomed large. In the first few days it also came out that a wolf and three of the seven vervet monkeys had also been ostra-cized by their groups and needed rehousing. Would we have any

animals left by the time we reopened? One well-meaning relative called to helpfully explain that I had made an elementary
blunder with the jaguars. "If you're going to run a zoo, it has to
have animals in it," she said. The sense of siege from all sides was
tightening, but I was sure that I'd made the right decision with
all the information available to me on the ground, and it only
made me more determined.

In these very early days a lot of time was spent clearing out
the house and grounds of junk, and burning it on a huge fire in
the yard. This was cathartic for us and the park as a whole, but
must have been hard for relatives of Ellis, like Rob, his grandson,
who had to help haul the now dilapidated furniture that he had
grown up with onto the pyre. I'd already agreed that Rob could
stay in the run-down cottage on site, and offered him anything
he wanted to salvage, but generally, he seemed relieved by the
process. Rob was extremely positive and helpful toward us.

But then, four days after we took over Dartmoor Wildlife
Park, while chatting with Rob about what to do with our surplus
stock, the unthinkable happened. In a catastrophic blunder, a junior keeper accidentally let one of the most dangerous animals on
the park, Sovereign, out of his enclosure. At about 5:30 PM I was
sitting with Rob in the kitchen when Duncan burst in, shouted,
"ONE OF THE BIG CATS IS OUT! THIS IS NOT A DRILL!" and
then ran off again. Now, Duncan doesn't normally shout or get
agitated, but here he was, clearly doing both. Rob disappeared like
a puff of smoke, and I knew he'd gone to get the guns and organize the staff's response. I sat for an increasingly surreal moment
and then decided that, as a director of a zoo, I probably ought to
go and see exactly what was going on. I started making my way
toward the part of the park where the big cats are kept. This was
one of the strangest moments of my life. All I knew was that a big
cat—a lion, a tiger?—was out, somewhere, and might be about

to come bounding around the corner like an energetic Tigger but not nearly so much fun. I saw a shovel and picked it up, but it felt like an anvil in my hand. What was the point? I thought, and dropped it, and began walking toward the sound of screaming. Was I about to see someone being eaten alive? I had images of someone still alive but fatally mauled, rib cage asunder, being consumed before a horrified audience. Then a car pulled up with Duncan and Rob in it. "GET IN THE CAR!" I was told, and gladly complied.

At the top tiger enclosure it was clear that the jaguar, Sovereign, was inside with a tiger, Tammy. Both animals were agitated and the keepers were shouting to discourage them from fighting. My first thought was relief that the animals were contained and no one was injured. I conferred with Rob, now backed up by his brother John armed with a high-powered rifle, and we began to build up a picture of what had happened. If the animals began fighting he would have to shoot one of them, and we decided it should be the tiger, because she was more dangerous and also the less-endangered animal, but he would fire a warning shot first to try to separate them. I asked that he only do this as an absolute last resort, as letting guns off would seriously up the ante for the assembled personnel, who at the moment were all tense but calm.

Suddenly the jaguar lunged at the tiger's hindquarters, and the tiger turned and swiped the jaguar's head, spinning him like a doll. At half her weight, Sovereign was instantly discouraged. From that point both animals stayed apart, encouraged by the coaxing of the keepers. But the tiger was reluctant to surrender her territory. Sovereign paced purposefully along the right-hand perimeter, tracking a keeper who was moving up and down the fence to keep his attention. Tammy took up a position on top of a rock and scowled and bellowed at Sovereign. Twenty minutes earlier I'd been having a nice cup of tea, and now I was witnessing an intense standoff that could only be ended by a dart from a gun. Unfortunately, the one in our gun room didn't work, and had never worked, despite being on the inventory as a working safety tool. We were only equipped to shoot to kill.

Soon the cat keeper Kelly ordered all available men to assemble along the bottom perimeter, and on command we shouted as loudly as we could at Tammy (she doesn't like men or shouting), while the cat keepers Kelly and Hannah called her to her house. All keepers, maintenance and ground staff, and even an IT expert, Tom, who'd been on a site visit to give us a quote and had been with Duncan up at the lion house, got caught up in the escape. Tom had a good bellow, as depicted on the TV series being filmed at this early time. A camera crew shadowing your every move can be a worrying thing, but we felt we had nothing to hide and, just to raise the stakes, I negotiated with Rob that the crew could leave the safety of their car and join us at the wall. The men commenced bellowing and the effect was immediate, like spraying Tammy with cold water. Her tail twitched, her ears flattened, and after a couple of minutes she cracked, jumped off the rock, and went into her house. There was an enormous sense of relief, but I called Mike Thomas and told him of my concerns. Although he was contained, Sovereign was not 100 percent secure because he was in an unfamiliar enclosure, and agitated enough to try something desperate. Mike agreed. "I've seen an ape jump forty feet when it was stressed," said Mike. "Which it's not supposed to be able to do. Luckily we caught her in the ladies' toilets." If Sovereign got out again, we were unlikely to be so lucky.

With all three tigers in, we decided the next obvious course of action was to try to lure Sovereign into the fourth tiger-house chamber, so that he really was contained. Unfortunately, this spare chamber was in disrepair, and was not secure. It needed lining with steel sheets and repairs to the slats on the floor, both tasks that could be carried out in-house in a few hours with materials and personnel on site, but the light was fading fast. And there was no light in the tiger house. Duncan stayed to oversee the refurbishment of the chamber, and I went off to try to buy some emergency lighting, with directions from the keepers to the nearest lighting emporium, in nearby Plympton. As I drove off into the dusk, I noticed some workmen on the main access road unloading transits with tools, but they waved me through and I thought little of it as I sped on in my quest.

After a couple of emergency U-turns I found a large garden center–cum–bric-a-brac emporium, selling myriad kitsch, but which had DIY and lighting sections. I sprinted up the stairs, grabbed an assistant, and asked for halogen floodlights. There was a long pause. Then, as if in slow motion, she said, "Well . . . I . . . think . . . we've . . . got . . . some fairy lights—" NO, no, no. Floodlights. Halogen floodlights, 500 watts. Completely different. Where would they be? As she drifted off to ask someone, I combed the lighting section again at emergency speed, eyes scanning systematically up and down the rows of frilly pink bedside lights, glass ladies holding a single bulb, and of course, fairy lights. I tried to broaden my mission statement; would any of this lighting detritus work as a compromise? I pictured our grizzled team working in a dank corridor with metal angle grinding machines, tigers in the next bay, and imagined their faces as I presented them with a Disney-character desk lamp. No.

And then I found it. In an unmarked box on a bottom shelf was a single exterior wall-mount halogen lamp, but no plug or cord. I grabbed it with both hands and shot down to the DIY section, past the emerging assistant, who was saying, "I'm sorry . . . but . . . we . . . haven't got—" It's okay. Got one. Thanks.

With no one around in DIY I found a plug and some cord, and finally raised an assistant to measure it out for me. It was taking too long, so I decided to take the whole roll. "I'll . . . have . . .

to . . . get . . . a price . . . for that . . . and Reg . . . is . . . on his . . . break . . ." Okay, measure it out and roll it back, quickly please, as I'm in a bit of a hurry. He got the idea and I was soon in the checkout line, restlessly shifting my weight and craning over the three people in front of me to see how long they were likely to take. Now, my tolerance for the dead time in checkout lines is minimal even when I'm not in a hurry. Over the years I have developed zazen breathing strategies, and trained myself not to focus on the inevitable sequence of minor ineptitudes that slow the line down and that could be avoided. But this wasn't working. I was in full emergency mode—a couple of hours before I was making life and death decisions for the first time in my life, there was a volatile big cat prowling around up the road in the wrong place, and it was going dark and I needed to complete this purchase so that we could continue working to get him contained. And this was not a proficient checkout. The cashier seemed bemused by her till, and everyone around me was moving as slowly as molasses. Then, as the first transaction finally meandered to its conclusion, the departing customer stepped smartly back into line and reached for a packet of marshmallows; "Ooh, I forgot these," he said. I very nearly cracked and went into manual override. My hand was twitching toward the bag of fatuous pink-and-white confectionery, and I fought the urge to snatch it away, throw it down, and demand to be processed next. But I didn't. Deep breaths. Eventually it was over, and I was speeding back through the darkness toward the emergency.

On the home straight an obstruction loomed in the head-lights. Unbelievably, the guys in the transits I'd passed earlier had closed the road between my leaving the park and returning. Concrete barriers were in place, and a sign said it would be closed for the next four months to build a power station. The diversion signs weren't up yet and my mental map of the area was scanty to say the least, and it was an additional half hour of getting lost down identical single track back lanes before I eventually tore up the drive and set off at a run for the top tiger enclosure.

A single 60-watt bulb had been rigged up, and I rapidly set about wiring up the lamp using the Leatherman tool on my belt. I've wired hundreds or so such lights in my time, but for this one I noticed that my hands were shaking slightly, and I wasn't doing a very good job. Doing it eighteen inches away from Spar, the elderly but massive and menacing Siberian tiger, didn't help. Sporting a small bloodied cut on his ear from an earlier encounter with Sovereign, Spar was naturally spooked by the afternoon's events, and didn't like unfamiliar people working in his house at strange hours of the day. He was as unsettled by my presence as I was by his, and kept up an impossibly low and ominous growl, occasionally reaching a crescendo with a roar and a short lunge at the welded mesh between us, his big orange eyes wide and locked onto me at all times. These noises travel right through you, resonating in your sternum and sending alarm signals to your primitive midbrain, which is already awash with worry, trying to suppress the distressing news from the eyes, and warning of massive predator proximity and imminent death. Perhaps understandably, in stripping the flex I cut too deeply into the wire, and the terminal connections were messy. But it would do.

When the light eventually flooded on, I confessed to Rob, our acting Health and Safety officer, that its wiring might have to be redone later under more conducive conditions. His drawn face smiled sympathetically and he said, "It'll do for now." John, Paul, and Rob worked quickly to finish the inside of the fourth chamber, with the unspoken efficiency of men who knew what they were doing and had worked together for a long time. Duncan had been exploring the dart-gun situation. The nearest zoo, Paignton, couldn't lend us theirs because it wasn't licensed for use off site.

Our park's previous reputation in recent years, and our much-heralded inexperience, can't have helped with their assessment of the situation, and this sense of fiasco, the public perception of it, and what it might mean for our prospects now had time to sink in.

Rob finally secured a dart gun and a licensed operator—Bob Lawrence, senior ranger at the Midlands Safari Park—who was prepared to travel immediately, but it was decided that because Sovereign was contained, Bob would come down in the morning. Opinion on the ground was, quite reasonably, that the cat was contained in an enclosure designed to contain big cats, and the risk was minimal. We began trying to lure him into the finished fourth cat chamber by placing meat just inside the door. Though the presence of meat had an almost chemical effect on this muscular predator, bringing him to the threshold several times, his instincts for self-preservation held him back. He was just too canny, and too spooked, to surrender his new territory in return for a free meal in a small box.

Mike advised that we keep a vigil from a car next to the enclosure, and at the first sign of trouble, such as Sovereign trying to climb the wire mesh fencing, call for the firearms. Rob went to sleep on the sofa in the keeper's cottage with the gun next to him, and I moved my mum's car as close as I could and settled down with a flask of coffee and a flashlight. Every half hour, Mike said, I should shine the light and make sure Sovereign was calm—and, most important, still there. "Don't get out of the car," warned Mike. "If he *has* got out, you won't hear him, and he'll be waiting outside the door." Unfortunately, as the evening wore on, sensible Sovereign decided it was safe to sit in the empty chamber, though he kept a watchful eye on anyone approaching the cat house. This meant I couldn't see him from the car, so every half hour I had to open the door, half expecting a hundred kilos of muscle, teeth, and claws to come bursting in. Then, when it didn't, I had to walk a few paces into the darkness, which may or may not have contained a large, angry jaguar, and shine the flashlight. My confidence grew with each sighting of the two reflective eyes staring back at me from the house. Sovereign wasn't going anywhere, and at 5 AM Duncan relieved me in the car. Bob Lawrence arrived at about 7:30 AM with the dart gun. With things hanging off his belt and an Indiana Jones hat, Bob was a very reassuring presence to have on site. If there was a rhino loose (not that we had any), you felt he could deal with it. The vet arrived with the necessary sedatives, and on the third attempt Sovereign was successfully darted, although unfortunately, it appeared, in the tip of his sheath, and he jumped around angrily until he began to slow down, scowling and prowling, glaring at us through the wire. You got the impression he was memorizing faces, so that if he got out again he'd know whom to punish for this indignity.

There was a danger that, drugged, Sovereign could fall into the moat and drown, so I sent for a ladder, mainly to use to push him out with, but I secretly decided that if it looked even remotely possible, I was prepared to climb down the ladder into the water to drag him out. But that wasn't necessary. Sovereign went down like a lamb, and we rushed into the enclosure to stretcher him out. Back in the safety of his own house—microscopically examined for flaws that could have contributed to the incident—Sovereign got a quick dental and general health check. It's not often you get to peer into this kind of animal's mouth without it being terminal, so the vet made good use of the time.

Carrying Sovereign on the stretcher, and touching him, was my first direct contact with any of the animals in our care, and it was an incredible initiation. One of the most beautiful as well as the most dangerous animals in the park, he required four men to be lifted. His exotic rosette markings watched you like eyes as he slept, his enormous power dormant, cloaked tight in a coat of deceptive beauty. As Bob Lawrence and the vet hauled this vast cat by the scruff like a sack of spuds clear of the welded mesh door, stepped out, and locked it behind them, there was a huge feeling of collective, euphoric relief. "The Code Red is now officially stood down," said Rob, which seemed to be his way of expressing it. But of course there were reports to write, and the precise timing of the incident would be critical, combed over by experts, and ultimately put into the public domain. Rob and Duncan interviewed Richard, the keeper responsible for not locking the shutter, several times, and eventually our statements and report were commended by the council as demonstrating that we had acted responsibly and professionally. We also got an endorsement of sorts from Tom, the bellowing IT consultant, who said as he left the next day that, "That was, without question, the most exciting site visit I have ever made."

But for now I was left with the horror, the horror of what it felt like to have Sovereign out, even for a second, and capable of anything. In buying the zoo, I had always thought that the concept of containment was a given—already fully under control, dealt with by experts using failsafe systems. The idea of one of these animals loose, marauding on the picnic area or going down into the village, brought to my chest a new residual level of adrenaline that has remained to this day. The prospect of a Code Red, what it feels like to be in one, and the potential consequences if it goes wrong, are there when I wake up, go to sleep, or walk about the park chatting to visitors. This level of responsibility has to be taken seriously. It's as though we're looking after guns with brains, a secured armory of assault rifles, but each one with a decision-making cortex and a series of escape plans. Sovereign had already successfully implemented one of his.

In fact, although we were exonerated by the subsequent council report, I think that our taking over the park may well have had something to do with that particular incident. Locking in the jaguar was always a two-person operation. It turned out that the junior keeper Richard had, according to his statement and in direct contradiction of an order to wait for the other keeper, "taken it upon myself to try to clean out the jag house on my own." This, he said, was in order to try to impress his line manager, Kelly, a notion that may or may not have been connected to the general sense of relief over the park's passing on to new owners and the animals' being saved. Of course, his line manager was not impressed, and nor was anyone else. That was Richard's last day. Clearly, zookeeping was not for him.

Another manifestation of this new atmosphere had struck me forcibly the day before, when I was talking to Rob out in the park. Suddenly his head spun around in the direction of an unfamiliar sound, with the urgency of a man used to having to react quickly to an escaped animal (an urgency I was soon to pick up). "What's that noise?" he said, and we listened intently. Then we realized it was laughter, coming from the staff room. Rob relaxed and his tired face cracked into a smile. "We haven't heard much of that round here for quite some time," he explained.

The day after his return to his house, Sovereign's anaesthetic had had time to fully wear off, and the fateful sliding gate was lifted. Sovereign, the epitome of stealth, committed his weight incrementally in ounces at a time across the threshold, slowly rolling forward on the lip of the sliding gate. His squat forelegs and bulky shoulders gradually bulged with the effort as he edged towards the outside—and food—ears flicking and eyes scanning the assembled personnel for signs of a dart gun or some other danger. "Sovereigngate," as it has never been known (and must never be in the future), was over, and the ramifications would begin. Our dream could have ended there but for the local council endorsement of our handling of the incident, which commented specifically on the professionalism of the keepers. I also was greatly impressed by their composure throughout a very difficult situation. I've never been in a war zone, but this definitely felt like seventeen hours on the front line, and with people you could rely on.

But as a family, our lack of euphoria was confirmed. In fact, a period of intense anxiety would ensue, as the grim living conditions, bad weather, and lack of money came home to roost. Dartmoor has one of the highest rainfalls in the country, and although we are in a slightly sheltered microclimate, the continual winter rain was an unwelcome contrast to southern France. My brother and I regressed to our roles from when we lived at home in the late 1970s, as we chopped wood for the big fireplace and jokingly did our best to undermine each other in front of our mum—"I picked you some of those flowers you like, Mum. Duncan didn't." "You only did it because you're adopted . . ."

But this became an increasingly difficult time. I swapped my role as negotiator for the zoo for the full-time job of fending off creditors and trying to raise money. We owned the place outright, but development funds of around £500,000 were urgently needed. The bankers and lawyers had a great time spinning it out, asking for yet more expensive surveys and more detailed predictions of our expenditures. "Can we have a specific breakdown of routine maintenance costs for August 2008?" asked the Royal Bank of Scotland, though that was more than eighteen months away, and utterly dependent on events between now and then. We'd made provision in our forecasts for £15,000 to be available for that month, but they wanted to know if it would be spent on paint, wood, tarmac, or lawn mowers. I could have made something up, but I told the truth: that there was no way of knowing the precise breakdown so far ahead, but that we had arrived at the £15,000 figure in consultation with other zoo and leisure facilities and with an on-site maintenance team (and relying on my experience in the building trade and as the author of The "Which?" Guide to Getting the Best from Your Builder), and that this amount would go a long way. But this became their sticking point, and after six or eight weeks of detailed and time-consuming negotiations—during which they sidelined other lenders with potential offers of reduced interest rates—they pulled out. So it was back to the beginning with someone else.

But all this was ahead of us. We still had the first week to get through, and the excitement hadn't stopped yet.

Driving Duncan and his business partner, Cameron, to the park from Plymouth station at about 11:30 PM on our seventh day, I slowed down just outside the village where the road narrows and is banked by stone walls, five to six feet high, backed by woodland. The problem seemed to be a deer in the headlights, leaning over the wall about twenty feet away, looking like it might be about to jump. Deer are silly enough to jump in front of a moving car, so I stopped to see what it was going to do. It was then that all three of us noticed simultaneously that this wasn't a deer. It was a puma. The human visual system works initially on a template system, drawing up a 2.5-dimensional sketch based on the available evidence, then finds a suitable template from a huge store in the brain, based on the individual's previous experience and the likelihood of a match within the context, which is why I'd thought the brown animal ahead was a deer. This is how many illusions and "tricks of the eye" work, eliciting the wrong template until your more detailed double-take sorts out what is going on. In this instance, the double-take took less than a couple of seconds, during which the harmless deer morphed into a muscle-bound, round-headed, cat-eared puma, including a distinctive gray dusting on the reddish coat, which deer do not have. "It's a ____ing puma," we all said, more or less together, and then it vanished into the woods. We burst out of the car and ran to the spot on the wall where it had been, in time to hear it padding off (not clip-clopping like a deer) into the undergrowth. We quickly ruled out trying to pursue it in the dark without flashlights over unfamiliar terrain, and raced back to check on our pumas. So soon after the jag escape, we were convinced of the much-talked-about possibility of animal rights saboteurs cutting the wire, like they had in the bottom deer enclosure six months before.

Heading straight into Code Red mode, we tore back to the park half a mile away and ran to the puma enclosure, armed with our biggest flashlight. And they were both there. But they were both definitely what we had just seen. There are many sightings of big cats out in the country, some cranks or mistakes—probably problems with their 2.5-D sketch—but some, I am now convinced, are real. Probably uniquely, we were in a position to confirm what we had seen with two examples of the exact same animal, because we had access to our own pumas.

The next day I told Rob, and Robin, who also acts as a volunteer of the Big Cat Sightings Society, expecting them to laugh in my face and mark me down as delusional. "Oh, there are pumas round here," said Robin. "You're lucky to have seen one so soon. I've been here seventeen years and only ever seen the tracks." Rob had more direct confirmation. "When I was living on site sixteen years ago, I opened the door of my caravan at about six in the morning and there sat a puma, watching me. I closed the door, opened it after a moment, and it was gone, but my God, it was definitely there." In captivity, pumas can live to sixteen, but in the wild the life expectancy is several years less. Judging from the size and condition of the one we saw compared to our more elderly females, this was a young male. Which means they were breeding. A credible groundsman a few miles away claims to have seem a mother and two cubs a few years ago, and all the sightings of big cats around Dartmoor are of pumas—not lynx, panthers, or servals, but pumas—a fact that we had no way of knowing before the evidence morphed into one before our eyes. Apparently the males come in off the moor to visit our females when they are in season (last sighting in the park was in 2003), giving us a unique opportunity to gather evidence on these elusive animals. Cats of a similar size, the European lynx, were once indigenous in the area, feeding on rabbits, rats, birds, and fallen lambs. They need never come into contact with humans, unless they decide to seek them out. This gave a whole new perspective to walking around the park at night. That Code Red feeling just wasn't going to go away. Never a dull moment in the zoo world, clearly.

4

The Lean Months

After that hectic first week, we had a little time to reflect. I spent my days on the phone standing on the spot in front of the house—a scene I had constantly imagined from France—with the walk-in enclosure sloping away in front of me down to the flamingo lake (albeit currently populated by only two elderly flamingos and a couple of rickety pelicans), and the tree line merging with the perfect rural English vista of rolling hills beyond, stretching like an organic quilt for five miles in all directions. The feel-good factor was—as I had told myself it would be—immense. But not quite enough to compensate for the content of those endless rounds of phone calls. Council officials, advisors, more lawyers, more banks and brokers, but above all, now, creditors, drip-fed my ear with increasingly bad news. With my feet planted firmly on my favorite spot, the thrilling and invigorating new zoo at my back, my mind raced ahead, scanning the possibilities and ever-decreasing options before me.

If my friends had been incredulous when I made the—admittedly surreal—announcement that my family and I were soon to live in and try to reinvigorate a run-down zoo, their bewilderment was nothing compared with our own in the first weeks we introduced ourselves to our new neighbors.

Back in France, the children hadn't quite believed it when I'd told them what I was trying to do. With the phone stuck to my ear I was constantly shushing them away, for six months, with the same refrain: "Quiet. Daddy's trying to buy a zoo." I could see that they thought I was deluded—silly Daddy makes us live in a barn in a foreign country and now he thinks he's buying a zoo. The trouble was, their naive insight struck a chord with a great many other people—pretty well everyone I knew—apart from my immediate family of brothers, sister, and mum. "I've got a really bad feeling about this zoo idea," one close friend had called to confide. "Are you still going on about that?" said another. "*Les tigres? Sacré bleu, c'est pas possible!*" said the entire village, in whose eyes my eccentricity had reached new heights. The trouble was that, having finally arrived, instead of being the smooth transition to spending our prearranged mortgage on clearly defined objectives, we were crisis managing on a shoestring.

But when the children eventually got there, after a couple of days of tiptoeing wide-eyed around the place, they adjusted much more quickly and fully than I did to the new life. Katherine brought them over from France after a couple of weeks, stayed for two days of huge culture shock (I already felt like a relatively old hand by this stage), and then had to leave for Italy for two weeks to be with her sister, Alice, who was having her first baby there. At first the children were tentative, and frankly a little afraid. I remember leaving them in the office playing with some remaindered stock toys while I cleared rubbish, and as I looked in at them through the window they were both square-mouthed, howling with fear at being left alone. It was quite a scary place at first, particularly for them. But they soon adapted.

When I decided to gently break the news to Milo that, one day, the park would be open and we'd have to share all this with hundreds of visitors, he replied, "Yes, but Daddy, they'll *pay* to come round." At last that naive insight was working *with* me.

My mum's two domestic cats, Pandit and Jow-jow, big black Bengals imported from Surrey, however, took much longer to see the wonder in our new life. Could it be the howling of wolves that troubled them? The bellowing of Solomon, our huge African lion, whose roar has been known to strike fear into golfers happily playing their course over two miles away? Or perhaps it was the time that they jumped up on a wall to discover the slobbering faces of three big brown bears staring back? Exploding into puff-ball parodies of frightened cats, they shot off back to the house at full speed.

Duncan, who had brought the cats down in his car, said that their first sighting of an ostrich was a unique opportunity to watch a process firsthand: their small, complacent brains burst with an overload of new stimuli as they desperately tried to adjust to the new concept of a bird bigger than a man. "Their necks stretched out as far as I've ever seen them go, and they darted their heads from side to side urgently scanning for as much information as they could gather from inside the car," said Duncan. "I sat with them for a while to let them get used to it, but they were still just as agitated twenty minutes later, when I took them into the house." The twenty or so peacocks who roam the grounds presented another psychological problem for the cats, who quickly developed a tactic of total denial of the existence of all these unsettlingly large and confident examples of a class of creatures they had only ever known as prey.

Of all the animals, my favorites initially became the three hand-reared Siberian tigers, Blotch, Stripe, and big Vlad, a male, and at more than three hundred kilos one of the biggest cats in the country. As I went around the back of the house in their enclosure for the first time, all three came up to try to cadge a stroke through the fence. No chance!

Tigers don't growl or roar, they *chuff*, which is a noise that sounds a bit like blowing a raspberry using just your top lip. But if you chuff at them, they chuff back, and having a three-hundred-kilo cat a foot away trying to be friendly is a uniquely uplifting experience.

For Milo and Ella, it was the otters that captured their imagination. Quickly they became smitten with the creatures, who make the most ridiculous squeaky-toy noises whenever you go past. This, naturally, elicited equally high-pitched squeals of delight from the children, who jumped up and down with glee until the otters realized they didn't have any food and scampered away. Sometimes the children do help feed them, but it's hard to fit in with the routines, which are varied to prevent the animals from habituating. The ferrets, Fidget and Wiggle, however, fit around the children. Katy, our first education officer, was getting them used to being handled, and so several times a week she fitted them with dinky little ferret harnesses and walked them around the park with Milo and Ella.

But it was standing on my favorite spot looking out across the valley in the first few days that I began to home in on the smell. A terrible odor hung over the park, the smell of rotting carcasses, which I recognized from occasionally helping drag them out of enclosures. Operating with a "skeleton crew" for so long, the amount of old bones in with the carnivores on the park had accumulated so that every enclosure was littered with rib cages, hooves, and miscellaneous bits of fur and skin, which it seemed were the root of the problem. Decomposing vegetable matter and uncleaned feces from the herbivores surely didn't help, but in fact the source was more systemic. It was the offal bins.

For food for the carnivores, the park relies on fallen stock—calves culled by local farmers, stillborn lambs, horses that have been hit by cars—brought to us and often prepared by the local "knacker" man, Andy Goatman, in our "meat room." This is basically a concrete loading bay with a sink, backing onto a walk-in deep freezer. The carcasses are stripped expertly by Andy, often assisted by butter-wouldn't-melt-in-their-mouths cat keepers Hannah and Kelly. To see these two mild-mannered, animal-loving girls straddling a giant carcass, boot-deep in entrails, brandishing big, bloodied knives and cheerfully chatting as they shuffle a horse's head into a freezer bin, was to understand fully that we had entered into a different world.

The bits that can't be fed to the animals—intestines, spines, and general entrails—are classed as Type I Matter and stored in offal bins, three large stainless steel hoppers, which are collected weekly and incinerated by a local licensed firm. Unfortunately, they hadn't been paid for quite some time, and wouldn't even pick up the phone to us without cash up front. The last time the bins were emptied was six weeks before we arrived, and the stench emanating from them was all pervading. Worse, for Hannah and Kelly, and everyone else who had to work in the yard, were the maggots. These writhing white grubs spilled out in a self-dissipating arc around the bins, crawling off toward the decaying matter around the gullies. Opening the lids of the bins, which I did a few times while helping to load them, facilitated the distribution of these maggots and opened up a world that Dante would have been proud to conjure. Empty skulls swam in a blue-gray fetid mush swarming with larvae, while the stench entered your bones. The keepers' work in these circumstances was truly heroic, though having gradually acclimatized over several years they wore their burden lightly. "This is nothing. It's much worse in the summer," John reassured me. Our flimsy domestic-pressure washer was, gratefully, deployed, but an industrial version was added to our wish list of essential but unaffordable machinery.

The dampness didn't help, coming up through the floor of the house via an ancient well—the ancient hand pump for which was now, sadly, defunct—to form mini-lakes on the worn topography of the stone floors. Many feet over several centuries had eroded the stones along the well-used pathways, and scuffed off the softer deposits to create valleys and dips, which now became tributaries and lakes in our living area. Water, and the effects of it, was everywhere. Overflowing cracked gutters, filled with years of mulch from overhanging trees, spread dampness into the walls. Mildew and algae blanketed everything outside the house with a dank frosting of green grime, symbolizing, and also actually indicating, profound decay.

And then there were the rats. "A plague of rats" would not be an overstatement. Everywhere you looked, even in daylight, big fat, gray rats scurried out of sight, and sometimes, arrogantly, didn't even bother. Right in front of your eyes they would dart into an enclosure and steal the food left out for the monkeys. Satisfyingly, these intruders received a terrible revenge exacted upon them by one or two of the enclosed animals, particularly Basil, the coatimundi (an amiable South American climbing animal related to the raccoon), whose powerful omnivorous jaws specialized in cracking the skulls of rats unfortunate enough to get caught in them. But this was an imperfect solution to the infestation. Rats carry disease, and also may be poisoned, if not by us perhaps by a neighboring farm. A few years previously an otter had died from eating a poisoned rat, so we had to tackle the problem carefully. We got quotes from three different pest-control firms, offering three different methods of gassing and poisoning, but the sheer scale of our problem—at least forty well-established nests over thirty acres, with a constant supply of food—was prohibitively expensive to address. Nine thousand pounds was the bottom line for the most thorough and exotic-animal-friendly method, and this was money we simply didn't have.

Peter Wearden and others regularly reminded me that eradicating the rats was an urgent requirement for getting our zoo license. But they didn't have to. I like all animals, including rats, particularly the ones in pet shops or those I worked with at university, studying social learning for chocolate rewards. Lab rats—at least the ones not exposed to vivisectionists—generally lead a happy and fulfilling life solving problems for rewards, and die with a substantially thicker cortex than their sewer-dwelling brethren. But wild rats give me the shudders. In my first encounter, in a flat in Peckham, I was filled with horror on discovering a big, brown, plague-infested rodent in a kitchen cupboard. And here they were again: in the kitchen, running over my mum's hand on the stairs one night, and even once jumping onto her bed. Luckily, Mum's cats, Pandit and Jow-jow, were also on the bed at the time, and the resulting commotion woke the entire household.

But I doubt they caught it. Those two stupid cats were nuzzling my legs one night as I moved in on some rustling emanating from a lower kitchen cupboard. With two feline predators at my feet I felt sure that if I flushed out a rat, they would catch it. Species-typical pest control. But it didn't work out like that. I crept stealthily in stocking feet on the hard-tiled floor, positioned myself carefully by the door, tried to attract the attention of the swirling, purring cats without alerting the rat, and then snapped the door open. The rat shot out and glanced off my leg, just as the blissfully oblivious, moronic, purring brother cats made another eyes-shut circumnavigation of my shins. It bolted under the dishwasher (which didn't work due to the low water pressure), at least revealing one of their entry points, a circular hole drilled through the two-and-a-half-foot-thick granite wall to accommodate a flue. John blocked this off with some balled-up chicken wire, but the rats still occasionally came into the house, and the effect was depressing. With systemic plumbing problems, sporadic electricity, disapproving friends and relatives, creditors, no money, responsibility for endangered animals and keepers' jobs, filth, decay and the smell of death wafting through the grim weather, the rat infestation probably completed the circle of psychological siege. It's fair to say that those first weeks passed like a dream. A very strange dream filled with fighting monkeys, severed heads, and carrion shipped in from local farms—but a dream nevertheless.

But it wasn't all bad news. For a start, we had the park. We'd finally overcome all the obstacles, seen and unforeseen, that had stood between us and this (with hindsight) slightly bizarre objective. And for once, Donald Rumsfeld, in the news at the time over the Iraq war, made sense to me: "As we know," he said, famously, "there are known knowns—things we know we know. We also know there are known unknowns—things we know we don't know. But there are also unknown unknowns—things we don't know we don't know." I knew exactly what he meant, and so far, we had navigated our known and unknown unknowns successfully. I only hoped that our strategy of sending a light force into a difficult operational area went better than his.

In addition, we had got the park against odds absolutely

stacked against us, against the "better judgment" and expectation of almost everyone involved. But this feeling was nothing compared with the invigorating thrill of actually walking around the park itself. The huge trees were sheathed with lush moss and ancient lichens that could only grow in an environment with good air quality (and high rainfall), and this pure, clean air filled our nostrils and lungs (when the wind was blowing the stench of death the other way) like a long-lost antidote to urbanism and stress.

I felt myself really coming alive as I moved around this—yes—species-typical environment for Homo sapiens. Merely showing a picture of a tree to an accountant in an office block has a small but measurable effect in reducing his or her blood pressure. Actually moving about among trees soothes us far more deeply.

Howard Frumkin is a professor of Environmental and Occupational Health at the Rollins School of Public Health, in Atlanta, and in between advising local governments on the use of public spaces, Frumkin researches the effect that the natural environment has on us. And in meta-analyses of countless studies, Frumkin has found that the natural world has a measurable beneficial effect on human physical and mental health. Prisoners in cells facing a prison courtyard, for instance, have 24 percent more sick visits than those in cells with a view over farmland. Postoperative patients with a view of trees need less pain medication than patients facing a brick wall, and were discharged one day earlier.

This all stems from the Pulitzer Prize–winning scientist Professor E. O. Wilson, founder of sociobiology and general god of evolutionary thinking. Wilson's "Biophilia Hypothesis" suggests that as a species we feel reassured in an environment that the animal within us recognizes. "It should come as no great surprise to find that Homo sapiens at least still feels an innate preference for the natural environment that cradled us," says Wilson. Over the last few hundred thousand years this environment has mainly been areas of sparse woodland, backing onto savannah, which has probably hardwired us with a preference for this particular kind of setting, the one we "grew up" with. "Early humans found that places with open views offered better opportunities to find food and avoid predators," says Frumkin. "But they needed water to survive and attract prey, and groups of trees for protection. Research has shown that people today, given the choice, prefer landscapes that look like this scenario."

That was now our scenario. Open spaces, groups of trees, watering holes stocked with exotic beasts. By some amazing coincidence, it turns out that almost all urban parks contain precisely the ratio of trees to shrubs to grass as the African grasslands of our ancestry. Big trees nearby, a scattering of shrubs, and open grassland into the distance, with occasional lakes thrown in for good measure. With some small part of your brain you are looking out for deer on the horizon, or a saber-toothed tiger amongst the trees—no wonder it heightens mental alertness.

The most amazing thing about our new environment of trees, open spaces, and lakes was that we actually did have tigers, lions, and wolves peeping through the foliage at us, giving us precisely that mix our ancestors grew up in. To be responsible for this uniquely intellectually, physically, and even spiritually invigorating environment—plus fulfill a mission to open it up and share it with the public for educational and conservation purposes (and get a free lunch in our own restaurant when it opened, as part of the deal)—seemed like a utopian quest.

And so we began to get to know our individual animals. Ronnie the Brazilian tapir seemed a good place to start. Ronnie is like a big pig, with the aforementioned wibbly nose, and while technically regarded as a Class 1 dangerous animal—the same category as a lion—is a huge softy. Keepers showed me photographs of other keepers from around the world who had been killed by these deceptively amiable creatures. *Tapir* means "strong" in Indonesian, and though usually placid, tapirs have a reputation for being able to power through chain-link fences as if they weren't there. This ability stems from their defense strategy against their major predator, the jaguar, who hunt them by dropping from the trees and hanging onto the backs of their necks. Evolution has furnished the tapir with a large gristle-filled scruff to absorb this bite, and also a propensity to charge forward through anything in its path in order to reach water to shake the jaguar off. Now, jaguars can also swim, so I have no idea how this strategy eventually plays out, but I suppose trying to fight jaguars on dry land has to be worse. Perhaps Ronnie, should Sovereign ever get out again and decide to come for him, was planning to crash through his fence to the emu lake and use his mini-trunk as a snorkel.

My first lengthy encounter with Ronnie was to help check his eyes for conjunctivitis, which he definitely had. Expensive medication from the vet—to whom we were already indebted by several thousand pounds—was a possibility, but so was bathing his eyes in a mild saltwater solution, something I had done countless times over many years with cats, dogs, and children, with equally effective results. The difference was that none of those creatures could suddenly decide to kill me if they didn't like it. But Ronnie was a pussycat. After we slipped him a few bananas and cooed to him in that way he seemed to elicit, Ronnie went along with his treatment stoically, even though he didn't like it, blinking and holding his head upright until I'd sponged the gunk from his eyes and expunged the traces around them. The trick, I learned, was to scratch him on the side of the neck so that he turned his head to the side, or—and this is a secret—to scratch his bum until he sat down.

Up close, Ronnie reminded me of a Staffordshire bull terrier, Jasper, I'd had for fifteen years: strong and solid but hopelessly soppy. Jasper was incontrovertibly and irrefutably gay. Early on in his adulthood he pushed past a bitch in heat to mount one of her male pups from a previous litter, and thereafter demonstrated a lifelong inclination as a "friend of Dorothy." Ronnie minced around his enclosure, which at the time was a narrow strip of almost entirely churned mud, with periodic access to the enclosure below, which contained a lake where he liked to defecate and mingle with the emus. As an ungulate—one of the cloven-hoofed persuasion—Ronnie didn't like treading in mud, which got stuck between his toes (Jasper was the same with snow, and would come limping up to me, paws packed with ice, which, once cleared, would send him speeding on his way again). Ronnie didn't have that option, and his narrow strip of an enclosure made it uncomfortable for him to walk around pretty well anywhere, except the hard earth surrounding his meager house. Even a trip down to the emu lake, which he was allowed every now and then by means of a gate at the bottom of his enclosure, was spoiled for him by the mud on the way there and back. I resolved straight away that we would give Ronnie permanent access to the lake, though this would require planning permission and relatively expensive new posts and fencing, and was a longer-term solution. Meanwhile, however, a simple answer was to dismantle the fence into the adjacent enclosure, which contained six miniature muntjac deer and was roughly twice the size of Ronnie's. These small deer were approachable and friendly, and could be left to roam the public access walk-in enclosure (containing the flamingo and pelican lake), which at the time was populated with a great gaggle of wild geese, strutting Bantam cockerels, and guinea fowl, who milled noisily, sticking roughly to their ethnic groups within the overall swarming population.

I asked Rob and John what they thought of this idea and they said they'd been waiting to do it for years, and also to take the fence away from the adjacent epic turkey oak tree to increase the size of the walk-in by a similar amount. This became a common theme: thinking of an innovation and finding that it was already on a wish list but that nobody had suggested it. This was basically because none of the seven staff we had inherited were used to being consulted—quite the reverse, in fact: they seem to have been trained to keep their mouths shut. I repeatedly reiterated that we were all ears, but this kind of cultural shift, naturally, takes time to sink in.

When Ronnie was let back into his new, triple-size enclosure, he tiptoed around exploring everything tentatively with his highly motile hooter. He seemed delighted, almost overawed, and it was a lovely feeling to have been able to implement such a simple but beneficial innovation. With fewer fences, the whole bottom area of the park looked better too.

Ronnie's one mishap was when he urinated on a newly positioned strand of electric fence, receiving about seven thousand volts (at a very low current) up the stream and probably into his bladder, via his most sensitive organ. The poor bloke apparently hopped and bucked around his paddock for half a morning, but he learned well from his mistake, as he has never peed incautiously near the fence again. In time we would take down the bottom fence and let him have permanent access to the flamingo lake, which would give him an enclosure many times the size of the industry standard laid down by BIAZA (the British and Irish Association of Zoos and Aquaria, formerly the Zoo Federation) for tapirs. Then we could start thinking about getting him a breeding female—or, if my animal gaydar was at all reliable, a boyfriend.

The subject of gay animals was one I had raised tentatively from the start, even with Nick Lindsay as we did our first walk around, and with Peter Wearden and Mike Thomas as I'd discussed our plans for the zoo in the early days. I'd read about a zoo in Holland that exclusively exhibited gay animals, and a recent exhibition at a museum in Oslo claims to have identified 1,500 species where homosexuality was clearly apparent—some opportunistic, like the notoriously randy (and highly intelligent) bonobo chimpanzee and bottlenose dolphin, while many others pair for life. Darwinian evolutionary theory has had difficulty with the topic of homosexuality, and from a sociobiological perspective it seems hard to explain. This apparent void has left the far-right homophobes and various religious extremists to be able to declare that it is a "crime against nature and God." In fact, theorists have built a compelling argument that a proportion of gay adults in a population—roughly one in seven humans, and about one in ten penguins, for instance—actually helps with group security and child rearing, because nonreproductive adults bolster the breeding efforts of the group as a whole. Two gay male flamingos, for instance, have been shown to be able to protect a larger territory and raise more successful chicks (albeit from pilfered eggs) than a heterosexual pair. This raises a tricky possibility of group, rather than "selfish gene," selection, but what is undeniable is that homosexuality exists almost universally across the animal kingdom. Having lived with a gay dog for fifteen years, over the course of which I met many owners of other gay dogs (roughly 5 to 10 percent of the randomly selected canine population of London parks), I am absolutely convinced that homosexuality has at the very least a strong genetic component, is perfectly natural, and nothing to get excited about. Unless you're gay, of course—or a homophobe.

I was encouraged that my proposals for some gay animal exhibits, for educational purposes, were listened to politely by all the zoo professionals I spoke to, including our own keepers, and not dismissed out of hand, though a bemused smirk often greeted them. But nobody said it couldn't or shouldn't be done, and several people were actively encouraging. I think they thought that if you're crazy enough to want to buy a zoo, you're going to have weird ideas. But as long as the result was educating the public about the natural world, it was okay.

Coco was another character who took me by surprise. Coco is a caracara, a large bird of prey with the coloring of a golden eagle. She stands majestically, almost haughtily, and her call is a rapid-fire staccato version of the laughing kookaburra, but delivered with an extraordinary head flip, in which her cranium jerks backward suddenly through 180 degrees until her throat is exposed to the sky and her eyes are momentarily upside down and pointing backward. The evolutionary origins of this call are hard to discern, other than that it throws the sound out in an arc above her, perhaps reaching a wider audience. All I knew was that it made my neck ache to watch her do it.

But according to a visiting falconer, Coco was probably the most intelligent bird in the park; she was once used in the falconry display, but quickly learned that by ignoring her lure and flying over to the restaurant, she could make a better living cadging french fries and sausages. Obviously, this brought her display career to a premature conclusion, but she remains a socialized and charming presence.

The falconer showed me that if you called her over she would come to the wire and bow her head to be stroked at the back of her skull. I wasn't surprised that her neck needed soothing with her surely spinally maladaptive call, but I was surprised at just how friendly and personable she was. Birds registered pretty low on my snooty animal intelligence perspective, though crows and some other birds have demonstrated problem-solving abilities and tool use that rivals the higher primates. This seems to be because they can deploy their entire brains onto a single problem, but the taxonomy of birds—which are among the few modern descendants of dinosaurs, and the eponymous inspirers of the term *birdbrain*—had previously been of little interest to me. Peacocks are definitely named for their brain size, and chickens and herbivorous birds do seem to be cursed (or blessed) with a very limited outlook on the world. But Coco has personality, and as Samuel L. Jackson said in *Pulp Fiction*, "Personality goes a long way."

Coco's dinosaur heritage is paradoxically coming home to roost, as caracaras, though effortless flyers, tend to hunt their prey by chasing them on the ground, like a mini T. rex, which is why her talons are not as pronounced as an owl's or an eagle's, who hunt by seizing from above. Coco spends a lot of time walking on the ground in her aviary, with delicate rather than overtly predatory feet. But her beak is formidable, curved like an Arabian dagger and designed for plunging into the vital parts of other animals. She is a raptor, pure and simple, and if you happen to be a small ground-foraging animal, she'll get you if you stray onto her patch. I once found her with a severed robin in her beak, chatting animatedly about it and looking pretty wild, but she still came over for a stroke. It was disconcerting venturing a digit through the wire to stroke a bird with bloodied evidence dangling from her beak; should she misinterpret the stimulus, I could be down to nine. "Coco's another one where you don't have to worry about rats getting in," said Kelly with some pride. "They don't come out again." Coco also tracks small children who run up and down in front of her, including my four-year-old Ella. At first I thought this was some display of affinity, but, learning more about Coco, Ella probably triggers an interest less benign.

Kevin also impressed me with an apparent personality where I had expected none. Kevin is a five-foot red-tailed boa constrictor whom we had moved from the unheated reptile house into the shop, which is heated and located in between the offices and the restaurant. Walking past him every day, I noticed he seemed depressed, if that's not too anthropomorphic. He was certainly lackluster, spending all his time curled up in his water bowl. Once, while on hold on the phone with some infernal institution, I asked Robin—the gray-ponytailed graphic designer, one of the seven staff we had inherited with the park—if I could get him out. He gladly obliged, and gave me a quick course in how to handle him. "Hold him gently but firmly, be assertive but don't make any sudden movements. Constrictors don't usually bite, but if they do he'll give you plenty of warning first, darting his head around. If he starts to do that, just stay still, and then pop him back in the vivarium." As Robin hung Kevin over my shoulder and free arm and made sure I wasn't going to panic— this was the first time I had ever touched a snake—the switchboard on the other end of the phone put me through. "And try not to let him get round your neck," said Robin over his shoulder as he went back to his work. So I began a slightly surreal conversation with someone no doubt suited and sitting at a desk, while I was wandering around draped in a snake whose muscular coils had instantly come to life. Kevin's head naturally probed for the dark warm folds inside my coat, but he also responded well—surprisingly well, I thought, for a reptile—to having his chin stroked.

The call finished, I continued playing with Kevin, warming him up under my coat and marveling at the symmetrical perfection of his head and his pure strength as he gripped my arm. Kevin is strong enough to stop the circulation in your hand, turning it purple, and if your hands were tied there is no doubt he could choke you to death. But he doesn't want to. He probably thought I was a tree, his natural habitat in the Amazon from which he hangs by his red tail and drops onto his prey (what with jaguars and boa constrictors falling from the trees, it sounds like the best place to look in the Amazon is up). Kevin's responsiveness to handling and stroking suggested he thought I was at least a very friendly tree. And I was surprised that after our twenty-minute encounter I felt elated for the rest of the day.

This could just have been the novelty of the experience, or perhaps an echo of Professor E. O. Wilson's biophilia, our positive physiological response to nature. I preferred to think that it was the latter. DNA analysis suggests that dogs broke off from wolves 130,000 years ago, which means they were adapting to human society long before we settled down and began practicing agriculture. During this time dogs perfected that big-eyed baleful look to help them get away with chewing up our slippers and manipulating us into giving them strokes and treats. This is something Kevin's locked features could not do, but we have certainly spent a formative part of our evolution surrounded by responsive, and not so responsive, animals, and I was delighted that this warm feeling Kevin had given me was something we would one day be sharing with the public. Kevin was part of the

Animal Encounters program, Robin informed me, and needed socializing as much as possible, to get him used to being handled by the children and adults, who, ideally, would be flocking around him at Easter, when we were due to open. I was only too happy to oblige, and regularly took Kevin over to the house to warm him in front of the fire—in the only warm room in the house—and introduced him to visiting friends and relatives. I liked this job.

Our two biggest snakes, both pythons over ten feet long, needed at least two people to handle them, because they could definitely get the better of you. I made several attempts to organize a session with these snakes, but in the fraught and hectic first few weeks, interrupting the keepers' routines too much seemed frivolous. Eventually, both snakes were given away to Paignton Zoo, thirty miles away and a pillar of the zoological community. Having just built a new reptile display, they had nothing to put in it and were grateful for our donation, which also demonstrated goodwill on our part and may help to facilitate future reciprocity. I secretly have my eye on some of their expensive flamingos (straight or gay). Scales for feathers.

The big pythons had to go because we had decided to turn the sparse, cold reptile house into a workshop, and the snakes, along with two four-foot iguanas, lived there in four large built-in vivariums that could not be moved. The concrete floor of the building and big double doors made it ideal for the large-scale heavy work that would be required to get the zoo back on its feet, and another barn, insulated and with a dirt floor ripe for installing under-floor heating, was earmarked as a future reptile house. When we had the money.

The existing workshop was simply unworkable. A cinder-block shack with a leaking, rusted corrugated iron roof, it was strewn with miscellaneous clutter, from elderly broken power tools to coils of rusted wire, and many, many other objects that were impossible to identify beneath what seemed like centuries of grime, the kind of rich, brown, oil-based filth you get beside railway tracks. And it was rat infested. A glance inside usually revealed an arrogant rodent or two, safe in the knowledge that before you could clamber over the detritus to get to them, they could be gone, having ducked into the impromptu tunnels and nooks among the debris that had lain long enough to shelter generations of foragers, and providing an important base camp for raids on the nearby animal food preparation room. The only tool in the whole workshop that actually worked was an old but serviceable bench-mounted angle grinder, though the lack of electrical supply and the position of the grinder, at the far end of the room across yards of grimy, rusting clutter, made it utterly impossible to use.

With relish we gave instructions to clean out the room and relocate the workshop to the reptile house, while relocating the few reptiles to the warmth of the shop. "That's a bloody good idea," said John, who was now our eighth member of staff. "I've always thought that room would make a good workshop." A grandson of Ellis Daw, John had been introduced to us by Rob as someone who could fix the floor in the front kitchen of the house. This was the room in which Ellis had for several decades stored his buckets of mackerel and chicks for the herons and jackdaws he fed in the mornings, the leakage from which had permeated the joists from the entrance to the back of the room. That was why it stank so badly, but the floor was also unsafe, so Duncan immediately commissioned John to rip out the floor, burn it, and replace it with new, fresh, sweet-smelling wood—which he did within a week. John was a tall, muscular, grinning man of thirty, whose four upper front teeth were missing and replaced by a dental plate with teeth much shorter than the originals, and whose canines were unusually long and pointed. This gave him a striking vampiric appearance, abetted by his posture, which is unusually erect. First encountering John in the dank mist with wolves howling in the background, I seriously questioned what kind of environment I had brought my children into.

But John turned out to be one of the most skilled, loyal, and levelheaded employees we could have asked for in those early days, able to do plumbing, welding, tree work, and carpentry, and also licensed for firearms, an invaluable skill on the park, and one we were to draw on several times in the coming months. When Rob first put him forward, he said to me, eyes down, "I'll tell you now, because you're bound to find out, that John's my half-brother." I had no problem with this, but it all added to the atmosphere of secrecy, with whisperings in the village about "things that had happened" at the park in the past, and the general sense that we had moved into the Wicker Man's backyard.

John, Rob, and Paul, Ellis's son-in-law, set about clearing out the old reptile house and converting it into a workshop. Again, a big practical change that also had the benefit of being cheap. The loft above was, as most places in the park, crammed with clutter (and rats), but some of it was salvageable. Old agricultural tools were put to one side and two huge workbenches were to be extricated and lowered down, when a path had been cleared for them. I asked John how he was anticipating bringing these enormous objects to ground level, and he held up a massive pulley wheel in one hand. "Rig this up to the roof joists, then call for some muscle," he said. As a reasonably able-bodied person, I waited for the call, but it never came. The next time I popped my head around the door, the benches were down and already coated with tin sheeting, ready for work. I clearly didn't count as muscle, which, as a lifelong hands-on sort of person, came as a bit of a shock. I was a director now, and it took a bit of getting used to. A small shantytown of sheds and cages containing rabbits and two ferrets was also cleared and the animals relocated around the park. And suddenly we had a workshop and a clear access yard. All we needed now were some tools.

Duncan masterminded the conversion of the old workshop into a vegetable storeroom. Every day Paul went off in the van to Tesco and Sainsbury's, collecting past-the-sell-by-date fruit and vegetables in sufficient quantities to reliably feed every herbivore in the zoo. Previously the produce had been stored alongside the meat preparation area, where fallen calves, horses, and occasional sheep were dismembered by Andy Goatman, the knacker man, and Hannah and Kelly, the cat keepers. The problem was that this is illegal, under the secretary of state's guidelines for modern zoos. Total separation between meat and vegetables is essential, to minimize the risk of cross-contamination, and a site visit from the environmental health officer, or worse, an inspector from DEFRA could close us down before we started. Duncan went into the legislation in detail, guided by Andy, whose encyclopedic knowledge of legislation around his trade has proved invaluable many times. A local builder repaired the roof with plastic sheeting at cost, and when the room was finally emptied, scrubbed, rewired, and illuminated, it looked huge. The back wall, it turned out, was made from local stone. Rob was impressed. "I haven't seen that wall since I was a little kid," he said. The process of accumulation of rubbish and subsequent general decline at the park had been long and gradual. But now we were turning back the tide. It was fantastic to be part of it.

The children were almost immediately absorbed into the local school, as one of our neighbors who had us over for drinks turned out to be one of the governors. They instantly took to the school, which had twenty-seven pupils and was only half the size of the school they attended in France. But the best news of this period was the arrival of Katherine, who had been winding up our affairs in France and then gone on to her sister in Italy. I'd left France around two and a half months before, packing enough clothes for a fortnight, in order to help my mum sell her house, and hadn't seen Katherine, apart from her fleeting visit to deliver the children to the park, for that entire time. Now she arrived for good, and it was very much as a force for good that her presence was felt throughout the park. Her learning curve was intense, partly through having spoken only French for so long, but also being plunged into a hectic, chaotic business environment which she knew nothing about and where everyone else was already rushing around with, if not absolute confidence, then at least a long way down the road toward discovering what needed to be done. But Katherine had been supportive of the idea of the zoo from a business angle since almost the very beginning. In the first week or so back in April, when I had begun to throw myself into the negotiations wholeheartedly, she had had her doubts. This was just another of my silly dreams that were a distraction from the daily necessity of earning a living and the writing of my book. This was her role in our relationship—I was the dreamer, she was the reality check—though I often argued that preparing only for the worst could become self-fulfilling. But generally she was right, I was wrong, and I was glad to have her wisdom to keep me in check.

Buying the zoo was only the second time in our thirteen years together that I simply overrode her—the first being the purchase of the French barns, which had involved selling our cherished London flat. In both cases I had an absolute certainty of the success of the venture, and was impatient to overleap any naysayers, no matter how well-intentioned. Within a couple of weeks, she confessed to friends, she could see me acquiring new skills in dealing with administrative problems, which were previously a despised terrain for me, and could see that I meant business. She liked this new me—I think she thought that the life I'd engineered for myself writing in the sun with deadlines few and far between was too cushy, particularly for someone with my personality (basically lazy). And as usual, she was probably right.

It's easy to idolize someone if you love them, but, though unrepentantly uxorious, I was not alone in thinking that Katherine was special. Her background was as a graphic designer, which, as with many professions, involves a period of proving oneself creatively before moving up the ladder into administration. In the world of glossy magazines, this meant becoming an art director. Though she went on to several other titles, ending up at *Eve*, the women's magazine, on *Men's Health* magazine, the glossy where we met, she was in charge of several staff and freelancers, as well as a budget, in the mid-1990s, of about £130,000 a year. This was more money than I had ever marshaled, but she did it well and diligently. "The thing about Katherine," a photographer once confided to me on a rare photo shoot where I was working with her, "is that she's good with other people's money." Many art directors succumb to the surface glamour of their industry and overspend on things like expensive lunches or endless rolls of film for costly locations and photographers. Katherine was different, ordering in sandwiches, partly to keep costs down but also to keep everyone in the studio, which charged by the hour, so they didn't have to be rounded up afterward. And she nurtured new talent. With an unfailing eye she could spot someone just starting out who would go on to greater things, get them cheaply, and then inspire their loyalty, so that they would often work for her in the future at reduced rates.

Her management style was simply to set an impeccable example, which other people felt obliged to follow. She worked harder than anyone else, often putting in twelve- and fourteen-hour days, which in our early time together had been a source of conflict between us. I, the indolent freelancer, though churning out work, would often do so from my "office" on a laptop on the slopes of Primrose Hill with Jasper, my panting assistant. At the end of the day I stopped and prepared our dinner, for which Katherine would invariably be late. I never actually left a note saying "Your dinner's in the dog," but many times I ferried in meals to her at 9 or 10 PM to find her doing something like organizing spreadsheets for other departments so that they could comply with new internal accountancy requirements. "THAT'S NOT YOUR JOB," I would rant, but it was a vital part of her to take up the slack where other people were prepared to let it slide.

Katherine's presence in the park was galvanizing—not least for me. She cleared a space in the (would you believe cluttered) office, fired up her PowerBook, in those days the most powerful computer at the park, and got down to business. Her roles, we had decided, were as money manager (getting a frivolous purchase past Katherine, as I knew from many years of trying, was physically impossible) and designer. Though we had a capable designer and illustrator in the form of Robin, he had other skills and predispositions, which we were beginning to unearth, and Katherine's unerring eye for simplicity and homogeneity, I knew, would be key to establishing the identity of this zoo as something separate from the mishmash of local tourist and animal attractions. A well-designed, understated, but slick visual image, homogenous throughout the leaflets, staff uniforms, advertising material, and even the signage for the animals, combined with my enthusiasm and that of the people we had with us, could make this place into a flagship twenty-first-century enterprise. Suddenly it all seemed not just possible, but inevitable, and the goals I had set for the future of the park loomed into the foreground as part of our business and development plans.

As success grew, the collection could be steered from its current 5 percent endangered animals toward the ultimate ambition of focusing on captive breeding of endangered species for possible reintroduction into the wild, like at Gerald Durrell's Jersey Zoo. Free-ranging lion tamarins, rare lemurs, Grevy's zebras, giraffes, and my personal holy grail, large primates. Bonobo chimpanzees are the smallest and most intelligent of the great apes, and also endangered, but gorillas are also clever and endangered, and available to zoos that have the right track record and appropriate facilities. With their habitat under threat and individuals still being killed for bushmeat or even apparently sometimes out of sheer spite by psychopaths in Rwanda and the Congo, these big gentle guys urgently need safe havens. And if we played our cards right, one day (in about ten years) we could provide one.

As an avid student of the work of Dr. Sue Savage-Rumbaugh's work with Kanzi the chimp and Dr. Penny Pattersons's research with Koko the gorilla, I know these big animals are capable of self-recognition, empathy, and arguably, humor and self-awareness. This is exactly what I am most interested in, my genuine "dream scenario," as my sister Melissa had first described the zoo—looking for language and humor in big apes in your own garden, and calling it work.

This scenario was still a very long way off, but I felt astonishingly fortunate to be at least on a road that could lead to it. With Katherine on board, it felt like we could go down that road. I'd always privately called her my Born Free lady, after Virginia

McKenna in the, for me, seminal film *Born Free*, about how Joy and George Adamson reared and reintroduced Elsa, an abandoned lioness, into the wilds of Africa. That seemed to me like a very good job to have. They lived in tents and log cabins in tropical sunshine, they were doing fascinating and worthwhile work, and they had a Land Rover. With a lion on the top. As a boy I'd always hoped to do something as exciting and worthwhile with animals in exotic locations. I could see it was a long shot, but also that I would need a special person to do it with me, and when I first met Katherine, I knew that I'd found someone who could meet that challenge. If I could create the appropriate circumstances, I knew she would go with it and be perfect at it, even though it wasn't, strictly speaking, in her initial life plan. After we got together I repeatedly warned her that one day I would be dragging her off somewhere exotic to do interesting things with animals. France was a staging post. Now we had made it to, er, Devon. But the project was perfect, engaging and harnessing her talents as well as mine.

Having Katherine back was the best thing. Our little family unit was functioning again, and here we were working together, in an environment in which I was fired up and Katherine was keen to engage as a business venture. In the absence of having any money to manage, Katherine set about organizing the office and, clutching at straws from the past to piece together, designing our logo. One big problem with this, however, was that we didn't yet have a name.

Mike Thomas, the reassuring voice of wisdom on the phone, finally materialized at the park, and ended up helping out considerably with this. It was great to meet Mike in the flesh, to shake his hand, and thank him for all his help in getting the park, without which it quite simply wouldn't have been possible. Mike and his lovely wife, Jen, had the solid, comforting air of people who knew what they were talking about. With his white beard, ready smile, and faded denim shirt, Mike looked like a cross between the British wildlife TV programmer Bill Oddie and the BBC's *Animal Hospital* host, Rolf Harris. In fact Mike's animal pedigree was far more impressive than those of these keen amateurs, as we were to find out.

Jen looked like a real "Born Free lady," someone who could bottle-feed a baby chimpanzee while getting on with her daily routine unfazed. Mike and Jen had both been through a similar experience to ours, more than a decade before, at Newquay Zoo. Now that we had time to chat, I asked Mike how he had managed taking over Newquay with no experience of running a zoo, as his background was in design and teaching. "Oh, I just called Gerry, and he was very helpful." Gerry? "Gerald Durrell at Jersey Zoo. You've heard of him, I hope?" Heard of Gerald Durrell? One of my heroes, as well as being a superbly evocative writer. *My Family and Other Animals* alone has probably engaged as many people with the natural world as David Attenborough. Durrell was the premier conservationist of his, or possibly any, generation. Founding Jersey Zoo in the teeth of opposition from the zoological world, Durrell then used it to change the center of gravity of that world toward active conservation, as opposed to simply exhibiting animals. Astonishingly, captive breeding programs of endangered species for reintroduction to the wild, and for learning about their breeding habits to inform our conservation and management of them in the wild, were still sometimes actually considered a bad idea as recently as the 1960s and 1970s.

According to Lord Zuckerman, president of the Zoological Society of London, addressing the World Conference on Captive

Breeding of Endangered Species held at London Zoo in July 1976, because extinction is part of natural selection we shouldn't interfere but merely document the process for the benefit of zoological science. "Species have always been disappearing," he said. "There will always be rare species." I remember that year's fantastic, sticky summer of glam rock, skateboards, and California sunshine making everything seem perfect, as an eleven-year-old at primary school, happily oblivious to the president of London Zoo's almost nihilistic perspective on animals. But even as a child I would have known he was wrong. I was probably sitting sweating and fidgeting in assembly as Zuckerman addressed the zoological community. Gerald Durrell was sitting, writhing apoplectically, in that audience. He was already a man with a zoo, and a man with a mission, and I expect that on hearing those words, from that source in that place, Gerald Durrell would have simply renewed his vows to himself for the thousandth time. When other people simply gave up, he just dug in deeper. He saw it through, against a lifetime of people telling him it wasn't possible. He was a conservation giant, a maverick, and a writer on a grand scale. And now it transpired that one of the main guiding lights on our final approach to buy the zoo, Mike Thomas, was a receptacle of Gerald Durrell's teachings. Wow. I'm not a religious person, but it did seem like the clouds had opened up a bit and our flimsy efforts were being endorsed from on high.

Mike and Jen helped us a lot in those crucial few weeks, as they had done when they steered us through the negotiations. This time they were more hands-on, frequently driving up from Cornwall to give advice and unpack endless boxes with Mum. One evening, around the old trestle table in the stone-flagged kitchen, with the dilapidated rusted range in the background, a legal document needed to be processed, which absolutely required us to come up with a name for the park. I have blocked from my mind most of the more depressing suggestions, but many were generated in the need to find something that echoed the mostly positive forty-year history and brand recognition of Dartmoor Wildlife Park, while distancing us from the bad publicity of the more recent past.

Staying "Dartmoor Wildlife Park" was not a good idea because of the previous prosecutions, and, shall we say, perceptions of it on the part of the wider zoo world and local suppliers. We needed a relaunch, and quickly. *Dartmoor Zoo* was ruled out because all our neighbors had already monopolized that, some would say predictable, format; Exmoor, Paignton, Newquay, and Bristol have already well tested the concept of local area plus *Zoo* as their title—which works for them. But we wanted to explore new possibilities. South West Wildlife Park, Dartmoor Wildlife Conservation Park, and all sorts of unsuitable horrors surfaced and floated around before finally being punctured by Mike, at our kitchen table, almost certainly with a glass of wine in hand. He suggested, "Why don't you call it Dartmoor Zoological Park?" It had continuity with the past, but also a clear reference to serious scientific activity in the future. I liked it; we all liked it, and that is the trading name we entered into Companies House, the official government register of UK companies. I was particularly pleased because, as well as establishing a new identity and ethos pointing toward the world of science, this gave us a *Z* in the middle of our logo.

Katherine seemed less impressed with this typographical development, and politely ignored my suggestions about how the *Z* could be used at three times the size of the *D* and the *P*, creating a Zorro-like dash. Katherine set to work with the brisk certainty of a skilled expert on home ground. She'd chosen her colors and collected examples of other logos from successful zoos, we'd discussed the broad outline of the brief, and I watched her go into her familiar routine of pasting up swatches of colors and fonts, fretting, squinting at things from arm's length, and working to tight print deadlines.

We had a "definite" lender in our sights, and, through Mike, even Gerald Durrell's vicarious blessing. DZP, as we now jauntily called ourselves, was going to work.

But in those weeks before the money arrived, things were still very strained indeed. The cold, wet winter weather exacerbated the feelings of despair and unreversed decline that we were supposed to be addressing. Very little real progress could be made because even the smallest tasks required some money. Everything we had or could borrow from credit cards was used to pay staff wages. My small income from my *Guardian* column and another in *Grand Designs* magazine was the only actual income for the park, and nowhere near enough to pay the wages of our not-so-happy little band.

Staff morale worsened, and the uncertainty that had been creeping in was now a full-time presence. I spoke to the NFU Mutual mortgage company every day, and their representatives assured me that everything was in hand, but the lawyers were taking their time drawing up the documents. The problem was that if they took much longer, the business wouldn't be there to lend to anymore, and we'd have to put it back on the market. There was a very tangible feeling that the lawyers behind the scene really didn't care whether this happened or not. They weren't going to be rushed, and if in the meantime the transaction moved from the active to the receivership pile, it just meant more paid work for them, or their kind.

Three days before the money finally arrived, a new secretarial employee on a month's trial opened up a statement from Lloyds, who had promised us a loan three times, only to withdraw the offer each time at the last minute. In the course of this charade, Lloyds had set up accounts in the name of Mee Conservation Ltd. (the name of our newly formed company), issued checkbooks, and begun sending us monthly statements. The problem was that the statements said things like 0.00, nil, etc., in row after row of austere columns, which, to the untrained eye of someone worrying about their job security, looks bad. This secretarial wannabe screamed across the office "They've got no money. Look! Look!" etc., waving the apparently incriminating paper around for everyone to see. The effect was not calming, and at about eleven that morning an unusually strained Steve, our brand-new curator of animals, visited me in the kitchen of the house, where I had just finished clearing away breakfast. "I'm really sorry to bother you," said Steve, and he clearly was sorry but also deeply concerned. "I think you'd better come over to the restaurant. Everybody is there." I looked longingly at my unsipped coffee, and headed over with him.

Everybody was indeed there, from Paul the van driver to gentle Robin the draftsman, all the keepers, and the new secretarial tryout, Sarah. They sat in a circle of chairs, arms folded, with an empty chair for me. It was an uncanny moment, with these normally polite and compliant people turning into inquisitors, and the unusualness of the situation emphasized its gravity. I wasn't nervous, but I knew I had to project myself or be overwhelmed by the sheer weight of uncertainty in the room. I explained as openly and honestly as I could about the promised money from the NFU, how I was expecting final confirmation any day now, that we'd signed the last of the last documents, and were now just waiting for lawyers to finish dithering. My frustration with the situation was every bit as intense as theirs, but more so, as I was privy to the intricacies of the mechanisms of procrastination. I told them that I was regularly promised the funds by a particular date, but that these arrangements were regularly broken. That previous Monday, for instance, had been a firm promise cast in stone, but had passed without even a communication from the bank. I hadn't believed the promise, so I hadn't told the staff about it, as it was frustrating enough for me without having to apologize for the bank to everyone else every time they let me down. "I didn't tell you about that deadline because I didn't believe it would happen," I said. "I will only believe it when I see the money in the account—and I do believe that it will come, but when, I can't tell you. But I will tell you when it's there. My feeling is that it will be within the next week. That's the best I can say to you."

I looked around the room. They were all looking intently at me, making economic decisions. Who was this young joker who had bought the place without having enough money to run it? Could he be trusted? What were the alternatives? The secretarial assistant had a question about her own wages, which I suggested was a separate issue for a private meeting. Her end-of-month review was coming up, and it was not going to go well. I looked everyone in the eye in turn and asked if they had any more questions. In the end I think it was John who stood up and said something like, "That seems fair enough." Other chairs scraped back as people got to their feet. The spell was broken. The inquisition was over. I'd got through by the skin of my teeth. Now I just needed to convince myself. I had been convinced before the meeting, and also during it as I'd managed to convince the others to hang in there. But afterward, the fact that I had been put in the position where the business was on the absolute brink of disintegration, by a bank, made me question whether they really were actually going to come up with the goods. I had believed Barclays, I had believed Lloyds, three times. I'd believed Arbuthnots, the Royal Bank of Scotland, and a host of others who had ultimately, utterly without compunction, let us down. I thought about the NFU. Their contact, Andrew Ruth, was clearly a nice, honest, and conscientious man, but he had no control over the backroom boys, who in this case were not the risk-assessment team, but the lawyers.

When institutions behave badly, it's easy for the little people like us to get caught in the machinery, which will not slow down as it grinds you up, repossesses your house, and sends the bailiffs in to evict your children. They are chilling people. All smiles when preparing to lend money, as long as your spreadsheets are in order, and you sign over all your assets as security. And their expressions barely change as they watch the prospect of you getting snarled up in the small print and everything ebbing away.

One problem we encountered was that we weren't borrowing enough. The amount, £550,000, seemed like a lot to me, but apparently that officially made us small fry. "Anything under a million takes time," we were told by one bank. "It's the highest-risk sector there is." I toyed frantically but briefly with the idea of asking for three million, but even my economically naive brain quickly realized that we would encounter spreadsheet difficulties quite quickly going down that route.

Having eventually found understanding lenders in the National Farmers' Union was reassuring, but the terrible uncertainty of having money promised but not actually available lasted for three agonizing months and had a massive impact on the business plan, the staff, and the idea of opening for Easter in April. When the NFU finally came up with the money, on 8 February 2007, our elation was tainted by the knowledge of the unnecessary damage already done by the delay, caused by our own brother's actions and the nature of financial institutions, which had made our target of opening for the all-important Easter bank holiday virtually impossible.

But far, far worse than this, for me, was the knowledge that the good news of the money arriving had been completely overshadowed by the very worst news of all.

5

Katherine

L iving together as an extended family—Mum, Duncan, Katherine, Milo, Ella, and me—would take some adjusting to. For the kids, it must have seemed like a huge adventure. It was going to be an adventure for all of us, a largely positive one, we hoped. But Katherine's illness changed all that. A few days before our first Christmas at the zoo, my wife and I received just about the worst news possible: her brain tumor was back.

In April 2004 we were married after nine years together. By June she had been diagnosed with an aggressive glioblastoma brain tumor, and given about a year to live. The excellent French medical services extracted the tumor and she underwent eighteen months of chemotherapy and radiotherapy afterward. When her body could physically take no more, the treatment stopped and she was monitored every month with an MRI scan to see if the tumor had returned.

Katherine celebrated the end of her treatment in her usual way, with a bout of intense hard work. Cleaning, sorting, gardening at a frenetic rate. I told her that the doctors had advised rest, but she said she felt fine, and sometimes it's better for people to feel good about what they are doing rather than lie low. One day

I went to the shops for supplies, and when I returned, Milo was at the gate to meet me. "Mummy's fallen over but she's all right now," he reported, obviously agitated but under control. I asked Katherine about her fall. She was looking dazed but denied it totally. Gradually we pieced together what had happened. While making some tea, she had suddenly fallen to the floor and started shaking all over. Both children eagerly performed vivid impersonations and pointed to the exact spot where it had happened. Ella had started crying because she thought she had died, but Milo pointed out that she couldn't have died because her eyes were open. "Then I tried to give her some bread to make her strong," he said. We phoned the doctor and went for another scan, where it was confirmed that this was her first epileptic seizure, which is why she had no memory of it. Epilepsy is very common in people who have had brain surgery, as the brain is a closed system and doesn't like being disturbed. Her anti-epilepsy medication was increased and tinkered with over the following months, as the combinations of drugs caused some quite serious side effects, including debilitating depression.

Eventually it was all stabilized, and we learned to look out for the symptoms, which could be brought on mainly by tiredness. I briefed the children on what to do if it happened again. The bread was a nice idea, but in fact you are not supposed to go near someone's mouth if they are having a seizure; with every neuron in the brain firing at once, the person can inadvertently bite your finger off. We told the children not to touch her if it happened again; she wouldn't hurt herself because she was unlikely to flail around, and the best thing to do was simply wait for it to finish. After her long months of anti-cancer therapies, Katherine had to endure perhaps the most frustrating treatment of all for her: taking it easy. She did this in her own way, by taking long afternoon naps and then working hard with a mattock in her vegetable garden as the day cooled. Gradually the naps grew shorter and her muscle tone began to improve. We dreaded the monthly scans, but with each clear result, our confidence grew. The epileptic episode was a warning shot, but it also gave us a less-scary interpretation of her occasional symptoms of giddiness or tingling in her hand.

Throughout that summer of 2006, I was on the phone negotiating to buy the zoo, and by October, that was finally achieved and I had moved in with Duncan and Mum. Katherine arrived about a month later, after tying up our affairs in France, and for me it felt like the last piece of the puzzle was in place. With Katherine on board, we couldn't fail. She never failed. She wouldn't allow those around her to fail either. Watching the budget with a beady eye, she also wouldn't tolerate overspending.

Just before Christmas 2006, shortly after moving to the zoo, Katherine developed a tingling on her right-hand side that didn't go away with the epilepsy medicine. I phoned the GP to request an MRI scan, and was amazed that one was scheduled in three weeks' time. In France a car would arrive to take you to the hospital the next day. I telephoned the hospital to get it moved forward and found that the faxed request from the GP had arrived on the desk of the wrong specialist, who was on holiday anyway. I called the GP again and explained to him what a glioblastoma was, what it could do, how quickly it grows, and gave him the fax number of the right specialist. And this time—good man—the doctor asked for an emergency scan and we went to the hospital two days later. There was a week to wait for the result, which we passed clinging to the hope of epilepsy, as the tingling seemed to lessen the more Katherine rested.

But it wasn't epilepsy. The MRI scan revealed a recurrence of the tumor. She quickly developed a speech deficit, leaving her unable to get past certain words, making her repeat the same word again and again, which was extremely frustrating for her and quite frightening. She lost movement of her right hand very quickly, and her right arm suddenly became an encumbrance. Around us, the zoo was lumbering on, and we were caught between two worlds.

The speed of the symptoms was alarming, but they were mediated slightly by the steroids she was prescribed, at ever-increasing doses, which alleviate intracranial swelling. I still felt optimistic because several new and less-invasive treatments had been developed since she was first diagnosed, and if the first line of conventional treatment failed, I knew there was a range of well-advanced trials, which I had kept in contact with. Before she underwent another craniotomy, I was keen to explore some of these newer, less-invasive methods.

The difficulty with treating problems inside the brain with drugs is the blood brain barrier (BBB), part of the body's own defenses. This is a physical membrane that restricts blood access to the brain, protecting it from blood-borne infections. Very few things can get past it, but a virus can, and a modified herpes virus was designed as long ago as 1995 to cross the BBB and carry with it an agent that targets cancer cells and kills them. The measles virus and scorpion venom have also been used in this way in experimental trials in the lab, though not in human trials, when I had last contacted them. Probably most promising, it seemed to me, was a German system of delivering iron oxide particles directly to the tumor site by injection, then agitating these particles with the MRI scanner, which is, after all, a giant magnet. This literally smashes up the tumor from the inside, which I liked the sound of. Best of all, it had been used on fourteen human glioblastoma patients in the previous year, all of whom were do-

ing well. I got in touch with the Germans to see if Katherine
would be eligible for their next trial.

Our first encounter with the neurosurgeon in Devon had not
been promising, however. Obviously anxious, we'd been led
through the neuro department to a small room to meet the man
who would be overseeing Katherine's treatment. He looked
reassuringly geeky, but then neurosurgeons usually do. He explained that the scan had revealed a recurrence of "abnormalities,"
and scrolled us through a 3-D computer graphic of Katherine's
brain, which showed six or seven small black specks across both
hemispheres, including inside the corpus collosum, which is the
bundle of nerves connecting the two halves of the brain. Around
each speck was a small white stain, like a water mark, which he explained was swelling, which would increase the symptoms asso-
ciated with each tumor site. This was the bit he could alleviate with
steroids, but the tumors were too widespread for an operation, certainly at this stage.

I asked if he could send the scan to our doctor in France so
that we could have her input? "No," he said emphatically, without looking up. "That won't be necessary." Would he please send
it, as she has treated Katherine for two and a half years, and we
would be very interested in what she has to say? "No, this is your
treatment center now." Rarely have I had such a strong urge to
punch someone's face in so soon after meeting them. Moments
before I had been respectfully listening to a skilled consultant
give us his considered opinion. Now I was fighting the urge to
snap off his pudgy fingers one by one before hospital security
took me away. However, I felt this would have been a bad start
to what was likely to be an ongoing relationship. This stubborn,
territorial conservatism in someone who held Katherine's life in
his hands was worrying indeed.

Then I asked him about future possible options such as the modified herpes virus, the measles virus, the scorpion venom, and the German iron oxide treatment, all of which had shown promising early results, some in human glioblastoma patients. He shut his eyes, shook his head and said he hadn't heard of any of them, but that there are lots of unproven trials that seem promising but always come to nothing. Then he looked at me and said, "I'm afraid this is a very dispiriting tumor to treat." Poor guy.

He prescribed a course of PCV chemotherapy, a three-pronged approach that is effective in reducing glioblastomas in about 20 percent of cases. To a glioblastoma patient, these seem like good odds. I telephoned our French neurologist and asked her to ask her English counterpart for the scan results, which she did, and fortunately he supplied them to her, so I could cross-reference treatment options with someone in whom I had some faith. She agreed with the initial treatment of PCV, so all we could do was wait until the NHS (National Health Service) was ready to start Katherine's treatment, on 7 January.

I only hoped they knew what they were doing, as these tumors are graded by their growth rate, and a grade 4 glioblastoma can double in size in a week. We had a quietly fraught festive season. It just seemed that no one was moving at the same speed as the tumor.

JANUARY

Katherine's condition had worsened in the run-up to the chemo, so we were glad when it began. It involved a short infusion and some tablets to take for the next week. By the time the chemo started, she was already debilitated. Her right arm was completely paralyzed, her hand bunching up with the tension of the tendons, and her right leg was beginning to drag. But she could still walk by herself with the aid of a crutch. With chemo there are usually a few days before the effects kick in, but she was weak, and still recovering from the effects of her long-term treatment in France. So, for the next three weeks she spent a lot of time asleep.

Meanwhile, I was still working at the zoo, in between popping back to the house to check on Katherine. Texts on my phone from that time reveal the usual concerns about wages, etc. But one piece of good news was that we interviewed a great candidate for the position of curator of animals. Filling this position was one of the most important conditions for getting our zoo license. We had to have someone who knew exactly what they were doing in all aspects of animal management—after all, we didn't. And Steve Pilcher came highly recommended from the much respected Newquay Zoo, Mike Thomas's old stamping ground, and before that he had worked with the orangutans at Jersey for several years. Orangs are among my favorite animals (though it might be a bit far-fetched to imagine them here within the next ten years), and Jersey is one of the best zoos in the world. Steve's interview went well. Mike Thomas came up for the day—after all, we weren't even qualified to interview a curator, as we didn't know what to look for. Mike led the questioning, and Steve came up with all the right answers, until we got to the question of Spar, the elderly, arthritic tiger up in the top enclosure, and whether he should be put to sleep. This is a contentious question, which divides zoological thinking. I knew from the vet that although Spar was wobbly, he was almost certainly not in pain. At nineteen, he was well past his natural life span in the wild, and his obvious frailty had occasionally upset the visitors at the zoo for the last few years. But the vet had told me he had been in Spar's corner for many years, and there was no reason why he shouldn't carry on until there was a real medical reason to intervene. Mike happened to disagree, and phrased the question in a way that made it obvious what he thought. Mike may seem avuncular, but he is also formidable, particularly to a younger candidate being interviewed for a senior position like this. The easy thing to do would have been to agree with him, but Steve didn't. "Well, he's not in the wild. He's in a zoo," said Steve. "No matter what he looks like, if he's not in pain, I don't see why he shouldn't live out his life until the vet says otherwise." Mike didn't like this answer, but I did. Apart from anything else, it showed a steeliness that he would need if he took the job.

Steve was married to Anna, another experienced zoo professional, who was currently lecturing at a university master's course on veterinary science in zoos. When her contract ended in a couple of months, she would make an excellent addition to the team. Both of them were seriously enthused by the potential of the site and brimming with ideas, backed up with the expertise to bring it forward. Suddenly it looked like we had an excellent upper-management duo, ready to take on the enormous challenges that lay ahead.

But in between us offering Steve the job and his arriving, Katherine's condition worsened considerably. When he arrived in mid-January, I had to tell him the news, and said that while I would liaise with him daily and give him full support on any changes he felt were necessary, my real attention was elsewhere. The situation in the zoo really required everybody's full attention, but with the arrival of Steve, already braced to face a huge task, I had to unload a lot of the responsibility onto him. Handing over to this poor guy, I could see him accepting the strain, but also that he wouldn't buckle under it. I thought he could do it, and there was plenty for him to do.

On the same day that Katherine started her chemotherapy, an article appeared in the medical journal *Cancer Cell*, which was not on my usual reading list. Duncan had heard about it through a review in *Scientific American*, which a friend had shown to him, and had been apparently mildly surprised when Duncan grabbed the brand-new magazine and insisted on taking it away with him. He showed it to me and explained it as I read. Dichloroacetate (DCA) had been used to treat children with a metabolic disorder for thirty years, with few side effects. What a team in Canada had just discovered, however, was that it would also dissolve glioblastoma cells on contact in the lab. Intrigued, they had infected some rats with these tumors, then given them open access to DCA, dissolved in their drinking water. Because DCA, being a very simple molecule, can cross the blood brain barrier, it finds cancer cells, enters them, and destroys them by reawakening the mitochondria. I've always liked mitochondria. They are the power plant of the cell, providing the energy, but they are not strictly human. They are descended from bacteria and have their own DNA, which is why high-altitude training kills off populations of them and produces new ones that can metabolize oxygen more efficiently when sprinting at sea level. What I didn't know was that mitochondria are also responsible for cell apoptosis, that is, the suicide of the cell, should it become infected. Naturally, as the cancer takes over the cell, one of the first things it does is to switch off the mitochondria. But DCA switches it back on. The experimental group of rats in the lab all had massively reduced tumors, and the control group, without the DCA, had great big fat life-threatening ones. So it can cross the BBB, has been tested on humans for thirty years, and it kills glioblastomas.

However, there were no human trials for glioblastoma specifically. It had only just been published, and at the time I was inundated by suggestions for cures from all quarters. My brother Vincent liked the scorpion-venom research, Katherine's parents advocated eating apricot kernels, and my personal preference was for the German method, which Katherine's sister Alice had uncovered and researched. If conventional treatment failed, one of the conditions of getting onto this trial was that the patient was not undergoing any other treatment at the time. Katherine's scan was already on its way to Germany, and I didn't want to do anything to jeopardize her eligibility. "If it was me, I'd be drinking gallons of DCA," said Duncan. But I held off for the time being.

Katherine came out of the chemo slowly, and we had to wait a week or so before she could be assessed for the next round. When she came back around, she came back worse. It had weakened her, as it does, but considerably. I only hoped it was having a similar effect on the tumor, but there was no guarantee of that. Her walking was worse, and she had to be supported on her left side, the good side, and the right leg wheeled into position for each step with a hip-to-hip roll of her whole body sideways. Once the right foot was in position, the knee seldom buckled if we kept the angle right. In time this awkwardly encumbered gate became more complicated, when the right foot refused to come up, and had to be flicked by the heel with my own right foot. This meant standing on one leg at a crucial part of the step with Katherine balanced on her own weakening left leg, so we decided it was more practical to get hold of a wheelchair, particularly for outings, which we wanted to continue while ever it was possible. Unfortunately, none of the different branches of the NHS with which we were by now in contact could provide a wheelchair. The application process was too long, and the kind we wanted, with the big rear wheels, was forbidden for triplegics, in case her bad hand slipped down and got caught in the wheel. But these were by far the most stable chairs, able to navigate the steeper unfinished paths of the park far better than the small-wheeled variety, which Katherine's brothers eventually managed to hire from the Red Cross. This did make things much easier, however, and I took her out into the park as often as I could, for fresh air and to remind her of the wonders that surrounded us.

She had never seen the tigers up close, so one day I took her behind the tiger house, where the three hand-reared tigers, Vlad, Blotch, and Stripe, would come right up to the fence and do their obviously friendly "chuffing" noises, wanting to be stroked. I'd asked Katherine if she'd wanted to do this, and because it's very much an "off show" area with poor wheelchair access, she'd waved her hand and shrugged, indicating indifference. But it is a profoundly powerful experience to be so near these huge, huge predators, and then to see them behaving just like great big house cats, wanting human contact. Katherine was not immune to this experience, and was visibly filled with wonder at the spectacle, which was lovely to be able to share with her.

Mum and Duncan provided enormous support for us during this time, looking after the children, helping Katherine where they could, and it would have been impossible without them. But as the person closest to her in her daily life, a position I now know to be formally called caretaker, I learned in more detail some of those little rituals she used to carry out with such graceful efficiency herself. Like the folding of clothes. I was dimly aware of it going on during our years together before, watching from the bed and wondering how it could possibly take someone so long to prepare for going to sleep (twenty-two minutes, over the years I'd noticed, was her average from entering the room to entering the bed). Now I understood the process from an insider's perspective. If you have nice clothes and you care what you look like, the key, it seems, is to treat them carefully and put them away after using them, rather than just leave them on the floor (my clothes are generally sloughed straight onto the floor and stepped out of, ready, often, to be reused the next day).

Though it was an outward and shocking sign of her increasing disability, with potentially sinister implications, caring for Katherine became in some ways the best part of the day. It gave us a chance to be together in a way that we couldn't manage while she had been the human dynamo in the office and the home, spinning more plates than I even knew existed. Those intimate hours in the daytime and at night as I helped her to the toilet, washed, fed, and dressed her were spent in laughter, and became a welcome break from my more public duties as a new zoo director.

As Katherine became more disabled, I spent more of my time with her. Initially I could get her up, washed, dressed, and breakfasted by about ten o'clock, and then leave her sitting or reclining somewhere with a stack of reading matter and remote controls. But this felt like abandonment, because for someone as naturally busy and as engaged with the outside world as she had been, this enforced leisure was a torture. I popped back as frequently as I could, inevitably delayed by myriad queries and problems that beset any novice proprietor of a run-down zoo. We were told that if, somehow, the tumors were successfully removed this time, her movement and speech might return, but again they might not.

In the meantime I began learning about the fastidious art of eyebrow plucking. If you need a magnifying glass to detect a bristle of an eyebrow, I suggested, then you probably don't need to pluck it. Someone across the room, or even a couple of feet away, won't be able to see it. But this cut no ice with Katherine. After careful positioning of mirrors, tweezer, and optical equipment enabling the detection of actual bristles, came the technique. This is no snatch and grab, but a much more deliberate and torturous method. Grip the offending millimeter of hair firmly with the tweezers, and slowly ease it out in what for most men would be an eye-watering agony. But female grooming breeds stoics, and never a flicker crossed even the good half of Katherine's face as I reluctantly conducted this torture.

Suitably groomed and plucked (Katherine, that is, not me), we arrived at the hospital for our next appointment—and had the most chilling conversation of my life. Our appointment with the oncologist to discuss Katherine's progress, and therefore prognosis, had a surreal breeziness to it, as the life of this most beautiful person was discussed and seemingly dismissed in a shitty little back room painted NHS blue, next to the toilets in the oncology waiting area. The big, doe-eyed oncologist began by discussing plans for the next round of PCV, but I was concerned that it had taken such a lot out of Katherine that we needed to be sure it was working before we continued, otherwise she would suffer needlessly, but also because she would be semi-comatose and unable to report symptoms at a very critical time, when we might need to switch treatments. It was a good thing I asked. "Well, actually, I have to say I don't think it is working," she said. "It reduces tumors in about twenty percent of cases, but normally by now we'd expect to see some slight improvement. And as you can see"—gesturing to Katherine—"things have got worse." Katherine sat in her Red Cross wheelchair, smiling her half smile, taking it in or not, shrugging a bit, unable to communicate the million things she must have been feeling inside. Then the oncologist turned to her. "You don't really want to be feeling poorly for a couple more weeks do you?"

Katherine, defunctionalized, unable to speak, probably unable to grasp the sheer enormity of what had just happened, smiled and blinked, and shrugged. It took me a while to grasp it too. I looked around the room. The medical student had clearly been briefed that this would be a death conversation. She couldn't do eye contact. The wide-eyed male nurse from Macmillan Cancer Support said nothing, but provided a foil for the knowing asides from the oncologist. I asked the oncologist if she'd read the DCA article I had forwarded. She rolled her eyes with a "silly me" smile, and said, "Oh, I haven't had time." *Cancer Cell*, I suggested, was a fairly serious journal that, one would have thought, would appeal to oncologists. "Mmm. It's a mitochondrial cell-apoptosis route," she said aside to the Macmillan nurse, who now seemed to be present more as security than for any benefit to Katherine. They laughed briefly. How silly of us to hold out any hope for that.

So what's the plan? I asked. Another shrug, another far-too-lightweight smile. There wasn't one. What about X, Y, and Z, and some other drug combinations suggested by the Americans? No, not available. I was rocked, and wanted to cry, but I wanted to stay strong for Katherine. Besides, at the back of my mind I still held out hope for the German iron-oxide treatment, or Duncan's DCA, which I genuinely believed could be fruitful, and once it was demonstrated to be working, the medics would back us up. But when the vast, imperfect but reassuring teat of NHS support is withdrawn, that is a cold feeling indeed.

It took a few days to adjust to the idea that we'd been cut loose from real treatment, and meanwhile the busy agencies of cancer care made it seem like things were happening. There were appointments with the district nurse, the Marie Curie people, the Macmillan team, the occupational therapist, and some people called the re-ablement team. After a bit, it occurred to me that a lot of people were arriving, sympathizing, and asking questions, but nothing was actually happening. Still no one could get us a wheelchair, for instance, because the NHS red tape strangled all efforts. No one could help me with lifting Katherine, as lifting is now against NHS regulations, but they all approved of my technique. One department gave us a load of blue nylon things that were apparently for hoicking Katherine around, but all of them seemed massively intrusive medicalizations of what can be a simple, friendly process. Someone else was looking seriously into the idea of fitting a stair lift. But I wasn't holding my breath.

Most of the physical disabilities, even if they became permanent, were things that I thought she could probably learn to live with. But I couldn't bear her looking confused. Offering, poker-faced, her leg to be put into a sleeve or a bra strap, reaching for a bar of soap instead of a toothbrush to brush her teeth, being surprised that the light is controlled by the light switch. But her humor was still there. Her laughter was readily available, which told me she was still in there. And her cool reproach if I wasn't doing something properly. Just one eyebrow raised (she could only raise one, but that made it more effective) told me I was still being critically assessed.

FEBRUARY

Katherine had become confused by the concept of spitting into a glass during the process of brushing her teeth in the bedroom. If you offered the glass to rinse and spit, she drank, then looked confused as to what to do with it once it was in her mouth. She often tried to quickly start brushing with a mouth full of water, which inevitably ended in a mess. But she more readily followed the concept of rinsing and spitting in the bathroom as it is a more familiar environment for teeth brushing, though the bathroom was logistically difficult to get to, and very cold. Yet despite this she was instantly amused if you pointed this out by mimicking her full-mouthed, wide-eyed perplexity. Her language seemed to improve at bedtime, briefly, when she could still be brilliantly dry and scathing. Having propped her up in bed with several pillows, which she indicated were working perfectly, I overeagerly searched the house for yet another. Propping it behind her, I asked if that was any better. "Marginally worse," she said, perfectly, after a day of being unable to discriminate between producing a yes or a no.

It got to the stage where, because I spent so much time with her, and already knew her so well, I had to be called in as translator for many simple interactions with other people. The trick was not to suggest too many things for her to choose from, and to realize that when she said yes, it could easily mean no, and vice versa. Once any word or gesture was out, it tended to be repeated. Watching someone new to Katherine's situation try to understand brought home how far she'd slipped. Usually I had to step in, but once or twice I left her at the mercy of a well-meaning friend or relative while I snatched a few minutes' catching up with things I had to do. Like when Katherine's lovely sister Alice was trying so earnestly to understand what she was trying to say, and offered a cornucopia of possibilities. Katherine appealed to me with her eyes across the room, and I knew exactly what she wanted. But for those five minutes, I simply smiled at her and shook my head, happily catching up on my e-mail. "You're on your own."

Before she almost completely lost her speech, Katherine was sitting at the table with all the family struggling to say something to my Mum. "Can I . . . can I . . . can I . . ." Have the salt? The butter? The vegetables? people helpfully suggested. A rare look of frustration passed across her face before she finally got it out. "Can I pass you something, Amelia?" With her one good hand, and seven tumor sites multiplying exponentially in her brain, she was still more attentive to others than anyone else at the table.

15 FEBRUARY: A GREAT ESCAPE

During this period, in the middle of February, I was still able to leave Katherine in the house for an hour or two at a time, propped up in front of the fire with some magazines, snacks, and the TV remote (which she never seemed to resort to, though I would have done). I didn't like to leave her for long, but I had to attend an urgent design meeting with a local firm to discuss whether they were able to carry on Katherine's design work, which she had so far, unfortunately, only sketchily outlined. Then the meeting was interrupted when I heard the news that a wolf had escaped (don't you just hate it when that happens?).

At first, I tried to carry on as if nothing had happened—I had enormous faith that the keepers and curator could handle the situation. Unfortunately, the wolf got past them, across the perimeter fence, and into the outside world. That was when the fun really started. Suddenly, instead of taking the odd call on the internal radio to keep in touch with the situation, I was stepping out of the meeting to do a quick interview on Radio Devon, and then Radio Five Live. The designers were very understanding and saw the funny side, but unfortunately, none of the journalists I was talking to did. Obviously it was a serious situation, and members of the public were also keen to point out on air that seeing a large black timber wolf running down their street was not conducive to a relaxing afternoon. Trying to explain to hostile journalists (don't you just hate hostile journalists?) that Parker, the number-two male wolf, was not a danger to anyone unless he was cornered, didn't seem to work. The truth remained that a Class I dangerous animal in our care was now running free in public, and that's not how things are supposed to be.

Phrases I used in radio interviews like "He's just a harmless scavenger," and "He's basically a big girl's blouse" have been quoted back at me derisively by friends who heard my torment. Other zoo professionals phoned to sympathize, saying that escapes were relatively common but for God's sake not to quote them on that. The meeting finally disintegrated as I liaised with armed police now two miles away, with Parker in sight, wanting to know exactly how dangerous this big girl's blouse actually was.

Then we got lucky. Instead of heading into woods, or across people's gardens, the black wolf turned left into a china clay quarry, which was a couple of square miles of containable basin, and most important, completely white terrain. Also in the WBB China Clay Works quarry were several redoubtable quarrymen equipped with local knowledge, four Land Rovers, and their own radio communications. As they liaised with our keepers on quad bikes (all-terrain vehicles) and the police, the tide turned toward the forces of containment. But Parker, not quite finished, ran the highly equipped humans ragged for an hour or so before finally succumbing to a keeper's dart. I waved to the parting designers over the heads of the mud-spattered keepers and police, and settled in for an evening of battle stories.

It sounded exciting, and part of me wished I'd been there. As it happened, a friend and former colleague of Duncan's was visiting at the time, and was a perfect person to join in the chase. Kevin Walsh is a rangy six-foot-four Cockney who worked for several years with Duncan as a private investigator. The nature of their work meant that they had to be adaptable, unflappable, and used to pursuits. Duncan and Kevin sped off down the road after Parker, in radio and phone contact with the police and keepers. "We just went straight into 'mode.'" Kevin laughed, clearly having enjoyed his day, and playing no small part in the recapture. At several stages, despite the manpower on the ground, only one person had "eyes on" Parker and was able to relay this vital information to the rest of the team. Kevin, Duncan, John, and a policeman had all held the line vitally in this way, in what sounded like a very near miss. If Parker had got onto the moors, or into built-up backyards, he would probably still be out there. "At one stage we were separated," Duncan recounted. "But I next saw Kevin riding shotgun—and carrying a shotgun—in the back of a pickup truck, in the thick of it." The vet who had been scrambled to provide the anaesthetic for the dart gun, apparently, was a fairly slight woman, who also had to carry a shotgun in case things didn't go as planned. With her other paraphernalia, this was proving an encumbrance, and she handed it to the capable-looking Kevin. "That shotgun was my golden pass to the center of events," said Kevin. "Everywhere the vet went I had to go, in police cars, Land Rovers and pickups." In the end Rob's sharpshooting with the dart gun meant that the shotgun was never used. Another close shave for us. And another satisfied visitor to the park.

It was deeply serious. It was absurd. It was not the first time the wolf had taken a shot at freedom. Parker had escaped once before, before our time, and had been collared, quite literally, outside the local pub. He seemed to have gone in search of Rob, who "scruffed" him and bundled him into the back of a van.

When I started down this road of running a zoo it was the psychological welfare of the animals that interested me most. The physical containment aspect, I assumed, was a given. Now I see that the two things are often closely related. Unhappy animals can take desperate measures, making them unpredictable. Parker, as number two, was stressed by the decline in Zak, the elderly alpha male, from whom he would soon have to wrest control of the pack. Rather than face his fear, he decided to try his luck elsewhere, and against the odds he pitched his bid when the electric fence was momentarily down.

The sleeping Parker was placed back in the wolf house on a bed of straw with some hot-water bottles scavenged from our house (Mum, Katherine, and the children would have to go without that night, because Parker's temperature regulation system was compromised by the anaesthetic). I popped back into the house and tended to Katherine, who needed a bit of help, while the keepers got cleaned up. Then I went back out into the driving rain to establish with Rob exactly how Parker had got out. There were a few theories flying around, and by now, everyone was absolutely drained—including me, from my difficult day of unplanned hostile questioning by the national media. The calls were still coming in, our reputation had been seriously damaged, and I could feel that one more incident like this would finish us. It was vital that we establish exactly what had happened and make absolutely sure it couldn't happen again, tonight or ever in the future. One possibility I had to eliminate was keeper error, which had been raised by an external professional who knew the design of the enclosure, and that the keepers were so used to working with the wolves, who scattered like, well, big girls' blouses, whenever anyone went in with them. This could have led to complacency, and Parker could conceivably have got behind them and fled before they reacted. The whole concept of going in with the wolves was something that needed to be addressed before our inspection with a redesign of the enclosure, but for now, my general paranoia at the end of another Code Red day led me to question Rob about this possibility. It was understandable, I said. There would be no recriminations. We just needed to know definitively. Understandably, he was not very pleased, but nor was I. I desperately wanted to get back inside to Katherine, so I insisted that he show me some evidence there and then that indicated that Parker had gone over the fence rather than through the gate.

In the woods behind the wolves, who were now howling and yapping in agitation in their sealed-off section of their enclosure—both of us drenched to the skin by the relentless rain—we shone our flashlights around the perimeter fence until we reached the section where the two halves of the enclosure are divided by a fence so that the wolves can be isolated from each other if necessary. Inexplicably, at this back corner, rather than meeting the perimeter fence at a right angle, the line of the dividing fence veered off obliquely, creating a triangular nook and meeting the outer fence at a sharp angle of about thirty degrees. Though protected by a couple of strands of "hot wire," or electric fence, this narrow triangle could provide purchase for an animal to climb, if the hot wire was down (there was no backup in those days) and the wolf sufficiently desperate. As it turned out, it was, and Parker was. "He'll have known straightaway when the hot wire went down," explained Rob, rainwater running down his face in the light of our flashlights. Many of the animals on the park apparently tested the fences vigilantly, not by receiving a shock, but by coming extremely close and somehow detecting the electrical field. This bothered me, as the old hot-wire system was one of the primary defenses against escape for many of the more "dangerous" animals, including the wussy but controversy-making wolves. Rob shone his flashlight on the overhand at the top of the fence, and there, without a doubt, were some tufts of dark fur that shouldn't have been there. It was from Parker's chest. The power was back on, but if it failed again, we were in trouble. The rest of the pack were to be contained in the secure half of the enclosure until the rest of it could be made safe. Relieved, I went back into the house to Katherine.

The council had ordered a cull of three of the wolves on the basis that overcrowding was causing the unrest, but once again I was reluctant to carry out this euthanasia without a lot of further research. The last cull several years before had apparently killed the wrong three wolves, all important in the hierarchy, resulting in the present instabilities in the pack. We employed freelance wolf whisperer Sean Ellis, a controversial anti-establishment figure, to advise us. He apparently performed a little dance that had all the wolves sitting at his feet, then recommended that we feed them a whole carcass instead of the joints of cut meat, because in the wild the hierarchy is established by who eats what. The leaders establish themselves at the feast, and then their urine smells different according to the bits they have eaten. Simple, and 100 percent effective. The pack calmed down, and after the electric-fence expert Roger Best had finished with the enclosure, motive, means, and opportunity for escape were reduced to nil. Once again, the orthodoxy was proved wrong, and some animals were saved.

I would have liked to have met Sean and seen his assessment, but by then I was with Katherine more or less full time, often out in front of the house if the weather was mild enough. Katherine would be wrapped up warmly, and I spent this time on the phone about treatment options and, while waiting for calls, renovating an old tabletop I had found in a refuse container and married with some steel table legs discovered in one of the barns on the park. The tabletop was covered with many layers of paint, which needed stripping off, and the legs were rusty, but these gentle DIY activities were normalizing for me and for her. For the thirteen years we had been together, I had spent an inordinate amount of time doing DIY. Partly because of doing up our flat and then the barns in France, partly because a significant portion of my income had come from writing about DIY as a columnist for the *Guardian* and other magazines, but also because, to be honest, I am an inveterate putterer. We settled into an almost familiar rhythm.

Unfortunately, during this time, the phone calls were not going well. The scorpion-venom trials and the measles and herpes virus groups all rejected Katherine, sometimes because they were not ready, and sometimes because she had too many different tumor sites—six or seven—and what they needed was one good primary tumor. Then, finally, a letter arrived from Germany to say the same thing. Because of their intracranial injection technique, her multiple sites meant that she was not a suitable candidate.

MARCH

Suddenly the options were drastically reduced. It might have been possible to find another experimental procedure in another country, but Katherine was not very well at all now—probably well enough to travel, but the huge upheaval of adapting to a new country, possibly a new language, at this stage on the off chance that it might work was not appealing. Duncan's DCA idea

now seemed like Katherine's best bet, particularly when a good
friend of mine from college days, Jennifer, who trained as a research chemist, also got in touch and said she thought it was a
good idea. "The Internet is absolutely swamped by this," said Jen.
"I've never seen anything like it. The researchers have closed
down their site and aren't taking e-mails, which is unheard of.
Everybody wants DCA." That didn't necessarily make it a good
thing, but I was already as convinced as I needed to be, and when
Jen said she might be able to get hold of some from her labora-
tory contacts, I asked her to please try.

Meanwhile, I contacted as many doctors as I could to try to
get a private prescription for what was, after all, a cheap, widely
available medicine that had been in use for the last thirty years.
The problem was, it hadn't been used for this condition before,
and so it was unlicensed. This meant that a doctor who prescribed
it was technically taking Katherine's life—and their career, should
anything go wrong—in their hands. And they would be personally liable, should I decide to sue them if things went wrong. I
know quite a few doctors from my medical journalism days, and
I contacted them all, and my GP. All, understandably, declined re-
gretfully, and I understood that it was a very difficult demand to
make on someone, and I think they understood how desperate I
must have been to ask. The one person I didn't understand was
the local oncologist in charge of Katherine's treatment. Her ideas,
which were officially palliative anyway (that is, designed to alleviate suffering or symptoms without eliminating the cause), had
not worked. She had not even tried to eliminate the cause, and
here was the possibility of a noninvasive treatment, successful in
the lab, known to have negligible side effects, which was actually
sitting in the pharmacy in the building where she worked. As with
all the other doctors I approached, I sent her the relevant pages
of the American Environmental Protection Agency toxicology re-

port, published in August 2003 to assess the use of DCA over the last thirty years. This clearly concludes that the side effects, even in long-term use over five years, were minimal: traces of peripheral nerve damage and minor toxic effects on the liver. If Katherine lived long enough to experience these symptoms, we would be delighted. Besides, she already had a lot more than peripheral nerve damage; she was paralyzed down one side and losing control of her other side day by day. As next of kin I could sign any disclaimers necessary. It had to be worth a try.

"No," she said. And I still can't understand why.

Duncan also knew a few doctors, and one in particular who might be prepared to step outside his comfort blanket. I thought he was too far removed from Katherine to go so far out on a limb for her, but I was wrong. A surgeon, he looked Duncan up and down, took his word, risked his career, and signed a private prescription. He wanted to liaise closely on dosage, which we worked out as best we could together from the existing literature, and he gave us a month's supply. Or rather, he prescribed it. Actually getting hold of an unlicensed drug that is at the center of an international controversy, even with a private prescription, is not easy. It took a further week of overcoming quite substantial bureaucratic and logistical obstacles, but unleashing Duncan onto a project is like unleashing the Terminator. Though his mission was benign, he'd be back when it was achieved. It was reassuring to know that he was out there, relentlessly tracking down this drug, which seemed like our absolute last chance to save Katherine. Even if it only slowed down her decline, the medics might take more of an interest and make it easier to get hold of, or, ideally, take over the treatment.

Finally, on my birthday (which we'd all forgotten about until I started opening cards in the evening), Duncan sat in a room in a London hospital with a still-suspicious head of pharmacy examining the paperwork in front of him. The two key elements were the prescription itself and his conversations with the doctor who had written it, and the diagnosis of palliative treatment only for Katherine. The pharmacist left the room and came back with a carrier bag full of bottles of DCA, but resumed probing Duncan about this unusual procedure. "As soon as I saw the bag," says Duncan, "I knew I was leaving the building with it, even if I had to take it off him and climb out of the window with it." Fortunately, this drastic action was not necessary, as Duncan answered the pharmacist's questions to his satisfaction and he peacefully handed over the DCA. Duncan leaped on a train down to Plymouth, handed over the bag, and we gave Katherine her first dose. It was, without a shadow of doubt, the best birthday present I have ever had. It gave us hope.

I drew up a chart so that I could monitor her progress, and added four doses of DCA to the ten or so different pills, such as steroids and anti-epilepsy drugs, she was still taking every day. The key with DCA is to soak the system in it, so that there are no peaks and troughs in concentrations; so, doses were administered every six hours around the clock. Her sleep was already disrupted, and it was easy to administer by mouth in the form of an almost tasteless liquid. If it worked, it was the least invasive of any of her treatments, and I scanned the notes I made every day looking for signs of improvement, or patterns of decline.

Despite everything, the time spent so closely with Katherine was enormously rewarding. We had our secrets. She was largely constipated by the steroids, which meant long and often fruitless sessions on the toilet, culminating in a successful launch about every four days. These heaving tribulations, punctuated by infrequent but periodic sweet success, were special times. We smiled and laughed at these bodily anomalies, with their involuntary contortions and novel procedures—such as the poo stick. By the time the poo actually exited "the building," it was so dense and turgid that it wouldn't flush. Previously, this had been an achievement only I had managed a few times in our thirteen years together. Now, Katherine was dropping whoppas that could survive several flushes absolutely unmoved. So we had the poo stick, specially sourced and cut to shape for breaking up poo into flushable sections. We giggled conspiratorially through these sorts of things as we stashed the poo stick (thoroughly cleaned, obviously) for future use where no one would find it, or if they did, would never suspect what it was for.

The children also took an active interest in toilet matters, perhaps because this was an area they had learned about relatively recently themselves. The best piece of equipment to come from the NHS was a mobile commode, a gleaming, new (small-wheeled) chair with a detachable seat, very useful in the nighttime but also at other times when conventional lavatorial facilities were just too far away. Several times on excursions with Katherine the children had witnessed us being caught short. Generally, I would go to the nearest shop and insist, with varying degrees of forcefulness, on using the staff toilets. They always agreed in the end, and we never had an accident. But the children both said about the commode that, "Now Mummy can be wheeled along and wee at the same time." Katherine smiled, and I had to explain to them that it didn't quite work like that.

With the DCA now our last hope, in which I still fervently believed was a genuinely possible route out of this nightmare, there was nothing to do but monitor her progress through my handwritten chart. Some days her speech seemed to improve. On 14 March, the entry reads, "Speech and movement slightly better." On the 15th, at the GP's, she eventually managed to say, "I understand everything." But the general trend was toward less movement, less language, and more sleep. Then her appetite rallied extraordinarily on the 27th. She consumed an entire meal of diced sushi, ate a whole basket of raspberries followed by half a bar of chocolate, and washed it down with a large glass of chilled white wine. "Superb. Superb," she said, giving enormous reason to hope for an improvement. But these were among her last words.

Toward the end of March, our good friends Phil and Karen came to visit, as they had been every few weeks, and we took Katherine out to the garden center in her Red Cross wheelchair. We were looking at adjustable recliners, a comfortable way to spend the day when you are triplegic. Katherine obviously liked the trip, looking at the scenery, and enjoying being out with us. When asked which recliner she liked, she shrugged and smiled and flicked her hand up to indicate that she didn't care. We settled on a silvery gray model that had real wooden armrests, as beautiful an object as possible within the confines of the genre and available market. When we got back to the house we maneuvered her into it; she was wearing the lovely fake fur coat that Phil and Karen had brought her on a previous trip down and that she had requested every day since. Katherine looked surprised by the chair, but was obviously delighted, and rubbed the armrest enthusiastically up and down, smiling to us to show her appreciation that we had got her the nicest chair we could. One week later, she died in it.

Katherine's breathing stopped at 3:30 AM on March 31, while I was a few feet away working on my computer. In the last few days her swallowing had become more difficult. I'd been expecting her to live at least a week or so longer, as my dad had lasted on liquids administered by means of spongy lollipops dipped in water for about two weeks. She never got to the spongy-lollipop stage, and the packet remained unopened. But

I wasn't completely surprised. In death, once again, she was absolutely beautiful. The puffiness of her face, which had aged her so dramatically because of the steroids, was gone, and the Katherine I knew was back. Except that she was dead. I woke my sister Melissa, who was staying with us, and then Katherine's two brothers, Dominic and Guy, and we stayed up, not really knowing what to do, as the shock set in.

Throughout the DCA treatment I had genuinely clung to the belief that it could reverse or at least arrest her symptoms, if we got the dose right. And then the medics might take an interest and take over the management of the treatment. Even if she was left utterly dependent, she was still Katherine, my friend, and able to communicate this through the confusion. But soon after that last proper meal three days before, she became unable to swallow, not even enough to take her pills, or the little squirt of DCA into her mouth, and I knew that that was it. Suddenly without hope, I was stunned. Melissa advised me that the literature recommends telling children before a significant death, if there is an opportunity, so that they can prepare for it. This seemed to make sense, so I took them out onto the picnic area of the park and sat down at a table to tell them the saddest news I hope they will ever hear. Mummy, whom they understood had been very poorly for a long time, was going to die. As soon as she had grasped the enormity of the concept, Ella burst into tears and climbed across the table to me. "I don't want Mummy to be dead," she said. But Milo stayed where he was. I told him it was okay to cry, but he just became very still as he took it into himself, and he said; "I don't want to cry. I want to be strong for you, Daddy." Everybody has their own way, so he just watched Ella and me cry.

At the funeral in Jersey, where Katherine grew up, it was odd being the focus of what seemed like such a communal loss. Everyone who knew Katherine quickly appreciated what a special person she was, and felt the appalling injustice of her, of all people, being taken away. Faces I'd known to be always creased into smiles and laughter were now all drawn and haggard, pained beyond endurance, with tears in every eye. The strain, the horror, the disbelief, the sheer agony no one had been expecting to face, confronting the inexplicable, unjustifiable, inexcusable loss of such a favorite person. She was the one person for whom nobody present had ever had a bad word or negative memory. The women looked at me with extreme pained sympathy, but somehow the men moved me most: big Neill, unable to speak, tears bursting from his eyes and rolling down his bearlike face; Tim, his fraught face full of fear and pain; Seamus, a school friend of Katherine's and now a local politician, so capable and composed in every other situation, stretched beyond any careful planning or considered charm. And while she had been alive, Jim and Mike, both big and strong, were so tender with her on their visits.

After the funeral, the full horror of the last three months began to sink in. With hindsight killing off hope, her decline looked different. But even within a few days I was able to appreciate that although this was a tragedy for us, it was not such an unusual one. Many people endure far worse. We were not in Darfur, or Srebrenica, or the Congo, where people have recently been eaten by rebels in front of their children. Katherine had had a good life in a wealthy country, and died peacefully and virtually painlessly in as measured and gentle a way as possible. We are designed to accept this loss—particularly children, who have had to evolve in groups where parental mortality was high. Daddy might not come back from the hunt. Mummy might die in childbirth. Different caretakers would take them in and they would either adapt or reproduce less well. We are mostly descended from those who adapted. This almost makes evolution sound like a religion, but I took comfort from these arguments. And, even amongst the luckiest people in the world today, we were exceptionally lucky. As well as being in England, with healthcare, laws, and privilege, and being surrounded by loving friends and family, we had a zoo out there. And one day soon, I'd get back to it.

In the meantime, I felt like I needed a mild sedative, preferably something organic, made from natural ingredients, like water, barley, hops, and perhaps about 5 percent alcohol by volume. Luckily, just such a sedative is widely available: Stella Artois. Just what the doctor didn't order, but in the early days, it worked perfectly.

6

The New Crew

A fter Katherine's death, I felt as if I might not give a damn about the zoo. But actually I did. Technically, I could see that the zoo was still possible—inevitable, in fact, or we were bust and the animals would be dispersed or killed— and this fact was bolted to my mind. And as far as I was con- cerned, other people who couldn't see this could simply fuck off.

Grief, apparently, according to the widely accepted Kübler- Ross model, generally has five stages: Denial, Anger, Bargaining (where you try to make a deal with God or fate, or in lesser cir- cumstances, the person who has left you), Depression, and Ac- ceptance. I feel as if I skipped the first three and went straight to depression and acceptance simultaneously. But the idea of anger intrigued me. I didn't feel anger as such—there was noth- ing and no one to feel anger toward for this random biological event, apart from some small-minded mishandling by some of the healthcare people involved, and they were just institution- alized cogs in a flawed machine. Besides, I didn't have the en- ergy for anger.

But I did feel a strong sense of disbelief that people could be so petty. I didn't mind seeing people arguing in the street, or not appreciating each other or frittering their valuable time in some other way. I could understand that they had drifted into this perspective and it was quite normal. What really got me, though, was the pettiness of many of the people at the park, particularly when there was such a clear and obvious common goal to reach for. I sat in on meetings and listened to endless silly bickering and power plays: "I can't work with so-and-so"; "He said this, so I said . . ." I stood out in the park in the rain impassively, awash with keepers' complaints about things like leaking wheelbarrows when they already knew that replacements were on order, and I wondered how anything in the world ever gets done. But these tiny, seemingly irrelevant preoccupations, I realized, were the stuff of life. People's daily experiences, what they had to deal with on the ground, were what it was all about—and that was somewhere on which I had to refocus.

Being part of the zoo had definitely helped, even in the most extreme times. Looking out of the window and seeing young keepers laughing as they worked, aware that someone was ill in the house and obviously sympathetic, but still knowing they had a job to do looking after the animals and getting on with it. Keeping the park going was participating in the cycle of life. Things were born, like piglets or a deer, and things died, like Spar the Tiger, or one of the owls. And Katherine. But no matter how devastating for me, the children, or Duncan and Mum, life goes on. It was like being on a farm, where it can't simply stop because one person isn't there.

For now, there was work to do: new repairs to make, new staff to hire, and most important, getting our license to trade as a zoo. This is a complicated procedure, whereby you have to give notice of your intention to apply two months before you do so, to allow objections to be raised, aired, and assessed. In our case we knew we could expect strong objections from animal rights activists who had targeted the park's poor practices in the past, but the local community was supportive, and the council was showing no signs of being obstructive. An inspection date would then be booked, after which a verdict could take another six weeks to deliver. So far, straightforward. But the problem was that if we failed this inspection, we couldn't just rebook one in a week or so; we would have to go through the whole procedure again, complete with the two-month delay and possible six-week wait for the result. If we failed the inspection, it would be catastrophic for the business plan, which relied entirely on maximizing the income from the summer season.

By early April we had already missed Easter, the first and sometimes biggest bonanza weekend on the leisure-industry calendar and a significant pillar of our business plan. As the winter progressed, we'd tentatively suggested early June as our opening date, backtracking our inspection date from there. But in view of the amount of work to be done, eventually we settled for July. Which gave us an inspection date of June 4. There was a clear deadline to meet, a certain number of tasks to be carried out before then, and as long as these were addressed accordingly, it was a done deal. Probably.

My participation was clearly necessary, but it took me a while to readjust to this already broadly unfamiliar environment. In those days, I needed to be alone to cry every few hours or so. I was lucky that the nature of my job, as roving troubleshooter and director, allowed me to be able to do this. I could steer a meeting or oversee the siting of a fence post, and then make my excuses and leave, ostensibly to pursue some urgent business about the park. More often than not, however, I'd hole up in one of my safe havens—the attic, the top of the observation tower, the fern garden—and let the tears roll. It was like a bottomless reservoir, busting at the dams, needing to be drained before any progress could be made.

While I had been watching from the house or the front lawn, Steve was recruiting two new senior keepers. Normally it would have been unthinkable that I wasn't involved directly in the interview and selection process, as I obviously have a keen personal interest in who is employed on the site. I want to know about their philosophies of animal management, their interpersonal skills, and see how they respond to the interview itself. I find that with the few staff that I have interviewed and then taken on, the interview itself comes up in conversation from time to time as an important part of the transaction between us. I may remind them of something they agreed to do, or they remind me of a commitment I made, or we laugh about some embarrassing moment. But the interview is critically important to me in establishing just who exactly we will be putting our trust in, and several candidates fell very wide of the mark. But as it was, I was distantly aware that the selection process was going on, and trusted Steve's judgment entirely.

And I was right to do so. The two keepers he recruited in that time, Owen and Sarah, had both participated in internationally recognized rare-animal breeding programs. And both of them brought useful contacts lists for exchanges with other zoos, and the personal credibility to back them up. In other words, each keeper carries a direct experience of breeding rare animals that follows them around. Sarah, for instance, has unique and direct experience of the fishing cats at Port Lympne Zoo, whose directors were so impressed with her that they said a breeding pair could come with her to DZP, as soon as we could build them a

suitable enclosure. Owen, a soft-spoken but assertive young Scots-
man who grew up on a croft, or small farm, also has a portfolio
of rare animals—in his case birds—which follows him around,
and his best idea was to cover the flamingo lake with a large enclosed aviary and put in a mangrove swamp to house some of his
more exotic future acquisitions. I agreed immediately, and then
asked how we would go about putting mangroves in. "I don't
know yet," said Owen. "But I'll find out and let you know." Then
it would be over to me to work out whether we could implement
it. Such are the challenges that face a zoo director, I was discovering. But these are enjoyable challenges, and being able to commission a mangrove swamp is a position I never thought I'd be in.

Owen and Sarah, who were now the senior keepers, were
several times referred to as "stars" by people in the zoo world,
such as Nick Lindsay and Mike Thomas. Owen and Sarah were
people they had read about in the literature, whose reputa-
tions preceded them. Even Peter Wearden, our local environmental health officer, seemed to have heard of them, or at least
appreciated the significance of us being able to attract them to
work for us. Owen, I'd been told, had turned down a place at San
Diego Zoo to work here. San Diego is a world leader in many
fields, including his, a place that could offer him almost unimag-
inable resources to pursue his interests. One day I asked him why
he'd chosen this run-down place instead, in an area with one of
the highest rainfalls in Britain, and not the resource-rich, sunnier
climes of Southern California. "When I walked round the place,
I obviously saw the amazing potential of the site," he said. "But
I also saw that there was a great sadness here, and that sadness
was something I wanted to reverse." He wasn't talking about
Katherine, he was talking about the effects of the long, slow,
twenty-year decline of the park, on the people, the animals, and

the infrastructure—piles of clutter everywhere, hoarded in hope that had gradually ebbed away, leaving a residue of fatalism and algae behind it.

Owen and Sarah may have been stars, but they were not prima donnas. They were physically tough and hardworking. Having both relocated from far-flung UK zoos, they initially had no accommodation and so they camped on site in the inter-minable rain, doing their laundry and washing up in the rest-rooms of the restaurant. I offered them use of the shower in the house, when it worked, but they were happier with their subsis-tence living—and besides, the hot water was more reliable in the restaurant. Out in the park in all weathers, they led from the front, and both regularly spent many extra hours until dark, mending enclosures, building new ones, and continuing the on-going project of the park without the need for constant guidance. And they fulfilled the license requirement of training the exist-ing staff in the ways of modern zoo practices.

This "trickle down" training was something we had been told we needed to do or else close down. Or rather, not open at all. The people we employed to look after the animals—Rob, Kelly, Hannah, Paul, John, and even Robin on occasion—were skilled and experienced, but they were not qualified. For all their hands-on knowledge and years in the trenches, there was barely a diploma among them. And these days, zoo-license-wise, paper qualifications are critical. I was delighted that these trickle-down processes were going on, because it was a vital part of our license requirement that we employed fully trained staff. Increasingly now I roamed the park believing that the impossible, which then became the merely improbable, had now, objectively, become the very likely. In fact, I had never had any doubt that we were going to succeed in opening the park, but increasingly, surrounded by so many pessimistic perspectives, I had begun to understand other people's perceptions and I hadn't liked what I saw from the other side. Even though I knew they were wrong, the sheer weight of numbers in the naysaying camp was almost overwhelming.

To be fair, they had some good points. For one thing, we needed sixty thousand visitors a year to break even, and at the moment we had nowhere to feed them. The restaurant, supposed to be a going concern, contained barely a single serviceable appliance. The dishwasher, gas hob, ovens, microwaves, and two of the three fat fryers didn't work. Luckily our new ideas for the menu, involving healthy, locally sourced food, meant that we wouldn't be needing the two broken fat fryers, but everything else needed to be replaced. I had a dream for the restaurant, which was to get it as smart as a Conran venue and open it in the evenings as a separate entity from the zoo. The figures for the last three years' trading, though in sharp decline, showed that the restaurant and bar were the engine of the park, accounting for more than a third of its total income. With its grimy Artex ceiling, strip lights, heavy dark-blue carpets and curtains, and a kitchen full of grease-coated scrap, it was going to be a long haul to get there. The other thing that the trading figures showed was that the month of August was absolutely critical, with combined ticket and restaurant sales accounting for approaching half of the annual income. August was make or break, and if we missed it, we were sunk. "I think that this August will provide about sixty percent of your income this year," Mike Thomas told me on one of his visits, sitting in the uninspiring environs of the restaurant. A quick glance around us left me in no doubt as to the scale of the task ahead. If sixty thousand people arrived over the summer wanting to be fed, we simply couldn't afford for them to walk out and find somewhere else to eat as we had once done, in the park's final open days last spring. As well as the requirements for the animals, this was a business, and the customer service side had to be treated with equal importance, or the vet bills wouldn't get paid and the worthy conservation plans would be unworkable.

So Duncan and I started going to pubs—strictly for research purposes, you understand—to observe catering operations in action. We put in many, many, dedicated, selfless long hours in this quest for catering enlightenment before settling in a carvery down the road in nearby Plympton that had an exceptional catering staff. The other interesting thing about this venue, though far removed from our aspirations for our own facilities, was that it was extremely well run. And always packed. A constant stream of local people came here to eat, so that a good-natured line almost always stretched from the restaurant to the bar. This meant that, in order to conduct our reconnaissance effectively, we had to loiter at a part of the bar forbidden to all but diners, which we did. What struck me was that, when a certain manager named Mark was on, we were always asked to move within about five minutes. Initially he was satisfied with our line, "We're waiting for some friends," but on about the fourth visit he laughed and said, "Are these friends of yours ever going to turn up?" Mark was everywhere: in the kitchen, amongst the tables, behind the bar, even facing down a gang of towering teenagers who had broken a window the evening before. I warmed to him, confessed that we were actually engaged in mild industrial espionage, and asked if he'd like to help us at the zoo. He didn't want to leave his job, but he agreed, and worked out some simple menu ideas that could be produced relatively easily using mass-market catering suppliers. These suppliers provided food for several well-known zoos, some of which I'd visited and sampled the food of, and it wasn't so bad. With minimum intervention we could tidy up the restaurant, provide simple food to get us through the all-important month of August, then revamp the place during the quieter winter months. It sounded like a plan, but a plan that worried me. Now we had the money for the redevelopment, though we were running out of time. By the time winter came, at the rate funds were flowing out, it was quite possible that the money would have been spent on other things. Mark visited us several times, brimming with enthusiasm, but because of his full-time job, his suggestions inevitably entailed a lot of legwork on our side. As the weeks inched forward toward crunch time, we had to decide whether to go for the holding strategy or the bold move, orchestrating a full revamp and a "hard" opening, showcasing our radical changes. What we needed was someone to take this problem in its entirety, run with it, and turn it into a solution for the other ills at the park.

And then came Adam. I was in a bad mood when I first met Adam, standing out by the otter enclosure in a large area of the park I had always wanted to dedicate to free-ranging monkeys, and to my father, Ben Harry Mee, who had provided the funds for the park—albeit unwittingly and posthumously, and absolutely certainly (had he been alive) unwillingly. I wanted more tropical trees populated with colorful birds, endangered, people-friendly primates running loose, and a modest monument to my dad somewhere, the Ben Harry Mee Memorial Jungle. It would have been the last thing he'd ever have expected, and I knew that despite his disapproval at the obvious folly of the misuse of his hard-earned capital designated for the future security of his family, he would have been quietly amused by this. I liked to picture him sitting down to read in a tranquil jungle glade to the sound of kookaburras and birds of paradise, beset by curious little monkeys, before finally snapping his book shut and saying, "It's bloody ridiculous." But he'd have kept going back, and one day we'd have found him feeding the monkeys with a stash of something he'd carefully observed that they loved to eat.

All this was constantly under threat from pressures within the zoo for other uses of the land. The petting zoo had to go somewhere, as did the education center involving a nature pond; between them, they would eat at least two-thirds of this space. That morning I had also endured an interminable barrage of phone calls from double-glazing-window salesmen; people who wanted to do marketing, advertising, and building work; and two companies that had a surefire way to reduce our business rates for a small fee (both utterly and obviously spurious), as well as a constant stream of personal callers, usually people who had worked in the park before and wanted their old jobs back, as long as such and such a person wasn't there anymore. I had had enough. And then Duncan came up the path, accompanied by a tall, fresh-faced man called Adam, who had sent me an e-mail a week or two before to offer his services as a catering manager.

Catering was one of the few areas we more or less had a handle on, it seemed to me at the time (though I was so wrong). "What? Yes, fine. I'll look at your CV," or terse words to that effect were probably how I initially responded, making a note to remind Duncan that the last thing we needed was a change of direction now. But Duncan was convinced by Adam. His story was that he had worked in retail and customer services from a young age until very recently, in his thirties, when his father had sold the nearby thriving Endsleigh Garden Center to a national chain, and they had both retired to pursue other avenues. In his father's case, this meant buying a yellow biplane and setting up another business in the sunnier climes of southern France (bastard). In Adam's, it meant buying a nice house in the locality and setting up a farm shop on the grounds of the garden center to sell organic produce for the more discerning market.

The more I delved, the more it seemed to make sense. Adam wanted to open the restaurant in the evenings—he had the bearing of the perfect maître d'—and he had excellent customer-service credentials and experience of the local market. And he wanted to start right away. After a week of dithering, we took him on, and it was as if a weight had been lifted on that side of the park. Adam wanted to go for the full revamp, and immediately set about pulling in quotes from reliable local tradesmen he had worked with before, ploughing through the administrative processes with the council, and even finding time to take a one-day licensing course so that he could be the named licensee for the bar.

Suddenly this tall man with the enthusiasm of a young pup, impeccably polite and diplomatic at all times, became one of our most valuable assets. Undaunted by the prospect of fitting out the restaurant, shop, and kitchen simultaneously, he also ran a computer business and was eager to fit an electronic point of sale (EPOS) till system which would give us instant feedback on visitor numbers, how much they spent and on what (the critical spend-per-head statistic that we really needed to get above £5 per person on top of their ticket price), and even their postal codes, so we knew where our market was coming from. We came to rely on Adam, and not just for his problem-solving abilities and propensity to take up any slack he saw, even if it didn't directly concern him. "Can I make a suggestion?" he would say, leaning in like a wine steward about to rescue an ignorant customer from the perils of a complicated wine list, whenever he saw a problem that wasn't being properly addressed. No, what I began to rely on most from Adam was his optimism. Having someone who said, "Of course, no problem. I'll get on to it right away," instead of "It'll be expensive, and you'll have to do X and Y first and that's going to be impossible," made all the difference. Optimism was undoubtedly Adam's most valuable contribution.

I once lost quite a lot of blood, about two pints, after a silly accident in a martial arts class (I walked forward when I should have stepped back, and took a precision blow to the nose that ruptured something deep in my nasal cavities). Sitting in the emergency room, dripping prolifically into a series of compressed cardboard trays, I gradually got weaker. Young(ish) men with skinhead haircuts and nosebleeds, particularly inflicted by some sort of violence, take a low priority in Accident and Emergency. There's always a car crash or a heart attack ahead of you, and it wasn't until my vision started tunnelling and everything went into black-and-white that I finally staggered up and informed the nearest nurse that I was about to pass out, then lay back on my trolley to do just that. Suddenly I was an emergency, and I was dimly aware of a phalanx of medical professionals bearing down on me, *ER* style, armed with drips and other bits of reassuring kit. Katherine, who had brought me in, didn't help by saying "Phwoorr," because at the head of the phalanx was a bronzed Australian orderly whose half-sleeve white tunic showed off his amply muscled forearms, as she had been pointing out to me for the last two hours. Just as my eyes closed and I started to be sucked into unconsciousness, they fitted a saline drip into my arm and gave me some injections, and the sensation was extraordinary. It was exactly like having an enormous thirst quenched, but instead of the relief spreading outward from the stomach, it was spreading from my arm. That was what it was like having Adam take over the restaurant at this difficult time. A seemingly peripheral piece of the puzzle was infecting the whole place with renewed positivity. The oil tanker of the park was gradually being turned around before it drifted onto the rocks.

The other thing that Adam brought in that cheered me up were builders, and good ones—well kitted out, hardworking, and versatile. Special mention has to go to Tim the carpenter, small but perfectly formed, and head of a small highly skilled team, which laid a solid oak floor in the three hundred square meters of the restaurant, built a curvy service counter based on a whimsical sketch I drew in three minutes on the back of an envelope, and clad the revolting bar in the leftover pieces of oak, on budget, and all in about six weeks.

During this time, materials were arriving, electricians were fiddling with new sunken spot lighting, and plasterboard gradually blotted out the Artex, that decorating crime against humanity, on the ceiling. There was floor sanding going on, painting, the first and second fix, all things I knew about and had witnessed many times, sure indicators of ongoing progress. Whenever I passed through the restaurant, it felt good, and I was drawn into discussions with conscientious experts in fields I also actually knew something about. Hell, I was a DIY expert, officially in print. I genuinely could make informed decisions in a familiar field, instead of having to learn everything from scratch as an outsider. Whenever I got the chance, I would join in a bit, usually during the lunch hour (even good builders have lunch hours, but I couldn't seem to justify the time). I remember one happy afternoon smashing the execrable tiles off the wall behind the counter with a large hammer and a bricklayer's bolster, and another using a belt sander to put a snub-nosed radius on the edge of the beautiful new oak-clad bar. These were fleeting visits to a simpler life, and I always had to reenter the general fray beyond sooner than I would have liked. But, like all good and righteous DIY interventions, they were good for the soul.

Peter Wearden made several visits to the park in the early days to see how things were going, give advice, and usually drop off interminable piles of unappetizing matter—I mean, essential reading—such as turgid ring binders entitled "Secretary of State's Handbook for Modern Zoo Practice," and "The Zoo Forum's Handbook." These, along with the health and safety literature, and food, drinks, and entertainment licensing forms, really are essential but not tempting reading. Perfect for dipping into relevant paragraphs in support of some application, or rapidly bringing on sleep at the end of a busy day.

But then one day he passed me something that nearly brought me to tears: a paper from the journal *Biologist* about why we need zoos. I really nearly could have cried. The big folders of nonsense merely added to the already enormous unfamiliar workload, joining pressing material from banks, lawyers, and creditors, which already overfilled my day. Suddenly, here was an academic paper I needed to read and digest, in support of future media interviews, press releases, or public debates.

Fifteen years earlier, I had taken a master's course at Imperial College London in science journalism, and since then I had been making my living to a greater or lesser degree by translating into English science papers exactly like this one, and many much more impenetrable, for publications in glossy magazines and newspapers and occasional broadcasts on radio and television. Seeing the paper felt like home, far more than the house we were sitting in. It was even presented on a stapled black-and-white A4 photocopy, a format very familiar, and handy for my pencil notes in the margin. For the last ten months I don't think

The new house takes shape.

Katherine translating for Karsan and the French electrician.

Ella strokes Dancer, who is sitting on Leon.

Building site on a building site.

Sausages on sticks for dinner.

Katherine and the children have a swim in front of "The Pretty Barn."

Dartmoor Zoo's most endangered animal, the new agouti.
Will Walker/Dartmoor Zoological Park

Juliette, the grouchy tawny eagle.
Will Walker/Dartmoor Zoological Park

Lazy Bones: Solomon, our African lion.
Will Walker/Dartmoor Zoological Park

Gilly, the dainty elderly serval.
Will Walker/Dartmoor Zoological Park

Zak, the patriarch (or alpha wolf).
Will Walker/Dartmoor Zoological Park

The largest rodent in the world, Mrs. Capybara, spends a lot of time in the pond
Barry Turner ©2008

Dilys, one of the new alpacas, has the brains of a rocking horse.
Will Walker/Dartmoor Zoological Park

Snowdrop, Asian short-clawed otter.
Will Walker/Dartmoor Zoological Park

Sovereign, planning his next escape.
Barry Turner ©2008

Three's a crowd, but the new black-cheeked love birds are breeding.
Will Walker/Dartmoor Zoological Park

Stripe smiles for the camera.
Will Walker/Dartmoor Zoological Park

Sovereign stalking.
Will Walker/Dartmoor Zoological Park

I'd looked at or even thought about a scientific paper amidst the pressing urgencies of zoo acquisition. Though I was by now already mentally, physically, and emotionally pretty drained, at last I was being asked to move back (at least a tiny bit) onto familiar territory, and this rare ray of positivity was not just a reminder of how life used to be, but an indication of how it could be again.

One of the main attractions for me in buying the zoo had been the prospect of conducting scientific research and writing about it in journals, books, and magazines. And this little sliver of science, carefully folded and put in my pocket next to the pencil that would soon be scribbling on it, reminded me that that was still possible—once we'd resolved that pesky matter of getting a £500,000 loan, spending it in the right way to get a zoo license, the license being granted in time, and then enough people coming through the door for the zoo to be able to support the interest payments on that loan. Piece of cake. Then I could think about research projects.

Another very welcome piece of scientific material, which came my way a few weeks later, was the Australian Regional Association of Zoological Parks (ARAZP) husbandry manual for the species *Prionailurus viverrinus*, or fishing cats. As an act of enormous faith in us, subject to getting our license of course, another zoo, Port Lympne, had offered us a breeding pair of these incredibly feisty, medium-size cats. Standing up to thirty-three inches tall and weighing over thirty pounds, they are taller than a whippet and heavier than a Staffordshire bull terrier, and far more dangerous than either. Classed as a "hazardous" animal to keep, in their native Asia they have been known to "fight off packs of dogs, carry off babies, and even kill a leopard." And, according to the IUCN (International Union for Conservation of Nature), they are "Near Threatened." Though only one category away from "Least Concern," this is also one category away from "Vulnerable," which would put it on the IUCN's Red List of endangered animals. Without sustained active conservation measures it is extremely rare for animals to move back down this list to where they are no longer under threat. What tends to happen is that they move up the list to Endangered, on to Critically Endangered, and then inexorably onward toward Extinct. Going, going, gone.

But there is hope. Conservation measures do work: in 2006, the number of species that moved up the list into a more critical category was 172, but 139 moved down to an improved status. And there is one other vital category for zoos: Extinct in Wild. Animals have been known to come back from this category, which nudges full-on, irrevocable Extinct, and even head right down the list and back out into the wild to Least Concern. It is an unusual but growing trend, and thanks to pioneers like Gerald Durrell, the zoological community is now increasingly focusing on captive breeding programs. These don't always lead to reintroduction to the wild; generally, creatures go extinct because there is no longer enough of their preferred version of the wild left to sustain them. But captive breeding does inform conservation measures in remaining natural habitats, also increasingly undertaken by zoos, by revealing the specific requirements that animals need to breed. Knowing exactly what conditions you are aiming for, rather than things you think they might need, can make that all-important difference between Critically Endangered and Extinct.

Fishing cats are quite tricky because they are so aggressive. The male sometimes kills the female, which is not a good way to continue a species. What prompts them to do this is not known, though as lovers' tiffs go, it is maladaptive in the extreme. But fishing cats have been bred successfully at Port Lympne and in Australia (hence the Australian husbandry guide—the European Endangered Species Program [EEP] is still drawing theirs up), several other places around the world, and with luck, at Dartmoor Zoological Park, before long. As their habitat shrinks, due to the encroachment of agriculture in northern India, Burma, Thailand, and Sumatra, if they do move up the Red List, at least there will be diverse seed populations in captivity, should their time come again. At least there will still be fishing cats.

This was scientific work that was directly applicable to what we were trying to achieve on the ground—it was even a license requirement that we launch projects such as these—and I avidly absorbed the entire document. The recommended minimum size for their enclosures, for instance, is 40 square meters. The Australians had provided 85. We could give them 160. Why not? We had the space. Better to look after fewer species well than cram in a load of disparate unhappy animals to pander to decreasing public attention spans. Besides, fishing cats are gorgeous, eye-catching creatures who warrant a sanctuary in their own right. Their markings are like a big tabby crossed with a leopard, on a background of golden greenish fur, and they sit by the side of streams intently until some hapless fish passes below, when they dive in headfirst and snatch it up in their jaws. Other cats, like tigers and jaguars, will go into water, but fishing cats specialize in it, wading around like fools even when they are not hunting, apparently indifferent to the fact that cats don't do that. I was delighted we were getting something so exotic and worthwhile, and though this was a project for the (not too distant) future, I kept the husbandry manual on my desk where I could see it, as a morale booster.

Another happy by-product of being given this paper was that it led me to discover, firsthand, what happens When Porcupines Go Bad. I always delight in being humbled by animals, something for which, happily, this job provides ample opportunities. One night I couldn't sleep because I'd had a "brainwave" about the fishing cats. The husbandry requirements told me that, among other things, these rare little beasts like to live with running water. Their wetland habitat, being reduced across Asia, is often converted to paddy fields: water based, but not moving water. Our site is awash with water running off Dartmoor, and there are several places where natural rivers seed, sometimes running into one of the two lakes or the two moated enclosures, but often just creating boggy ground in underused areas. With these rivers formalized into proper waterways, they could be made into features, and even be a source (on a small scale, for lighting perhaps) of hydroelectric power. They would also benefit the fishing cats, whose enclosure could be built to follow the contours of a living stream.

I had a hunch where the best place for this would be, in what I still liked to call the giraffe field, but is now "the small cats field," where it borders the walk-in enclosure containing the flamingo lake. This is where Owen wanted the mangrove swamp for his birds, and the husbandry guide informed me that fishing cats also love mangroves, which are, I'd discovered, themselves "Threatened," according to the IUCN. At this crux between enclosures, a natural spring bursts out from boggy ground to babble into the lake amidst a thicket of brambles and overgrown exotic plants. It was for this thicket that I set out at three in the morning wearing a headlamp and carrying a notebook, to do a feasibility study for a snaking fishing-cat enclosure, ending in a continuation of Owen's mangroves for his birds in the flamingo lake (obviously the mangroves for the birds and the cats would need to be segregated, or the tenure of the birds, and indeed the birds themselves, would be short lived).

After an hour or so of getting my feet wet and my arms scratched, I retired, satisfied that this was an ideal place to work back from to instigate a small river, which could in turn run through a futuristic, twenty-first-century fishing-cat enclosure. I stood in the field and sketched a few ideas by the light of the headlamp, and stretched and yawned, knowing that now I could sleep. But I thought I might make a sedentary detour to the top corner of the walk-in, where the porcupines live (another enclosure in need of revamping, but adequate and some way down the list). I had been in with the porcupines a few times with several different keepers, most recently with Steve, the curator, helping to haul some huge pieces of fresh wood on which these glorified rodents like to gnaw, to keep their constantly growing beaverlike incisors in check. Every time, in daylight, Mr. and Mrs. Porcupine, as they are known, had kept to themselves and stayed in their house while their enclosure was cleaned or revamped, their natural shyness and nocturnal lifestyle keeping them indoors, so that the door never needed to be secured during our forays into their backyard.

I nonchalantly vaulted over the fence to collect some of their many fallen quills littering the ground, which often rotted into the earth before they could be salvaged. Porcupine quills are particularly lovely objects, almost like politically acceptable, harvestable ivory. Some are twelve inches long, narrow with perfectly symmetrical bands of cream and brown, others as small as three inches, fat as a pen in the middle and virtually monochromatic. No two are the same, except that each one ends in an exceptionally sharp point, with a small barb that leaves it sticking into your skin, as I had previously discovered from cleaning them too carelessly under the tap. They are sometimes used for the tops of fishing floats, or by calligraphers to mount nibs, or just a handful in a jar as decoration. They were once sold in the park shop until health and safety fears prevented it, but I was collecting them because, if you get one the right size, the blunt end that used to attach to the porcupine's skin makes a particularly good stylus for a modern mobile phone. I'd lost my original stylus and broken the last quill I'd used for the job, which I'd collected from the enclosure, cleaned up, and cut down to size.

Now it was my turn to be cut down to size. As I rummaged nonchalantly in the dirt, Mr. Porcupine came bustling out of his house, his bristling quills shimmering in the lamplight. I was surprised at how active he seemed, but unflustered, as I had been in the enclosure several times before without incident. But that was in daylight, when Mr. Porcupine had better things to do, like snuggle up (carefully, I presume) asleep with Mrs. Porcupine. Now I was on his patch, in his garden, on his time, and he didn't like it. As he paced up and down I gave him more space, with the result that he soon had me herded into a corner. At which point he turned his back to me at a distance of about three yards, then reversed at high speed, brandishing his motile array of beautiful barbs like a lethal Red Indian headdress. I just had time to register the extent of his displeasure, and the unacceptable consequences of staying where I was, before it was time to act, and I found myself scrambling backward in the dark, over the fence, and falling heavily on my rear into a patch of nettles on the other side. The nettles went up my sweater and stung me comprehensively before I could scrabble myself away. Ouch, ouch, OUCH. I stood up and laughed with new esteem for this pint-sized animal pincushion. I had been totally trounced by what is technically an elaborate rodent. Mr. Porcupine, one; Mr. Zoo Director, nil. Respect.

"Tourette Tony"

I was introduced to Tony perhaps a week after Katherine died, while I was walking around the park with the children. This was before Katherine's funeral, and everyone was giving me lots of space, but a couple of people from the film crew who had shadowed me since before the purchase, and who were booked to stay until after the opening day (should it ever arrive) came over tentatively and said that there was someone, if I felt up to it, I ought to meet. We'd hired a digger, a full-size JCB excavator, and the operator, Tony, who had been on site for about a week, had been making a good impression with everybody. The zookeepers liked him, the maintenance guys liked him, the film crew liked him, and he could handle the digger like it was an extension of himself. Clearing huge swathes of scrub and rubble with deft efficiency, then moving it into apparently inaccessible areas with the grace of a ballerina, and without damaging anything, deploying the vast half-ton bucket on the mechanical dinosaur arm to carry out a procedure delicate enough to make a heart surgeon miss a beat. So he could handle a digger. He could also handle people, and by now, people issues were beginning to surface.

The new crew wasn't getting on that well with the old crew, whom they regarded with suspicion as potential collaborators in the alleged transgressions of the old regime, rumors about which were rife in the zoo world. None of the new people had ever worked in a place like this, which was pretty Wild West compared to the pristine, regimented environments through whose ranks they had progressed. But Tony had. During his seventeen years as a hired digger hand, Tony had worked in much worse, and was making no secret about wanting a full-time job with us. And we needed a head of maintenance. John was multi-skilled and able to fabricate or repair pretty well anything on a shoestring, but by his own admission, paperwork was not his strong point. We had to have someone in charge who could cope with the order forms, file receipts, and manage a budget, which goes with running a busy maintenance department in a modern zoo. I spoke to John, who said, "If that bloke wants a job I'd vouch for him and be more than happy to work under him," which seemed positive. Tony was also a trained mechanic, welder, marksman, and an assistant Olympic archery coach, keen to set up lessons at the park should there be a demand. Having not been around, I asked various people what they thought, and it was unanimous. Everyone wanted Tony, and I did too. The film crew asked if they could film me from a distance talking to him and taking him on, so I conducted an informal interview next to the JCB to sound him out, making sure that his approach to handling people fitted in with our needs, then took him on with a shake of the hand. Immediately Tony became an invaluable member of the team, cheering people up, nudging them along, and using his technical skills with great efficiency.

And after he started, it transpired that Tony had another special skill: swearing. From my time working on building sites many years ago I'd noticed that prolific swearing was basically the dialect in which the building trade operates. It's even in the terminology. Cement is *shite*; nothing is "not straight," it's *pissed*. Swear words are even used as fillers when people can't think of what else to say, as in an example I remember from my first day on a bricklaying training course. The man working next to me asked, "Can you pass the, er, fucking, the, er, fucking, the fucking hammer?" That seemed about par for the course: roughly one in three or four words was a profanity of some sort. Tony, as a senior veteran of the game and former soldier, had got his average swear rate up to one in two on occasion, though he sometimes lapsed back to one in three.

Tony's speech is not just littered but positively crowded out with expletives, but if you accept that and listen carefully there is an almost poetic quality to some of his utterances. Once he cornered me to share his concerns that our advertising strategy needed to be wider than the medium of print. What he actually said was "Not every fucker reads the fucking paper. I was in the fucking paper the other day, I thought, fuck me every cunt's going to be taking the piss. Fuck me if only one fucker did. I thought, fucking hell." Not quite Guild of Poetry, perhaps, but pithy nevertheless. He was christened "Tourette Tony" (or sometimes simply "Fucking Tony," to distinguish him from "Kiosk Tony," who came later), and appointed himself "Chairman of the DZP Tourette Club."

Before Katherine died, I would be out there, listening to everybody, trying to build bridges, trying to make sure that everybody got talking again. After Katherine died, I was out there again, eventually, watching from close up but at what seemed like an extreme distance, not even able to muster the energy for contempt at the pathetic bickering, which daily demonstrated that even Milo and Ella exhibited more self-awareness. There was so much to do, and such a clear, straight line in which to proceed, and to squander so much energy on such petty issues seemed like a crime. Everybody with any business experience that I spoke to assured me that "staff" were always a big headache, but in my acutely distanced state, this seemed to me ultimately like a crime against the animals. Yet, in any kind of crisis, all pettiness was put to one side and everybody pulled together with resolute, practical professionalism.

Like the day they came to get the two jaguars, and it very nearly all went wrong.

One day early on, it was time to move the two female jaguars. This was a momentous occasion for us, because it was something I had agreed to with Peter Wearden at the council and Mike Thomas, and I knew that the entire zoo community was watching. It could never have happened under the old regime, and though it was a difficult bullet for us to bite, the two beautiful jaguars were going to a purpose-built big-cat park, where they would live in a brand-new enclosure, owned and run by a senior member of BIAZA. We were paying our dues. The jags would be better off, and we would be better off without the constant risk of their escaping. According to what people said, we may even get some zebras in return, somewhere down the line. And when it was over, the keepers would get to demolish the much-hated, dilapidated wooden house for the jags, which they had been wanting to do for so long.

It had been mooted by one or two people that we could actually sell the jags, worth several thousand pounds each, to a private collector who could hold them perfectly legally, with the right facilities, under the Dangerous Wild Animals Act. Much as we needed the money, we also wanted to do the right thing. Under such scrutiny, now was not the time to deviate from the script. I was also looking forward to seeing how another team from an established mainstream zoo, Thrigby Hall, in Norwich, would operate—and initially, I was not disappointed.

An immaculate, anonymous white van arrived, exactly like a plumber might use (though these guys arrived when they said they would), and two unbelievably grizzled rangers emerged from it, clad entirely in green, apart from old brown boots, the mandatory dog-eared Indiana Jones hats, and leather pouches on their belts. Their weather-beaten faces and clothing made them seem a part of the woodland around the jag house, almost as if they were covered in moss, or a wren might fly out of one of their beards. Like Bob Lawrence, who had come down from the Midlands to dart Sovereign for us, these two looked like they'd seen it all before and could cope with anything.

So we were surprised when they produced wooden crates from the back of the van, which didn't look quite up to the specifications for holding jaguars. Rob, as head keeper, raised this with them. "Don't you worry, we've moved countless jags in these crates," they assured us. One of the boxes was newer than the other, made from heavy-duty marine plywood, and this was deployed first. Positioned inside the jag house against the solid steel gate into the enclosure, it was nailed in place with big battens to prevent it moving should the first jag not enter cleanly, or begin to struggle. Kelly called her with the usual promise of food in the house, the gate was raised, the cat jumped in, and the door of the box was shut behind her. As simple as that. There were no windows in this box, but a heavy-gauge mesh door to provide light. We carried the box down to the van and loaded it in like removal men carrying a tea chest of crockery—easy does it, but no problem at all. The only difference was that you really had to concentrate on keeping your fingers away from the mesh on the door, or they'd be ripped off and eaten in an instant.

The ease of this move gave us confidence, though the second crate looked less suitable than the first. It had a window about a foot square in the roof panel, secured with two layers of wire mesh: one on the outside, and one on the inside. Again the construction was marine ply, though much older and more worn. Again Rob raised his doubts, particularly about the strength of the mesh on the window, which looked bent and was of a lighter gauge than that on the door. "Are you sure these boxes aren't for pumas?" he said, but again was reassured, somewhat tetchily this time, that everything was under control. We consulted with each other and decided to give the rangers the benefit of the doubt, even though the jaguar is much stronger than a puma—stronger than a leopard—and had the most powerful weight-to-jaw-strength ratio of any of the big cats. This enables them to bite through turtle shells and hunt larger prey such as deer (and if you are unlucky, man), by puncturing the skull directly with its canines. We really didn't want her to get out of the box.

The same procedure of lining up and nailing down the box was followed. Kelly called the cat, who, anxious for food, readily jumped in, and the door was closed behind her. And then it started to go wrong. This was the grumpy sister, and she wasn't at all pleased about her confinement, or being tricked, or us peering down at her through the window in the roof panel. Immediately she began thrashing around with that almost supernatural strength of a wild animal, and began using her primary weapon, those awesome jaws, on the mesh that separated us. Upsettingly, the first layer began to yield right away. Her teeth, her flashing eyes, the primal guttural noises emerging from the box, which was bucking—though not buckling, I was pleased to notice—suddenly all seemed reminiscent of the scene at the beginning of *Jurassic Park*, where some large creature exerts far stronger forces on its holding bay than anticipated. Somebody dies in that scene, and though we were a long way from that possibility at the moment, it would definitely raise its head if we didn't get the next bit right. In fact, our worst-case scenario was simply to open the door of the crate and let the jaguar back into the enclosure so that the men of the woods would have to come another day. But if we delayed too long, it looked like the jag could definitely burst out of her window to be among us, and may not be tempted by the prospect of going back into her enclosure. Before that happened, the four or five people in the jag house could, obviously, clear out in time so that the house could be secured—if not, the redoubtable John on firearms would have to shoot her, which would not be a good result. This was a plan that could conceivably go wrong at some stage—those unknown unknowns again—and we had to act decisively to minimize the risk to the people and the animal, who could easily hurt herself if she continued chewing on the mesh.

Time shrank down so that every second was precious, eked out in a serious group analysis of the situation. If the first mesh went down, we would open the gate into the enclosure and exit the building, closing the door behind us. Before that happened, though, we had time, we calculated, to reinforce the window, so that the transfer could proceed as planned. It was not a full Code Red yet, but it had all the ingredients needed to become one.

Someone suggested sliding some metal slats under the top mesh, to be gripped by the bolted fixings securing it, and I ran to the workshop, fortunately only a few yards away, with Paul and Andy Goatman, the young knacker man, who had been making a delivery and is always good in a crisis. It was a good thing the workshop was now functioning, at least to some degree. Paul quickly found some suitable metal slats and began cutting them to length with the newly relocated bench-mounted grinder, pretty well our only tool. Andy and I rummaged amongst the old agricultural miscellanea in the three-quarters cleared loft for a hook, or something that could be made into a hook, to pull the top mesh on the box clear of the plywood roof and to insert the slats underneath without losing a finger. I think in the end we used one of the slats, modified at the end to make a hook, and it was successfully deployed. Somebody strong hooked it into the wire to raise it the necessary millimeters, and the slats were inserted one by one. As they went in, the *Jurassic Park* scenario still loomed large, but the jaguar gradually became calmer, and so did we. When the light went out above her, she stopped thrashing entirely, though continued her low, disturbing growl. The rangers said they were happy, and we loaded her into the van without further incident.

As they drove away I marveled at the fact that rear-ending this particular white van could potentially have terrible unforeseen consequences for the average unsuspecting motorist, unleashing two extremely unsettled middleweight predators onto the hood of his car. Armed police along the route had been alerted, but their response time, measured in minutes, would not do much to reassure those possibly already injured people on the scene. But that was now no longer our problem. In fact the nine-hour journey would go without a hitch, the two jaguars would be successfully relocated to a much more suitable environment, and we would be left with a tranquil, empty enclosure that had previously been a source of much concern.

During the fray, with the cat box bucking in the background, I had joked to Andy that if he had any extra guns lying around, now might be a good time to deploy them. Afterward, as everyone was packing up, Andy showed me that in the midst of the situation he'd slid his .357 Magnum revolver into his trouser pocket. Issued for killing livestock above a certain size, four of the six chambers were blanked off by law, because if you can't kill a bullock with two shots from this piece, you're in the wrong job. These two enormous slugs, in the hands of someone who could hold his nerve, were, retrospectively, intensely reassuring to me. I liked the fact that should things go wrong, there were people equipped and prepared to intervene. If somehow everything had all gone pear-shaped, and if John had slipped in the wet leaves at a critical time, it was good to know that somebody like Andy was there.

Officially, Andy was not a designated firearms officer for the site, and the correct procedure, should the cat have got past us, would have been to notify the police, whose nearest firearms unit was about five miles away. I preferred knowing that we had backup on the ground, but this was yet another entirely new world for me: real guns, big ones, deployed in the routine procedures of everyday work. With guns come danger, both in their handling and in the nature of the reasons for their deployment; if you need guns, something pretty heavy must be going down.

I cornered Andy and asked him to show me his gun. He pulled it out of his pocket, checked the safety, and slipped it into my hand. It was a solid steel .357 Magnum with a three-inch barrel, iconic from countless crime and cop films, here battered and worn, used as an agricultural tool. And it felt like a tool, heavy with precision engineering, unremittingly purposeful. Much as it scared me, I could see that to do this job properly I would have to get my firearms license. I trusted myself to be able to shoot a tiger on the loose without panicking (until afterward), and we needed all the cover we could get. And I also made a mental note never to get into an argument with Andy Goatman.

LICENSED TO CULL

When we arrived in October, the vervet monkeys were fighting—kept in a tiny cage with a concrete floor and a few old bits of rope covered in years of grime. Two rather truculent adolescent males were being ostracized by the alpha male for not showing sufficient respect, and out of a little bit of preemptive vindictive-ness on his part. They risked serious injury if they remained in such a small enclosure with him. We tried to find homes for them, but nobody wanted them. Vervets are common—classed in South Africa as vermin—so two boisterous young males are very difficult to rehouse in Western zoos. The ethical review process—whereby the vet, the council, a senior employee from another zoo, and some of our own employees meet to discuss the best course of action—concluded that we should resort to euthanasia: basically, taking them somewhere and shooting them in the head.

"Absolutely not," I said as the solitary non-zoo professional but the one with the deciding vote. *He'll learn*, I could see them thinking, but I was determined that the two monkeys shouldn't die for the sake of convenience. If necessary, we'd build another enclosure, an idea that went down like a lead balloon, since it would take resources from other, more exotic animals we could get in the future. The two monkeys were rehoused temporarily in the large cinder-block molting sheds, known as Conway Row, which were part of the license requirement to house working birds of prey so that they can shed their feathers in comfort. As we didn't have any of these—our eagles, eagle owls, and Coco the caracara were all long since retired from public duties—the huge sheds, four large, terraced chambers, were free. One was made monkey proof and decked out with some branches and straw for enrichment and warmth, and the two ostracized adolescent males were netted, transported in cat boxes, and introduced to their new home. It wasn't ideal, and it presented me with a new front in resisting the orthodox opinion—which felt like a thin line to tread in the circumstances.

But at least the monkeys wouldn't be killed, and I was absolutely certain about my position. It gave me the confidence to realize that, though esteemed and impeccably well-intentioned, the zoo community was not necessarily always right, and if I felt morally obliged, I could and should challenge it. The last thing I wanted to do was create the impression of an amateur maverick who wouldn't listen to the experienced professionals around me, but there were some things where I simply felt I had to draw a line in the sand. "Those monkeys are standing between you and your license," I was told on numerous occasions from all my most trusted sources. But I countered with ideas of two separate communities of vervets, in different areas of the park, which could then be studied for differences in dialects, for instance. As it happened, a paper on dialectic differences in vervet monkey calls had just been published, and I was able to argue that we could keep one troop roughly where they were while developing another group, out of earshot, who would be exposed to different stimuli. Like the eagle display, which could fly above their enclosure. That would teach those naughty adolescent troublemakers to form their own troop properly and get with the program.

This may sound cruel, but it is normal for a vervet monkey to be exposed to predators—from the ground, from the trees in the form of snakes, and from the air, several times a day. It is their species-typical environment. This is why they have evolved clearly distinct calls to indicate predators from above, causing the troop to take cover, or from the ground, triggering a mass exodus to the trees, or for a snake in the tree, which tells everyone who needs to know to get down onto the ground. These calls—their frequency, accuracy, and dialectic nuances—are currently being investigated, and by running two populations of vervets separately exposed to different stimuli on the same park, there is every chance that we could contribute something useful. More important for me, however, was that we had inherited these monkeys and there was no way that we were just going to kill them because we had been told by "experts" it was "for the best."

This argument fell on deaf ears but was met with tacit compliance. In the absence of funds to establish a second monkey enclosure, the two monkeys were fed, watered, and housed in Conway Row throughout the winter and spring of 2007. When I emerged from the house to start work in the park again in April, it was still part of the keepers' routine to feed and care for these monkeys, but still disapproved of roundly at a senior level, though the junior keepers continued to work tirelessly to find new homes for them. It seemed as though there was no way we would get a zoo license if the National Zoo inspector found that we were indefinitely storing these animals off show in an enclosure not built for that purpose. The Conway Row sheds are each nearly as large as the enclosure left to the rest of the monkey troop, with branches inside to climb and a window the length of the front wall that gives a view over hills and trees. But they couldn't stay there forever. With the amount of work we had to do to get the zoo ready for the inspection, it was impossible to build them a new enclosure yet, so the date for the euthanasia of the monkeys was set for the week before the inspection, and the issue ran like a sore with the experienced keepers, who felt that animals in improper accommodation should not be kept, and I was simply staving off the inevitable and prolonging their suffering.

But as it turned out, a few weeks later, well inside the inspection deadline, a small but well-run monkey sanctuary unexpectedly stepped in to take them on, and the monkeys got to live happily ever after, after all. I felt vindicated, and ratcheted up another notch of confidence in my overall approach, which was to listen to all the expert opinion, then make the decision which required the least intervention in the delicate ecosystem of the park, complete with all the animals and staff we had inherited.

Initially, it seemed, this was a continuing theme; I had the impression of being constantly enticed to cull from all quarters, both animals and staff. Several of our early advisors had recommended sweeping the board, both of a majority of animals (to redesign the collection from scratch) and the staff. The ongoing problem with the wolves had resulted in an order from the council to cull three of them to reduce overcrowding, which I was resisting. And as well as the monkeys, there were two tigers in the frame, one of whom was ill with chronic kidney disease, another simply very old. As well as the old guard of employees, most of whom were constantly presented as mandatory candidates for dismissal from some quarter or other. But I didn't want to do this. There was a guiding principle at stake. There would be no deaths of animals, and no sackings if I could help it, and everything we had inherited should be tampered with as little as possible in order to achieve what we needed. As in any ecosystem, everything was interdependent, and until we understood exactly how it all fit together, it was foolish to presume we could make sweeping changes without unforeseen consequences.

Even moving "inconvenient" animals had to be treated with caution. Although provisional homes had been found for a majority of the animals during the protracted process of the sale— and these were the animals it was suggested we rehouse in order to establish a new identity—I felt that we could easily go too far, and most of the animals could be happy where they were. Apart from that, there were local favorites; people often phoned to ask if the otters, or the foxes, or the lynx or pumas were still there, because when we opened they would be back to see them.

And then there was the pressure to change the staff. Because of their tremendous devotion to the tigers, and their occasional forays into sentimentality, Kelly and Hannah, who had stuck with the animals through some extremely testing times, were denounced by senior zoo establishment figures I was in contact with as "bunny huggers." This dismissive term is applied to zookeeper wannabes who don't understand some of the harsh realities that the job actually involves. But, hey, neither did I, and I'd been proved right with the monkeys already (and was later to be further vindicated on the wolves and the tigers—and most of the staff I defended). When I looked at Kelly and Hannah I saw dedicated zookeepers, unqualified perhaps, but absolutely invaluable holders of knowledge about the specific animals we had, and whom they had looked after, for several years in often intolerable circumstances. They were loyal (to the animals rather than us) and extremely hardworking, and I was going to keep them and get them trained up.

Another member of staff who came into the crosshairs a few times was Robin. Lovely Robin, who I had first met when he challenged me and Nick Lindsay on that first formative walk-around, was difficult to pigeonhole. Having worked on the park as a bird and reptile keeper as well as graphic designer, in later years he had been used as Ellis Daw's personal assistant in writing his memoirs. For the last two years, this had largely meant sifting through four decades' worth of dusty local papers and magazines for clippings that mentioned the park. Robin had set about this with due diligence, but I think it is fair to say that it had worn him down. When Duncan first met Robin, he came to me afterward and said, "I think Robin is clinically depressed." Duncan had gone over to Robin, still processing old newspapers, on our first or second day and asked him what he was doing. On hearing the explanation, Duncan put his hand on Robin's shoulder and said, "You can stop now. You don't have to do that anymore." With a half-turned page in his hand, it took Robin more than a moment or two to absorb the enormity of these words, and us a bit longer to work out where he could be fruitfully deployed.

It turned out that Robin had many useful skills, which were soon unearthed, and one of the first was administration concerning the license application. He was offered a place in the office to work, but preferred to spend his time at a table by the restaurant instead. Though a horrible room, it was spacious and had good views and natural light, which the office lacked. He got on with his new work at his own pace, which was efficient if not frenetic, stopping for his half-hour lunch break every day with his thermos and radio at exactly one o'clock.

Now, one day early on, Katherine, accompanied by my mum and Jen, Mike Thomas's wife, had decided, in that way that strong women do, to take matters into their own hands with regard to the restaurant. A huge open space for three hundred diners, it was choked with old Formica display cabinets for leaflets, the scattered remnants of those leaflets, the piles of old newspapers, yellowed fallen light fittings, tables stacked on top of each other amidst piles of chairs and a stuffed tiger, all coated in a layer of airborne grease. As these three female whirlwinds of industry set about clearing up and sorting out, working up a sweat, their certainty enhanced with every radical decision they made and every heavy piece of furniture they lifted, one of them was finally moved to ask Robin, on his lunch break looking out of the window, exactly what he was doing. "Well, I'm just counting the peacocks out on the drive," he said, before helpfully adding, "There are twelve. But it was fourteen yesterday." This was very much the wrong answer. I have been around enough fussing strong women—sue me—to know that you never admit to any kind of whimsy when they are working and you are apparently in repose. What he should have said was, "I was calculating how long we had to submit the license application for the established business plan to remain viable." But the damage was done, and Robin was unceremoniously added to the list of endangered creatures on the premises.

But by now it didn't matter. I was used to opposition. It was the natural state. Robin turned out to have, among other things, draftsmanship skills, which have so far saved us thousands of pounds, as well as a knowledge of the park and certain animals within it, which is irreplaceable. He is now comfortably employed in a site of his own choosing, a loft adjacent to the maintenance room called Robin's Nest, where he fabricates small items like signs and cages for small animals, draws up architectural standard plans for new enclosures, and answers several otherwise unanswerable queries a day through the two-way radio system. He seems happy. And we are happy with him.

This sort of holding on to the past while acknowledging the future is the balancing act we must play. Our little ecosystem is now part of a global network of conservation facilities and programs, and it is up to us in the longer term how much of a part we play in it. Starting almost from scratch as we have done, with an amateur-enthusiast eye, we are in a good position to innovate. And on the ground, the rewards of sharing this environment with tens of thousands of people a year are uplifting.

Many of my friends from London are unrepentant urbanites, buying designer woollies to visit and only putting them on again to go to a WOMAD or Glastonbury festival. But all are uplifted by their visit in a way that transcends simple excitement at seeing such a big project moving forward. It's the animals and the trees that reach into a part of them that cannot be stimulated in Soho.

Woody Allen said, "Nature and I are two." Funny, but wrong. A surprising amount of this archetypal urbanite's dialogue is delivered in walks through Central Park, which has, unconsciously or not, been designed to simulate our evolutionary species-typical environment. I felt, and continue to feel, a missionary zeal about exposing as much of the population as is feasible to this experience.

7

The Animals Are Taking Over the Zoo

W hen an angry lion roars at you from less than a foot away, it is impossible to remain impassive. Late one night I was making notes and sketches for the new jaguar house—which is situated near the lion enclosure—nonchalantly sitting against a post and working by flashlight. After twenty minutes I'd finished, and stood up to find all three lions—two females and a magnificent maned male called Solomon—right up against the fence next to where I'd been sitting. The fact that three such large and dangerous animals can get so close without your noticing is impressive but chilling. Watching their intent faces so close to mine I realized that Solomon was about to roar at me, something I'd witnessed from afar, and the impact of which I'd seen on other people (usually total involuntary full-body spasming and retreat) but never experienced directly. Okay, I thought, I know he's going to roar, but there is a lion-proof fence in between me and him. I'll hold my ground, stay calm, and stare him down by the light of my headlamp. My plan worked well for the next few seconds of eyeballing, until suddenly he roared and lunged at the wire, and I instantly leaped backward three feet into darkness and unseen brambles. It's impossible to remain impassive in the face of a charging lion. There's something in your primitive midbrain that tells you it's just not right to be that close to something that can eat you, and the amount of adrenaline dumped into your system at such times is truly primeval.

As a new zoo director I am privileged to be exposed to such experiences fairly regularly. This also helps explain why zoos, with their captive breeding programs, mandatory conservation measures, and outreach educational programs, have such a vital part to play in the promotion of biodiversity in the twenty-first century. David Attenborough (may his name be praised) can educate and promote on a bigger canvas, but even he cannot replicate that visceral, direct experience of physical proximity to these magnificent creatures.

I'm not saying that all visitors will get roared at—though a few might, if Solomon is showing off (stumbling on the path in his line of sight sometimes triggers him). But having now shown many people around, from surveyors, lawyers, and bankers to friends and neighbors, the euphoria engendered convinces me that the direct viewing of exotic endangered animals is one of the best motivators for future involvement in conservation.

As I am discovering, there are many complicated arguments for and against zoos, from those extremists who think that all captive animals should either be released back into the wild or killed, to those who see no harm in any kind of containment for entertainment. The conservation argument to me seems unassailable, with a long history of important species saved from extinction by zoos over the years (the South African white rhino, the Mauritius kestrel, the golden lion tamarin, the Père David's deer, the condor; the list is long, though shorter than it should be).

But high standards in zoos are needed, which is where conservationists should concentrate their efforts, ensuring that each animal is held for a good reason, as close to its species-typical conditions as possible, and that its educational potential is maximized. Then if you're lucky, you can feel that moment of sheer physical terror in a safe environment, which can't be synthesized. Toilet facilities are available nearby should they be required.

I had had a dream. Dartmoor Zoological Park was going to be a massive, thriving success, with the potential to become world class, and contribute in some small but tangible way to the effort to reverse, or slow down, or at least in some way mitigate, humankind's inexorable, self-destructive onslaught against our planet. There was now enormous reason for hope—for the park at least. We had money in the bank, a definite plan, and all that stood between us and achieving it was a lot of hard work. Which is a happy position to be in. Throwing yourself into worthwhile, fruitful hard work that you believe in, as much as you can handle and more, is a kind of luxury not everyone gets to experience. It is also exhausting.

My days were incredibly varied. They always started with getting the children ready for school between 8 and 9 AM, which often saw me in pajamas and dressing gown also having a quick simultaneous kitchen meeting with Tourette Tony (always on his best behavior in front of the children), or Steve, Adam, or a combination of the above, while brushing hair (not my own) and dishing out shredded wheat and orange juice.

A scrawled note from that time reads:

Reallocate office space to Robin, Rob, Sarah and Steve. Clear own desk and set up computer. Speak to Katy, education officer working as keeper until facilities arrive to reassure. Let down by absentee, re-organize rota to cover. Council representative arrives for preliminary health and safety audit. Pull necessary people off jobs to accompany,

*spend two and a half hours on [more than mildly irritating
and demoralizing] walk around. Conduct three media interviews, ambivalent, relying on extremist animal rights activists' views for "balance." Research and then fax absolutely
final, last piece of paper to lawyers regarding company set-
up. Speak to BT again about delay in providing more lines.
Resend request to two-way radio company for new frequencies. Fetch children, get them changed, pass to grandma. Re-
solve argument about new stand-off barriers for tapir. Help
install fence posts. Listen to keeper concerns at end of shift.
Chop wood for fire. Do school admin and homework. Eat.
Answer phones. Kids to bed. Answer more phones. Bed.*

Some days were more exciting, some less. But it was always nice
to get a call from an urban friend when I'd just done something
decidedly unusual. A phone call from someone in magazines
once went like this: "What are you up to?" "Well, we've just darted
the jaguar and he's gone down okay, so I'm about to go into his
enclosure and stretcher him out." Short pause. "So your day's turning out much the same as mine then."

Whenever possible I took the opportunity to go inside the
enclosures, to see what it's like from the other side of the wire
and wonder what can be improved. One of the first enclosures
I worked in that spring was the lion den. My mission: to deliver
a collection of gruesome severed heads while perched on the end
of a branch fifteen feet off the ground. The heads, from farmers
culling young bullocks, are regularly hung from the trees, or
wedged into branches to give the lions a puzzle to solve to get a
treat: crunchy on the outside, chewy in the middle. The lion enclosure is a disturbing place to be: one keeper error or lock mal-
function could release three hungry cats expecting food and
finding us as a live bonus. And I knew the lions would not mess

about. At Christmas we had made a full-size cardboard zebra for them, filled it with bits of meat and left it in the enclosure. Four seconds after they were let out, one of the lionesses was onto its back, dragging it down, while the other closed in from the front. Captive bred, but instincts undiminished.

While Kelly and Hannah cleared out the old bones and un-eaten bits of skin from the lions' last meal, I looked around try-ing to find imaginative places that would challenge the lions and give them something to think about. The girls, being busy—and being girls—didn't have quite the same enthusiasm for climbing trees as I did, so I set about showing off a bit and placing the heads a bit higher than they usually had time for. I shinned up a suitable tree, and edged out along a branch about fifteen feet off the ground. One of the lionesses had apparently taken a heron in flight at a similar height, so I knew it was possible for them to reach this branch. When I was in a good position by a solid fork, I called down to Kelly, who stretched up as I stretched down to receive my first head. This really was my first-ever head. Kelly handled them nonchalantly, as tools of her trade, and I knew I mustn't appear squeamish or I'd never live it down. She held it by the neck, its glazed eyes askew and its slippery purple tongue uppermost. I could only just reach it but I didn't want to grip the tongue in case it slipped (not through squeamishness, you under-stand), so I asked her to pass it ear first. I just managed to reach the blood-soaked ear, like wet leather, hauled the head up onto my perch, and wedged it in the crook of the fork. Jumping down I sited several more heads, one from a rope, which involved pierc-ing the ear with a knife to thread it through, then helped gather the last remnants of scraps into the barrow.

Looked upon by my wide-eyed children, I'd braved the li-ons' den and managed to hide my fear. But the best bit was that it took the lioness three days to get that head down. Throughout that time, she never relaxed or stopped thinking about it. She paced underneath the tree, climbed up it a bit and then jumped down, and prowled around irritably, trying to solve the problem. This was real enrichment, giving her the sort of tricky issue she might have to solve in the wild—stumbling on a leopard's kill stored up a tree, for instance. Whenever I went up to the enclosure, she was there, fretting about it. How she got it down in the end I don't know, but I bet that bullock head was one of the best she'd ever tasted.

Despite these intense distractions, I was frequently snapped back into vivid memories of Katherine, often from the most unlikely or mundane sources. During a meeting in the house I popped into the downstairs toilet, and realized that this was the first time I'd visited this room since I used to prop Katherine up in there, its wobbly unsecured base an extra hazard for someone who couldn't keep her balance unaided. It hit me like a train, but I had to leave that room and go straight back into the meeting looking like I was concentrating and on top of things.

Other triggers from the mundane world included things like opening a cupboard and finding a half-full box of her favorite herbal tea. A trip to Tesco was also fraught with peril. After walking past the wheelchairs that she had so enjoyed being spun around in, there was aisle upon aisle of reminders from our years together, when I used to hunt her out a treat while doing the shopping. Côte d'Or chocolate; chocolate truffles; sushi; navel oranges; magazines like *Elle*, *Vogue*, *Red*, or the one she had begun writing for, *Eve*; the makeup aisle, easily avoided now but once a surefire way to brownie points via the latest wonder cure antiwrinkle cream; Bombay mix; cashew nuts; herbal teas—the list was endless. And it didn't stop in the supermarket. Being in any part of London; black cabs; Converse

All Stars, Jimmy Choos, Prada shoes and bags, coveted and un-affordable; people wearing old Birkenstock sandals; costume jewelry shops where she could pick out a gem and make it look like the real thing; Muji; John Lewis; kitchen and bathroom showrooms; tile showrooms; drapers' shops stacked with bolts of shot silk; haberdashers; Apple Macs; yoga mats; Ian McEwan novels; flower stalls; health-food shops; passports; any sad music; good graphic design; stationery shops; book-making suppliers; speaking French; seeing the children, our bed, and the chair where she died.

Against this backdrop, very little out in the zoo itself reminded me of Katherine, because she was hardly there. The new information signs going up about the animals, though informative and capably drawn up by our education officer, were a mishmash by Katherine's standards, and a vivid illustration of her absence. But I didn't know what to do to put it right, and each time I contemplated tackling it left me feeling like I was running across the Sahara in lead shoes with a plastic bag over my head. But putting heads in trees, driving the dumper truck, breaking up concrete with a road drill, dealing with keepers' needs and seeing sales reps had no such connotations, and I knew I was lucky to be able to lose myself in these nonassociative tasks.

Having the camera crew around also helped a lot. Getting them on board, in the early days of negotiations for the park, had been the final persuader for me, because this was one of the few other things I knew a bit about and could see the enormous benefit of. Careful readers will have noticed that there were several final persuaders for me: the Nick Lindsay/ZSL endorsement of the park; talking to the thirty or so other big attractions in Devon who raved about the site and offered their support; Tesco persuading me that we were within the reaches of civilization—all were mini-tipping points in the final cascade. But this development, I could see as a journalist, was not just a chance to air a great story about animals, but, cynically, it was also going to have a positive impact on the business plan.

Frustratingly, though a huge coup for us, none of the early potential lenders even registered it. The backroom boys barely looked up from their calculators: after all, there was no tangible money coming in as a result, no change in front of them to our wonky bottom line. It needed a tiny leap of imagination to comprehend it, and leaps of imagination were not how they got to be backroom boys. The TV series was one of those things that were dependent on us getting the park in the first place, so no benefit would be felt unless we had already succeeded. Therefore, by their strange but immutable logic, there was no benefit.

I put all this to one side and concentrated on the positive, and suddenly here we were, in the middle of myriad (resolvable) crises, a great breaking story, all being filmed for BBC2. The crew, from Tigress Productions, natural-history specialists I had worked with before, were inspiring. One camera operator/director, Aidan, who had shadowed Mum and me since before the purchase, had just returned from seven months in the jungles of Cameroon, filming gorillas orphaned by the bushmeat trade, and was quite unfazed by anything about our predicament. Max, a charismatic, clear-blue-eyed reprobate, had a host of natural-history filming experiences and countless stories to go with them.

Another tremendously knowledgeable person at Tigress Productions was Jeremy Bradshaw, M.D., whom I had worked with briefly in the past. When I'd lived in France, I'd once spent a few days making a pilot with Tigress, and during my one ten-minute meeting with Jeremy, had thrust my book of DIY columns from the *Guardian* at him, with a short pitch about how it would make a wonderful series. He had taken the book politely, and even read it, and every few months we exchanged e-mails about ideas of how to develop it—basically, whenever I was desperate or disheartened by some obstacle to my work. To a freelancer pitching is routine, as is having the pitch rejected or simply being completely ignored. But Jeremy was impeccably courteous, and would always return an e-mail after three weeks or so. For someone in his position to someone in mine, this was outright encouragement, even though they were almost always one-liners saying he was very sorry but he hadn't managed to think of an angle yet, and if I ever had any other ideas to let him know. A reply of any kind other than an outright negative is gold dust to a freelancer, and this tenuous direct line to Jeremy had felt like an enormous asset—though I'd known it could evaporate fairly quickly if I failed to come up with anything of interest over the next couple of years.

But I had been happy writing my book and doing my columns, until the zoo came up. I happened to mention this development to Jeremy in an e-mail fairly early on in the negotiations, and was amazed by his response. He came back the same day with an effusive reply about how he had heard of this zoo (he is a Fellow of the Zoological Society of London and had read about it, whereas I'd just received the real-estate agent's details from my sister), wished me luck, said it was an enviable way to spend one's life, and urged me to keep him informed.

He began contacting me about once a week. Suddenly I had his mobile number and he was calling me on Sunday afternoons. I could see that he was keen, and this could be very good for the zoo, if we managed to buy it. I had always hoped that as a journalist I would be able to partially support and publicize the zoo by writing about it—I had a skill to be deployed in the modern marketplace, and in this case it was for a good cause. My ambition had been to switch my *Guardian* column from the family page, to which it had migrated from the magazine, to writing about the zoo. I knew the *Guardian* reader market, and that their level of ignorance (and squeamishness) on animal matters was roughly equivalent to their position on DIY; after all, most of my friends read the *Guardian*.

But Jeremy was talking about a different level of exposure. "I think it's a quintessentially English story," he said in his soft Oxbridge accent, which is, objectively, only a couple of notches down from Prince Charles's. "Completely mad and eccentric, but with a very wide appeal. I wouldn't be surprised if we can get BBC2 to do a series. Keep me posted." *Dream on*, I thought, but I kept in touch, adding Jeremy to the loop of phone calls I made from France, and he always provided a supportive and encouraging ear.

And so one day, it turned out, I was showing Jeremy around the park we had just bought, and he was discussing the timing of the BBC2 series he had recently been commissioned to make about it. Jeremy's knowledge from a lifetime in natural history was comprehensive, and most of our animals were of species he had filmed in the wild, often with a celebrity presenter. The tigers reminded him of his direct experience of them while filming a documentary with Bob Hoskins, the lions with Anthony Hopkins, and my aspirations for orangutans (Julia Roberts) and chimpanzees revealed that he had twice filmed Jane Goodall at her world-leading chimpanzee research and conservation center in Gombe. But my favorite remark was as we walked past Basil, the coatimundi, the South American climbing raccoon I had barely heard of before we arrived. "Oh, you've got a coati!" He beamed. "Wonderful creatures. You see them in the canopy in Ecuador all the time."

I was humbled by the entire film crew's knowledge and their professionalism, and uplifted by their enthusiasm for this project—our project—which simply involved filming us while we learned about just exactly what we had got ourselves into. But it was a relief from time to time to be recast as the relative expert, for instance when the *Guardian* sent down a photographer to cover a feature on the park I had written for the magazine.

As a journalist and feature writer, much of my time for about ten years was spent working with photographers. I'd be sent on some hare-brained but marvelous assignment, like horse-riding in Spain, swimming with dolphins in the Florida Keys, or snowboarding in California, and a photographer would come with me to document exactly how badly I messed it up. It was a wonderful way to earn a living, but a large part of the pleasure was working alongside another professional with the same objectives, out on our own overseas. Photographers are practical people. They make the best of situations, they improvise, they have gaffer's tape. As another pair of eyes and ears, a photographer is useful in spotting good people to interview, and I was also able to help by drawing out and distracting people while they were photographed. Working as a complementary duo like this was enormously satisfying, and it was one of the things I missed most when I fled to France to write my book.

So it was a very welcome relief from the myriad unfamiliar pressures of the zoo when the newspapers got hold of the story (after Sovereign and Parker made the nationals, they could hardly miss it), and started sending the odd photographer down to capture developments. This was something I was used to and knew all about, from the demands of the picture editor to the backdrop and the light, but more than that, it was a chance to dip back into that world of journalism where I had spent so many comfortable years. During my time working in London I was always the person most likely to mention animals or to suggest an animal story (usually rejected), or be disgusted with the shallow industry obsession with fashion and other matters of extreme inconsequence. At the zoo, around the many dedicated professionals who have devoted their lives to exotic creatures, I am practically animal illiterate, unable to sex a snake, tell a Bengal owl from a European eagle owl, or dismember a horse for the tigers.

So when some fashionably dressed Soho-junky with a cappuccino habit and totally inappropriate footware arrived asking all the wrong questions, I found it enormously refreshing. Julian, from the *Guardian*, arrived in Italian calfskin brogues with designer jeans trailing on the ground, both instantly sodden in the long grass of the walk-in enclosure, where he wanted to get some shots of me with Ronnie the tapir. On being warned of the dangers of Ronnie, who is a Class I dangerous animal easily capable of killing a man with gruesome efficiency, his reaction was to ask the stony-faced keeper supervising us, "Wow. So who'd win in a fight between a tapir and an anaconda?" As soon as I could, I took him away on my own, so he didn't upset anyone and I could enjoy his hopelessly out-of-place remarks.

Trying to lure a peacock onto a picnic table for a shot, Julian approached the problem pragmatically, as photographers do, by laying a trail of bread that ended in the tabletop, but he didn't factor in the tiny pea-size brain of the bird. After twenty minutes with the light fading, he snapped. "Come on, you total fucking spaz. You're not a peacock you're a peac___." When he met Ben the brown bear, who at three hundred kilos is bigger than Vlad, our male Siberian tiger, his instant reaction was, "So who'd win in a fight between the bear and a tiger?" His "animal maths" theme continued all day, culminating in, "What about four rats against a swan?" I was sorry to see him go back, by his own admission, to the land of trivia and inconsequence, but it was probably for the best.

Meanwhile, there was plenty of work to be getting on with. And again, for a change, some of it was stuff I was used to. Like demolition. It is marvelously cathartic to wield a pickax or a sledgehammer in times of stress, though I did find that visualizing a particular lawyer, banker, or some other source of frustration often led to an overenthusiastic work rate, unnecessary damage to surrounding infrastructure, and occasional personal injury. Like when I lost a thumbnail to my new, heavy-duty crowbar while thinking about a certain high-end bank. Demolition is not just randomly smashing things up—though there is, occasionally, room for that—but is more a systematic, if brutal, dismantling in the most efficient way possible. My most enjoyable project was stripping out the vet room, into which we were sinking thousands of pounds to convert a fetid former stable into a modern animal operating theater. In the deeds, this was already officially the vet room, and animals had in the past been stored here when there was an urgent need for isolation. But in reality it was a series of four dank interlocking chambers with flimsy partitions, lethal wiring, and a constant splattering trickle from the faulty plumbing running across the ceiling. Smashing this stuff out, sifting the lead and copper for salvage, piling up the hardcore barrow by barrow for use under the concrete base of the jag enclosure, was a luxury I allowed myself two or three hours a day while it was going on.

The best discovery was a room that had not been opened for fifteen years. A former workshop, its doorway onto the vet room was blocked with the subsequent decade and a half's worth of damp junk, so the easiest way in was taking out the rotten window frame. Inside, it was like a small museum of artifacts from

another time. There was a mini dilapidated range like the one in
the flagstone kitchen, and the walls were bedecked with rusted
two-man lumberjack saws and other agricultural implements
from the nineteenth century—plus, of course, the mandatory
piles of grimy miscellanea, here including many decomposing
rats, covering the floor so that not one square inch of it was exposed. Sifting this lot for scrap and interesting artifacts was a welcome distraction, particularly when it came to ripping out the
ancient rotten tongue-and-groove paneling with the aforementioned heavy-duty crowbar. Insulated from the world by a
breathing mask and goggles, covered in sweat and grime, I could
wield heavy implements and avoid calls and callers for a couple
of hours a day, while performing useful work and also saving
money on gym membership. But inevitably, a line would build
up outside and I would have to engage with them. Well-dressed
young reps—women in stilettos on the uneven grimy surface of
the yard, men in gray suits—would stand clutching clipboards
with things for me to sign, always (enjoyably for me) surprised
that the man they had come to see was the person loading the
skip they had assumed was a laborer and turned their noses up
at before we were introduced.

Reluctantly, when it was fully gutted, I had to hand over the
vet-room resurrection to a team of outside builders, who were
remarkably proficient in transforming this shell into a white-
tiled medical facility. They worked well, though the expense for
an off-show area was worrying, as the money, so hard-won, was
hemorrhaging out in all directions, and front-of-house issues like
pathways, enclosures, and the kilometers of stand-off barrier to
be replaced seemed at least equally as important. But investing
heavily in an off-show facility like this would benefit the animals,
who wouldn't have to be moved so far to undergo veterinary pro-

cedures, and it would demonstrate to the authorities that we were serious. The new crew of builders took over, and seemed to know what they were doing, so I moved my recreational focus to other areas of demolition.

Like digging out enclosure fence posts from concrete with a road drill, pickaxing loose concrete wherever I could find it, and transporting rubble in the dumper. All too soon—though not quite soon enough—this stage of the operation was complete, and the only jobs to be found were restorative. Again, as long as they were not too complicated and something I could dip in and out of to make way for the other myriad demands of my new position, I gladly got involved. In the absence of a budget for much needed tarmac for the car park and paths, Adam had organized deliveries of road planings. These are the bits they trim off the tops of roads before resurfacing, with that huge machine like a giant electric razor without a guard, a whirring wheel with blades that chews up and spits out the chips of the old tarmac onto a conveyor belt behind it. The conveyor belt deposits them into lorries, and the lorries, if you're quick enough and know where they are working, will come and deliver them to you for a token price of about ten pounds a ton. We secured about a hundred tons, which was left in the bottom car park in vast piles, and which needed to be transported up the drive (a fifth of a mile) and deposited on the pathways for Tony in the digger to rake out, and then someone on the steamroller to flatten down.

We had tried for some weeks to buy reliable machinery ourselves, but this meant thumbing through *Farmers Weekly* and other magazines dedicated to the sale of heavy machinery. These quickly became compelling, and many times I had eagerly dropped what I was doing when Tony or John came striding up with a folded-back catalogue in their hand saying, "I've got a lovely dumper/digger/tractor here for you, Ben." I even took to thumbing through back issues to get a feel for what was out there. I soon learned to tell the difference between a Massey Ferguson and a John Deere at a glance, and easily identify a mini-digger as a one-, one-and-a-half-, two-, or three-tonner. But what I couldn't seem to do was buy any of them at a reasonable price. Good ones tended to be locked in some place like Dundee, where the transport costs could double the price of the machine, and there was that delicate trade-off between getting something cheap, within our relatively measly budget, and getting something that was going to work. This meant visiting the nearer ones with Tony, pulling him off whatever he was doing, invariably to find that what was on offer was either not good enough or too expensive. Everything decent, in this heavily agricultural area, was quickly snapped up. Canny farmers were always there before you, bidding against you, knowing exactly what they were doing. (I still pine after a particular John Deere with a front loader, which was stolen from under my nose by a neighbor of the vendor just before we got there. It would have been perfect but, alas, it wasn't to be.) So we ended up hiring equipment, much too late in the day for Tony's liking, who was then further harassed by the weather. English summer was starting, and so of course, was the rain.

But eventually, with only a few weeks to go before the inspection, two diggers (a one-and-a-half- and a three-tonner, as it happens) and a thunderous steamroller arrived, and everybody in the park set to work as one. Minor differences and big egos were forgotten as keeping-staff, maintenance, directors, and everybody else worked like a human conveyor belt, shifting to whatever was needed at the time with the alacrity of reckless troops volunteering indiscriminately for dangerous missions. And sometimes it was potentially dangerous. Once I had taken some time out to escort a local journalist around, and I noticed that the steamroller was reversing slowly down the path toward us, leaving a flattened carpet of planings before it. I noticed too that the driver was being duly diligent at keeping his distance from the wall to his right, which was just as well, because one wrong move from a machine this size could send it crashing through that wall, and that would be a terrible shame because it was a wall of the tiger enclosure. So far, reassuring. And then I noticed that the driver was Duncan, who, I knew, had only learned how to drive this machine the day before, and I hurriedly ushered the journalist out of the way. But there were no accidents with these potentially lethal machines, and the Health and Safety officers Rob and Adam took their roles very seriously. The first accident recorded in our accident book was a cut finger months later, sustained during an incident involving some stationery.

In the middle of this park-wide blitz of manual labor, Steve had to think about pressing animal-welfare issues. Like where were we going to put Sovereign the escapist jag while we renovated his enclosure. Twelve of the posts in his enclosure needed replacing, as did the rotten slats in his house, and a few other adjustments needed to be made to his living area, which Sovereign would simply not tolerate if he was around. He had to be moved, and it was decided that the best idea was to reinstate the old quarantine area, once a bear pit, and before that a cottage that the Brownies (junior Girl Scouts) had apparently used as a meeting place during the war. Unfortunately, nobody had told Brown Owl (the leader) about the rudiments of structural engineering, and she had cut away the pesky A-frame timbers supporting the roof to enlarge the loft space for a table-tennis table. While Plymouth naval dockyards succumbed to the Luftwaffe, this fifth-columnist children's paramilitary organization got their badges for bringing down the roof of what was then a farm cottage seven miles away. But they left the walls and gables stand-

ing, which provided a suitable enclosure for temporarily hous-
ing dangerous animals.

With Sovereign, however, no one was taking any chances.
As soon as the electric-fence specialist had finished his long (and
expensive) refitting of the wolves' enclosure with a new system
and a backup supply in the event of a power failure, he was
moved onto this project. Too much was just right for Sovereign,
who scared everyone, particularly me, with his propensities for
forward planning and timely, decisive action. The place was lat-
ticed with electrically charged deterrents to climbing the walls,
scratching at the door, and using the internal window ledges as
platforms for leaping onto the high iron gantry across the middle of the building, presumably installed for viewing the bears
it once housed. As the security measures closed in, this shell of
a house with its wired-up observation gantry became a disconcerting place to stand. As our minds prowled around the potential purchase points—rolled steel joist sticking out here, a brick
chimney projecting in there—for a single-minded cat to use to
climb out, they were closed off one by one. But we were also creating a holding chamber from which even a human, with fore-
knowledge and ingenuity, could not escape. Inevitably, this
sparks images of maximum-security prisons, and worse, human-
atrocity-standard containment where detainees are thwarted in
their desire for freedom and utterly controlled. This in turn raises
questions of animal rights, and just exactly what we were doing
containing such an animal who longed to get out. The answer
always, honestly, was absolute.

The International Union for Conservation of Nature
(IUCN) says that jaguars in the wild are "Near Threatened," and
the good news is that they moved down the Red List from Vulnerable in the 1990s as protection measures kicked in. However, habitat destruction has pushed them into increasingly

isolated pockets of forest, bringing them into conflict with ranchers whose cattle they eat, and hunters, for whom they represent competition for food, and mortal danger if they are attacked. Despite being protected, jaguars are frequently shot on sight, and are already extinct in El Salvador and Uruguay. It is expected that at the next audit they will be moving back up the list to Vulnerable again. We inherited Sovereign; he can't be reintroduced to his diminishing native habitat, but he is top of the stud book and his excellent genes are underrepresented in captivity. We will be breeding from him as soon as we can.

Eventually there came a time when the wires in the new enclosure were in place, the locking mechanism on his gate had been quadruple-checked by every available pair of eyes, and it was time to introduce Sovereign to our new dart gun. This enormously expensive piece of equipment (£3,000) is able to deliver a dose of anaesthetic at any distance from a yard to fifty, and we spent a day having a fairly strict tutorial from the Austrian supplier, who set up a target for us in the unfinished restaurant. This dart gun is a Dan-Inject, the preferred industry standard, a top-of-the-range model often brandished out of the sides of Land Rovers in wildlife documentaries as they chase down and dart rhinos and lions. Its laser sight also enables you to shoot from the hip, because many animals seem to recognize the raising of a rifle as a sign of danger. Firing from the hip, even I was able to hit the bull's-eye at thirty yards.

But such minor deceptions cut no ice with Sovereign. The second he saw Steve with the gun he began to pace and spit in his house, careful not to present his flank, as he has been darted before and knows that this is the target. Eventually his agitation got the better of him, he turned slightly, and Steve darted him in the thigh, a perfect hit. We all retreated, as planned, for fifteen minutes while the vet monitored the progress of the drug, and

Sovereign gradually went down. These operations were carefully planned in advance, with only the people who were directly involved in the vicinity. Everyone had a role, which was rehearsed in meetings—a bit like a benign bank job—ceaselessly, until everything was clear. The crate was ready, the van in position outside the jag house, and the exact route to the new quarters established. But even so, it is always a moment of high drama when the door is opened into the cage where the sleeping cat lies.

Even in his sleep, something like Sovereign—in particular he, in fact—is scary. Your brain is telling you to keep back. It may be a trap (you almost suspected this cat had hid an antidote pill inside his mouth like some secret agent). What if he just springs up? I feel it every time, that I am not supposed to be close to an animal like this. But he was genuinely out, and the only thing to remember was that it was a light dose, for safety's sake—his safety, not ours—and that jerky movements and loud noises could trigger an adrenaline response in him that might, conceivably, counteract the drug. Which you don't want. So the atmosphere of total silence—radios and phones off, only essential commands whispered—greatly adds to the tension of the occasion. As we successfully maneuvered him onto a blanket and manhandled him out of his house, I noticed that in our efforts not to jostle our lethal patient, I had somehow ended up with the head end, while the other three porters were carrying the rear legs. Not only was my end much heavier, it's much scarier, too. His head is as big as a medium-size Halloween pumpkin festooned with real fangs, the most prominent being his two two-inch canines designed for puncturing skulls. I'd just noticed the proximity of my delicate-seeming wrist to these gaping jaws (remember the jag has the most powerful jaws of all the big cats), when the vet's phone went off. As the ringtone (a Kylie Minogue track, incongruously) boomed and echoed in the narrow concrete corridor, the vet did a pantomime horror retreat to turn it off, and hissed over to me, "Put the blanket over his head." I gladly complied, but had little faith that this flimsy material would do much to lessen the sound, or protect my wrist, particularly with Kylie singing her little lungs out trying to wake him up.

But he didn't wake up, and we got him into the crate, and the van, and his new quarters without a further hitch. It was a great moment. Our new equipment worked perfectly, the new team performed impeccably, and we had successfully transferred a very dangerous animal without incident. We could now get on with the license requirement of renovating his enclosure and re-lining his leaking moat, which meant more demolition work for me, and more welding, fence work, and rendering for people with better skills.

Unfortunately, the next move did not go quite so well. This time it was for the much-anticipated relocation of Tammy the tiger, who, you may remember, had been fighting with and had needed to be separated from her sister for about five years, since they both had hormone-changing contraceptive injections. After tireless efforts from all the keepers, eventually a home was found for her in France, and a date set for her transportation. The procedures were run through as before, and minor adjustments made to the plan from small lessons learned. The Frenchies arrived the night before, ready for an early start, and we spent an enjoyable evening in the local pub getting to know each other. I had been looking forward to speaking a bit of French, perhaps to translate some crucial information at a critical time, but these vain hopes receded quickly when it emerged that both of them spoke English as well as I did.

On the morning of the move, the first little thing to go wrong was that the van couldn't get as close to the tiger house as we had liked. It was further up a long steep slope than the jag house, and that slope was now covered with road planings, which don't give much purchase for an empty two-wheel drive van trying to reverse. No problem, the vet was confident that she would be out long enough for us to carry her the extra fifty yards to get her safely inside, so we carried on. Tammy was less canny than Sovereign and easier to dart, but she made some hellishly frightening noises after she was hit. After the requisite time, a delegation went in to have a look, and it was deemed she needed another dose, so we waited again. After the vet flicked her ears for a bit, he decided she wasn't going anywhere, and we maneuvered this considerable animal onto another blanket (we still hadn't been able to afford a stretcher). Six of us carried Tammy—again, under a code of silence—watched over by John on firearms with the big gun, which could kill her with a single shot should things go wrong. And then, go wrong they did.

Halfway down the path, which is about three meters wide, with lions on one side and tigers on the other, Tammy woke up. The first sign was her tail, which started moving and then wrapped itself tightly around someone's leg. Then she just stood up, right out in the open, scattering people like gunfire in a shopping center—or, indeed, a big cat in a crowd of people. She was incredibly groggy and could barely stand, but she was still a big girl, upright and on the wrong side of the wire. People evaporated from the scene over the stand-off barriers backward—not too close to the lions though, because they were suddenly very vocal in their objections to seeing Tammy so close (Duncan's policy of putting the other cats away during these procedures had been overlooked, with potentially volatile consequences). I noticed that several people had somehow managed to climb the observation tower, despite the bottom six feet of rungs of the ladder having been removed to make it inaccessible. But mainly I noticed Tammy, less than three yards away, standing, then slowly wheeling round to face me. I decided to stay still. Her eyes were glazed, but I knew that they are hypersensitive to tracking movement, and could easily be triggered by signs of a prey animal in front of her (i.e., me), trying to escape. I didn't have to look to my right to know that John would have raised the rifle ready to fire, and I did my best to remain utterly motionless. There are people who claim to be able to withdraw their aura inward and become almost invisible, certainly less noticeable, an idea I had previously thought was ridiculous. But under the circumstances, I was willing to give it a try. In fact my brain did it for me, because I was not afraid. I was beyond fear, to total calm, as if something even more primitive than the fight-or-flight response had been triggered, and my body knew I couldn't be trusted with the release of that much adrenaline; perhaps it would cause me to move, or some sensitivity in the tiger would pick up the increased electromagnetic activity from so close. I concentrated on seeming like part of the stand-off barrier I was leaning against, or maybe a tree, or some other inert and routine stimulus. It seemed to work, because Tammy's glazed gaze swept across me without registering, and she wobbled slowly off down the path towards the van.

John, as firearms officer, was responsible for everybody's safety, and he would have been within his rights to kill Tammy the moment he had a clear shot. I was half-expecting this, though my perception of the situation on a second-by-second basis was that there had as yet been no need. And he didn't. John held his nerve, as I knew he would, and maintained eye contact communications with Steve the curator and the vet, who fed back that he should hold off. Everyone held their nerve. Tammy staggered a few more paces, then lay down, unfortunately right next to the dart gun, which was the only means of administering more anaesthetic. There followed a tense few moments as the vet prepared a dart and Steve crept towards Tammy, covered by John, to

retrieve the dart gun. With animal stealth—it doesn't get more animal than this—he moved to within four feet of her, conscious
that as the seconds ticked by, the drugs were wearing off. Without the dart gun we would have no choice but to shoot to kill as
she became livelier. Steve reached the gun, tiptoed over to the vet,
and he gave Tammy another dose.

Now we had to wait again for it to take effect, this time out
in the open, a stark period which could have been a minute or
twenty, but was probably nearer five. By the time Tammy was declared under (again), my adrenaline had kicked in. But we desperately needed her in the crate in the van, and no amount of fear
could prevent that happening. I remember feeling decidedly uncomfortable as we hauled this incredibly dangerous thing, the
trigger of so many primal fears, who had already demonstrated
that she could wake up, into the crate. Once again I had the head
end—though not alone this time—and I didn't like it. Tammy's
head is bigger than a very big watermelon, and though the move
only took about thirty seconds, I was constantly expecting her to
show signs of life with disastrous consequences. As soon as I had
pushed her head clear of the crate door, which slid down and
bolted her to safety, I felt the anger rising. Anger that I, and all the
staff, had been put through this.

The lessons learned immediately were that a move can't go
ahead unless the vehicle—ideally a four-wheel-drive—is right
next to the animal's house; and other animals in the area should
also be shut away, every time. Then Anna, our Zoo Collection
Manager, and Steve began investigating that most salient question: why had Tammy been able to stand up? Exhaustive inquiries
to about thirty zoo vets and other professionals revealed a universal consensus on the drug of choice to sedate big cats during
these procedures. Unfortunately, it wasn't the one the vet used.
He had chosen a horse tranquilizer, which can work, but is thought

less reliable. And so it had proved. Anna and Steve lobbied hard (though they didn't have to) that in future, all major moves and medical procedures should be managed by an external specialist organization, the International Zoo Veterinary Group (IZVG), a freelance organization that does only exotic animals. What they don't know about zoo animals, nobody knows. Obviously, they were decidedly more expensive, but this was not a consideration, and I agreed wholeheartedly. The next move we were going to attempt, when the vet room was ready, was transferring three big predators in one day for long-overdue dental procedures, and we couldn't afford for any part of it to go wrong. Regardless of the cost, we were going to use the IZVG.

In the meantime, on the back of so many other unsettling incidents, this one was probably irrevocably formative. Duncan and I discovered that we were no longer fully relaxed out in the open, particularly around here. Once, we were up at the reservoir for the zoo, a misnomer since it really is just a big manhole cover at the highest point in the park, above the bore hole that supplies the water at the rate of about four thousand liters a day. Unfortunately, it leaks, which means that every ten days to three weeks the water pressure drops, so that the otters' supply dries up, one of the artificial ponds starts to drain (through another as yet unidentified leak), and the pressure in the restaurant drops below what is needed to keep it running. But far more important to me, at eight in the morning when you tend to find out about it, is that the shower doesn't work. The shower, as described before, is not a haven of luxury even when it does work. A yellowed, fractured plastic upright coffin installed in a shower-wide, partitioned room directly in front of the only window, the mechanism is fine (though festooned with live mains wires immediately behind it), and once you are in it, when it is working, this can often seem like the best part of the day—a short period of time in touch with our aquatic roots, almost guaranteed not to be interrupted. Almost. Milo and Ella still regard you as fair game in the shower, and I have also been called out from it a few times to attend to various emergency meetings, but generally, this imperfect sanctuary is as good as it gets. Until it doesn't work. When it fails to deliver hot water, or even any water at all, the denial-tinted spectacles come off and you see it for what it is: a miserable piece of shit that we can't afford to replace yet. Like a TV or laptop that suddenly doesn't work and is no longer a conduit to the center of the universe, but just a shoddy plastic box.

What you have to do when the water dries up is go into the woods behind the wolves and above the bears to the reservoir, armed with two yard-long wrenches, and tinker with some heavy-duty valves to bleed the system. Early in the morning, before school, this can only be described as a bummer, so we try to preempt it, which is how Duncan and I found ourselves up there one Sunday evening, chatting about the day's events, relaxed as we tried to remember the exact sequence of things to turn and pipes to connect to each other. Suddenly there was a large animal rustling around less than twenty feet away, and we both spun around, gripping our wrenches and ready for mortal combat. Both our stances were wide, ready to fight or flee, and we cast wide-eyed glances around looking for good trees to climb in the nanoseconds before we assessed what we were up against. It was a cow, on the other side of the fence. At the edges of the park, we forget, other people have large animals like cows, horses, and sheep, that are not about to rip your limbs off and eat them. But you can't be too careful, and it took us a few moments to relax and get back to the job in hand.

Another time I was out in the open crossing a carefully assessed empty field belonging to a neighbor, when a plastic bag reared up out of the long grass and sent me into a similar spasm of panic. But the scarier moments are at night. The first time was while collecting wood for the fire, in what I'd vaguely remembered was a virtually empty enclosure containing some ground-based birds, the biggest of which was a turkey, who was sometimes aggressive but not insurmountable. I looked up from my bow-sawing to see several sets of mammalian eyes reflected in my headlamp, all small and narrowly spaced, indicating little animals. But if they were little cats, I had a big problem. Then I remembered that we don't have any little cats, apart from Jilly, the elderly serval whose enclosure was some distance away, and that these were in fact the innocuous miniature muntjac deer who were desperately more afraid of me that I should be of them. Even so, my rattled reasoning told me, they have little spiky antlers, and I was careful not to upset them as I completed my foray for fallen wood.

The most recent occasion of nocturnal fear was while walking the dog, Leon (more on him later). Out in the corner of the giraffe (all right, small cats) field, which backs on to the pumas, on a clear but moonless night, I heard something big moving very slowly toward me. The dog was busy some distance away, but my anxiety was based on the fact that the female pumas were in season and calling out with their giant, strangulated *miaoww*, which is thought, along with their pheromone incentive, to draw young male pumas from the moor. And that was the direction this animal was coming from. I hesitated, hoping that the idiot dog would pick up on it, and, ideally, challenge it and be eaten by it rather than me. But he remained oblivious, selfishly snuffling around the many animal scents of the long grass a hundred yards away rather than volunteering to sacrifice his life for me. There was a firm breeze coming from behind me, so I knew the animal knew exactly where and what I was, and still it slowly crunched through the undergrowth in my direction. Finally I cracked and snapped on my headlamp, half-expecting to see a fleeing puma and partly dreading the other alternative, that it wouldn't flee. The eyes that stared back at me were wide spaced and didn't flee. They didn't do anything, which I gradually drew comfort from, because predators tend to make snap decisions. Taking my time, and finally enlisting Leon as moral—and potentially sacrificial—support, I moved toward it. As I did so, it gradually became clear that this was another harmless, dumb-assed cow, newly introduced to this normally empty field, stalking me because it presumably thought that I was the farmer, breaking the habit of a lifetime by bringing it food at 3 AM.

These sorts of incidents, though actually quite exciting, serve to reinforce the sense that to live here is to exist in a state of perpetual impending emergency. For the time being, though, most of the emergencies were false alarms, or at least manageable, all made more bearable by the influx of money from the NFU. Now the sensation was more like riding the rapids on the way to a waterfall, as the money flowed out and the deadline of the inspection for our license loomed inexorably nearer.

With the vast amount to be done, we were working at a frantic pace, and every problem that came up seemed to require an expensive solution. The van, an old transit that had done a remarkable 260,000 miles, suddenly gave out when a strut from the chassis snapped and punctured the floor in the back. There's no coming back from that, so a gleaming new (well, with only 80,000 miles on the clock) replacement was bought. The dumper, a giant yellow monster with the wrong engine and a gearbox that looked like it had come from prehistory, blew up one day, necessitating further outlay. These two vehicles are the backbone of the operation, used for fetching and distributing food for the animals and materials of all kinds throughout the park.

The new dumper, on hire, was enormously popular, mainly

because it actually worked, and did a great deal to improve not just the work rate but also morale. But the cost of everything loomed into focus sharply and again made me miss Katherine, because I knew her budget-management skills would have saved us money, but she would also have brought a sense of control that in her absence, seemed to be slipping away. However, it was a one-way journey we were on, and most of the problems we faced, for once, really could be solved by throwing money at them. I was just acutely aware that once the money was spent, there wasn't going to be any more. And if we failed to get the park open with it, the level of disaster would be unthinkable. Probably many animals would die, and many people (including those who had left good jobs to work for us) would be unemployed. And the family assets, which my parents had worked so hard all their lives to build up, would be in tatters.

"But at least no one's shooting at us," my mum would say. Brought up in Sheffield during the war, as a child she had endured nightly air raids, culminating in one where she emerged from the cellar to find that the family house, indeed the whole street, had been destroyed. The family simply walked to their nearest relative's house, an aunty seven miles away, past the rows of bodies laid out on the roads until they could be dealt with. These sorts of experiences gave my mum's generation a profound grip on reality, and though she had spent the last thirty or so years in relative suburban opulence and didn't relish the grim living conditions and constant stress of gambling everything on a crazy venture that was in no way dead certain, Mum knew from direct personal experience that things could be considerably worse.

Mum's strength and sense of adventure were absolutely vital in pursuing the zoo in the first place, and in continuing to fight for it once we were there. We were always mindful of the sacrifice Mum had made in buying the zoo, and did our best to make her comfortable and reassure her. But she didn't need mollycoddling. The plan had been that she could continue her life of making pots and painting, with the zoo as a sort of thriving backdrop. But when Katherine died, when Duncan was away, she ran the place. This was no small step up for a recently widowed lady whose husband had impeccably run the family affairs for the previous fifty-three years. Dad used to marvel at Mum's lack of proficiency with figures—he would read books like *Mathematics Made Difficult*, and pass his thirty-minute commute doing complicated mental arithmetic. But Mum was not entirely alone. Adam had put us in touch with Jo, a clear-eyed, perspicacious, and matronly bookkeeper who gradually wrestled the accounts under control, skillfully juggled creditors, and provided daily bulletins on our financial health.

With so many unexpected expenses—particularly in the restaurant where everything from crockery to cookers had to be replaced—many projects became too expensive and had to be shelved. Like replacing the demolished jag house, which had been priced at £27,000. By simply not doing this we could afford all kinds of other things, like a new lawn mower, a forest of new fence posts, and the staff wages for another month. Mum's determination to get to grips with the nitty-gritty of the business undoubtedly saved it at a difficult time, and won her the respect and admiration of the staff and many more. As I emerged from my self-imposed exile, I found that Mum was at the center of most things that were going on, despite recent doctor's orders to avoid stress, following a heart scare. One of the few places in the house where we spent money was in fitting out the old kitchen (the formerly smelly one) with a new floor and turning it into a pottery studio. When it was finished, we tried to get Mum interested in going back to her lifelong hobby, at which she excels, talking in detail about selling her pots in the shop. But she wasn't—and still isn't—having it. While ever there is work to be done, Mum will do it. And trying to ease her out of the loop of stressful decisions simply doesn't work. She has spies everywhere. If she feels she's getting bland reassurances from management and at department-head level, she just taps into another staff network to find out what's really going on. Although the television series was called *Ben's Zoo*, in more ways than one, it should have been called *Amelia's Zoo*.

8

Spending the Money

What a difference the sun makes. I have a theory that a disproportionate number of expatriates who leave this country to seek a place in the sun have seasonal affective disorder (SAD) to some degree. I'm sure I'm on the continuum somewhere, as I crave the onset of spring from the first moment the leaves turn brown in autumn. When the sun finally did start coming out, in late April and May, everything looked a hundred times better. The liberal sprinkling of snowdrops gave way to a host of daffodils, and the optimism in the air was palpable, and no longer only coming from me.

The workshop was churning out newly welded metal enclosure posts, big machines were laying new pathways before our eyes, and the restaurant was a teeming hive of activity. Spring was definitely in the air, and with it came the need for some reversible vasectomies, as we didn't yet have the paperwork or facilities for many of our animals to breed. First in line was Zak, the elderly alpha wolf, whose problem actually looked more serious. One testicle had swollen to the size of an avocado, and though this can happen to wolves for short periods, Zak's had been engorged for several weeks and the vet thought he needed to be opened up. The vet room was still a work in progress, so the shop beside the restaurant was sterilized and some tables pushed together. On the allocated day, Zak was darted and went down easily. Though the van was in position, the vet and Steve decided it was just as easy to carry him the hundred yards or so to the mocked-up operating theater. In truth, if Zak had managed to get up and do a Tammy, no one would have been very scared. At nineteen years old, even on his best day you could probably walk faster than he could run, and he maintained his grip on the pack now, not with brute force, but through sheer charisma and experience.

They arrived slightly breathless, and Zak was placed on his back, cradled by two large plastic blocks with a semicircle cut out of them, a bit like a headsman's block, specifically designed for keeping animals with ridged spines steady on their backs. The blocks were well worn, and this procedure was fairly routine, though I asked how many actual wolves the vet had done. "Oh, quite a few by now. Don't worry. No different from an Alsatian." Like anyone being prepared for an operation, Zak looked painfully exposed and vulnerable, and as he was shaved and washed in the relevant areas, waves of empathy from the men watching went out to him. The women present found our discomfort hugely amusing.

Once he was opened up, the avocado-size testicle was instantly declared cancerous, and its black and purple striations clearly indicated the presence of this malign nemesis of so many animals and people. Luckily, even when advanced, dogs and wolves hardly ever get secondary cancers from the testicular region—unlike humans. But the sound of a vas deferens, the small strand of connecting tissue between the testicle and the body cavity, being cut, is not a pleasant one. There is much crunching of gristle, and much wincing and crossing of legs in the audience. His other testicle, pinkish white and normal size—more like a big conker in the shape of a kidney bean—was also declared a potential health hazard, since it could have been contaminated by its neighbor, and the second set of crunching and cutting was far worse, as it was into healthy tissue. When the second ostensibly healthy testicle clanged into the metal dish, it was a poignant moment, and every man present felt something, though exactly what, it was hard to pin down. Mainly, probably, never to let the medical profession anywhere near your gonads. Though we had saved Zak so that he could live to lead the pack another day, it could hardly be described as a good day for him. But he made a full recovery, and worries that his empty scrotum might impinge on his leadership abilities were unfounded, as Zak went on to provide his pack, and his successor in waiting, the slightly pathetic Parker, with guidance and leadership for several more months.

Next in line was Solomon, king of the beasts, the hugely impressive male African lion. This really was a routine reversible vasectomy, as one day we will probably try to breed from him, but at the moment the production of a lion cub would have been seen by the zoo world as irresponsible. Although slightly smaller than Vlad, Solomon is arguably the most impressive cat we have. At around 230 kilos, or more than five hundred pounds, he, his mane, and his roar are truly epic. Tigers don't roar, but this awesome sound is high in Solomon's arsenal of weapons of terror. I feel it is worth reiterating that, in nature, you don't generally get to hear this sound from so close and live. As Solomon blasted Steve with his Death Roar from the confines of his house, his lips curled back revealing dagger teeth, presenting highly alarming visual as well as auditory stimuli, I watched Steve brace himself and resist the temptation to back to the far wall of the narrow corridor. Steve bided his time and soon got the dart in Solomon's flank. When I next visited the scene, Solomon was out cold, the door was open, and the vet was stitching up the lion's back end,

utterly undaunted by the sheer scale of his patient. I was not undaunted, however. Solomon's flanks were absolutely huge, and
the gory procedure going on in his most intimate region would
surely be a source of displeasure should he wake up. John was
there on firearms duty, but otherwise there was an open door between him and the park. When Kelly, positioned at the head end
inside the enclosure (the other lions were locked away in their
parts of the house), started to report that he was blinking—i.e.,
that the anaesthetic was beginning to wear off—I looked for
signs of panic, or at least increased work rate from the vet. After
all, doing what he was doing, he'd probably be number one on
Solomon's hit list should he come around. But the vet remained
unperturbed, and continued his methodical stitching as if he were
operating on a house cat in the comfort of his practice. A few minutes later, it was done, and the vet and others stepped in with
Solomon to microchip him and move him clear of the door. This
was also performed with nonchalance, though perhaps now just
a hint of urgency. Then, mission accomplished, everyone stepped
clear, the door was closed, and normal security levels were resumed.
And Solomon bounced back from his ordeal to happily fire off
his blanks, in accordance with our license requirements.

The final vasectomy, which I didn't witness and was a little
uncomfortable about, was Vlad's—again, carried out in his house,
decreed from on high in case he impregnated his two sisters, the
absurdly named Blotch and Stripe. These three tigers were bred
illegally and hand-reared, despite an obvious genetic defect in the
line and overrepresentation of this strain of Siberian tigers in the
gene pool. This was one of the reasons Ellis, the previous owner,
had run afoul of the authorities, and all three tigers were classi-
fied as "Display Only," and not to be bred from. This I didn't
mind, but what bothered me was that tigers are particularly sus-
ceptible to dying under anaesthetic. Vlad's brother, Ivan, had died

during a routine procedure some years before, and Tasmin's heart had stopped some months before, while she was being investigated for an ongoing kidney problem. In that instance, only Duncan's fast response in alerting the vet, who was walking back to his car at the time, saved her, and she was quickly given the antidote to bring her round. As Vlad's amorous efforts with his sister had so far, in seven years, resulted in no illegal offspring, I was reluctant to have him tampered with at the possible risk of his life. I liked Vlad a lot—he is a nice, friendly boy—and the machinery of state intervention, coupled with a mild snobbery about his lack of strict zoological value, I felt, was exposing him to unnecessary risks. But by now I was a bit battle weary, and with my stand on the wolves and monkeys and various other issues, it was probably a good time to let a few slide past. The operation was a success, and Vlad returned to duty the next day.

The money was ebbing, but at last we had an inspection date, set for 4 June, which gave us an all-or-nothing deadline to work toward. Everybody pitched in, occasionally getting a little high on resources, sending out for new tools or equipment with relative abandon. The core staff we had inherited were brilliant improvisers—they had had to be for many years as the fortunes of the park declined. Instead of buying new metal bars, for instance, I encouraged salvaging existing ones that were liberally scattered around. There was an estimated acre of scrap behind the restaurant, for instance, containing old cars, even lorries and the long-forgotten husk of an old dumper truck, as well as perhaps twenty fridges, innumerable tires and wheels, bits of wood, and a thousand other things "stored" for future use at some indefinite time in the future, which never came. We did a deal with a local scrap merchant, who arrived with a large flatbed truck with a grabber on it and a mini digger (which he kindly lent to us when he wasn't using it). The deal was that he could have everything, except the choicest bits of metal that we could recycle, in exchange for clearing the site. "No problem," he said, delighted. "It'll take about five days." Nine weeks later, he was still loading up his lorry every day with more metal objects dragged from the ground. Although 95 percent was pure, unadulterated rubbish, in the meantime we had salvaged all kinds of useful things, including double-glazed panels of glass miraculously unbroken, some perfectly useable fence posts, and enough scrap angle iron to fabricate a small enclosure. The first object fabricated entirely from the salvaged scrap was a trailer for the keepers' new quad bikes that John made in less than a week, using wheels from an old sit-on mower. That trailer is still in service today.

The quad bikes, however, are not. Or rather, one of them is, just. Duncan's idea to buy cheap quad bikes as a morale booster for the staff backfired at first, when the wrong people ended up using them for the wrong reasons. Instead of Hannah and Kelly's workload being lightened, they still seemed to be pushing heavy barrows of meat or bedding up steep paths, while junior maintenance staff and casual employees thrashed around the park on the bikes doing minor errands. The quad bikes deteriorated rapidly, and spent more and more time being fixed or waiting for parts. This caused a lot of bad will, and several meetings were held where strict protocols were implemented for the use of the quads. The person who was least happy about it was probably Rob, head keeper and long-suffering grandson of Ellis. "What's wrong with walking?" he'd ask. "It's part of what working in a place like this is all about." Though well-intentioned, the purchase of the quad bikes taught us a lesson about tampering with the ecosystem we had inherited.

My own gift to the keepers was on a smaller scale, and caused less controversy. Ten headlamps, distributed throughout the staff, had made working in the dark winter evenings, in the absence of exterior lighting (and even lights inside some of the big cat houses) safer and more bearable. "I haven't heard a word said against them," said Rob. Though by spring, every one of them had been lost or broken. On a lighter note, in the lighter evenings we didn't need them.

The peacocks were another welcome part of that spring, pouting and preening their quite unbelievably over-the-top plumage for all they were worth. Peacocks seem to have been designed by a flamboyant madman, probably of Indian extraction given the fine detailing, though with more than a nod toward the tastes of Liberace. Even in repose they are stunning, their impossibly blue heads and necks suddenly giving way to equally unlikely green and gold feathers laid like scales from halfway down their backs. These in turn abruptly change into their famous long tail feathers, many of them around a meter, easily three times as long as the males' bodies. As if this is not enough, as an afterthought their heads are embellished with more blue-tipped feathers on narrow stalks, which blossom out in an animal parody of a Roman centurion's helmet. *And why the hell not?* you think. They've gone this far. It seems the only limit to their opulence is the almost boundless confines of the imagination of their Indian Liberace designer.

In the sunshine, watching these extravagant birds, I found, was uniquely cheering. Their sheer physical beauty was uplifting, a symbol that, even striding around with a mobile phone stuck to my ear, I was somewhere unusual, worthwhile, and with a hint of the exotic. And they were highly amusing, too. These pea brains would launch their shimmering fan at anything that moved, and quite a few things that didn't. The older males, with their magnificent tails, shimmered in the sunlight, flashing their wares at the ducks, cockerels, and moorhens, who studiously ignored them or walked away embarrassed. But they also targeted picnic benches, footballs, plant pots, and even the cats (which upset these still slightly nervous felines no end). Only occasionally, it seemed, did they actually display their wares to the correct subject, a peahen, who is supposed to be so impressed with this array that nothing less will do. But they didn't seem impressed either, and often wandered off leaving some hapless male shimmering away at nothing, abandoned as if halfway through a promising first date. In the whole mating season I think I witnessed only one successful copulation, and there was certainly only one pregnant female by the end of it.

I also loved the peacocks because of their place in evolution, or rather in the explanation of it. As an occasional writer on evolutionary psychology, particularly regarding male behavior, I often used the peacock's tail as shorthand for some elaborate and expensive male display designed to attract females. There are strong arguments in favor of the idea that the entire human cortex—metabolically the most expensive organ we possess—evolved with mate attraction in mind. Similarly, humor, hunting, risk taking, and red Porsche 911s can all be shorthanded as peacock's tail–type phenomena. You look for other examples, often toward the birds of paradise, but their elaborate displays and one-off shock-tactic plumage, though certainly ridiculous, have nothing on the sheer extravagance of the encumbrance the peacock has landed himself with. The point of the tail is that it is very expensive to produce and maintain—like the Porsche, or cortex—and having one is a definite drain on resources. A human neocortex requires 40 percent of our calories, and a Porsche costs a lot to buy, and, subject to legal action pending at the time of writing, may become almost as costly to drive in central London, where most of them surely live. But the peacock's tail really hampers him, drawing massive attention from predators and making evasion much more difficult. The weight impedes take-off, and you rarely see them attempt more than a wing-assisted hop when in full plumage. This point was illustrated graphically a few years previously, when, according to Robin, the bears were moved into their new enclosure in woodland frequented by peacocks. "Yes, it took them a while to get used to the change," said Robin mildly. "The bears ate mainly peacocks in the first week." Having landed, the birds were startled by and then poorly equipped to evade the three fast-moving, voracious predators, and this lesson in natural selection is fascinating to me. Watching them parade this incredibly expensive display so poorly, and at such inappropriate objects, while children play football around them, I have to think that, having gone to all that trouble, squandering the display on a camera bag or a tree stump seems marvelous in its profligacy. It really does say to me, to borrow Dawkins' phrase from his famous book on Darwinian theory, that the Watchmaker was blind. Just an extra gram of neural tissue, you would think, would be a better investment, but not when the market, evolved through rigorous sexual selection, is in expensive tails. I had a soft spot for the peacocks. So I was disturbed to learn that Owen, our star bird keeper, had taken it upon himself to cull four of them, citing overcrowding. I suspected there was more to it than this, because Owen, like Sarah, had told me that he didn't see the zoo as a place where non-exotic animals, or more specifically, "animals of no zoological significance," should be kept. Most of the hundred or so birds in the walk-in enclosure—mainly chickens, geese, and ducks—had gradually disappeared—culled apparently by some systemic parasitic infection that was too advanced to treat and that was a health risk to the more zoologically significant rare birds we had and planned to acquire in the future. But several neighbors and farmers were contacted and invited to take the birds, subject to their own health check, and many were saved, going on to produce many eggs for many other people. Adam in particular occasionally taunted me that he enjoyed a particularly fine duck egg for breakfast. This culling, deemed necessary, particularly upset Mum, who had enjoyed being followed around by this raggedy brood while feeding them, an experience, standing in her own park, which seemed a daily reminder of the remarkable distance she had traveled in her life since childhood. It upset me too, and indicated a level of disagreement with the new keeper-staff, which was to culminate in a fiery meeting about the direction of the park a few weeks down the line. More of that later.

In the meantime, I went along with this and other, to me, quite radical measures, simply because there wasn't time to contest everything, and nor was it wise to challenge the orthodoxy on everything I felt uncertain about. Zookeepers are a little bit like paramilitaries. They wear big boots and combat trousers, they communicate with walkie-talkies, and they do a dangerous job that sometimes involves firearms. To come up through their ranks requires a lot of discipline and dedication, as well as conformity to the established orthodoxy. I couldn't do it. Arguably, I have a modicum of self-discipline (though I can imagine my dad snorting with derision at this assertion), but external discipline often seems to rankle with me. Duncan tried to be a zookeeper once, for about six months in the reptile house at London Zoo, and it wasn't for him either. "I remember my first day," says Duncan. "The man in charge of me held up a broom, told me what it was, and then showed me how to use it, by putting the head on the floor and then pushing it out in front of you repeatedly. It took a while for it to dawn on me that I was standing here being shown by a grown man how to sweep a floor." Having been fully trained, he thought, in these esoteric cleaning arts, after a few days he made an innovation. "The head of the broom kept falling off, so I popped a nail into it and trebled the efficiency. But the bloke was livid. 'Who told you to do that?' he yelled, and with good reason, it turned out." Apparently the head was left loose because it was sometimes necessary to go in with the alligators to clean around these slow-moving throwbacks, and the broom was the keeper's main defense. "The idea is that if an alligator ever made a move for you, you offered it the broom and it would bite the head off and retreat, thinking it had got something. And then at least you still had the handle, instead of it being yanked out of your hand and thrashing about the place." So there was method in this apparent madness (though this arguably most important part of the training had been lacking), but some of what Duncan encountered just seemed like plain madness.

"The Galapagos tortoises had beak rot and weren't breeding, so I decided to use my lunch hours to look into it," he says. London Zoo is home to one of the most comprehensive zoological libraries in the world, but as a trainee keeper in the early 1980s, Duncan wasn't allowed access to it. "They made it really hard, and it was as if they genuinely didn't understand what I wanted to do in there." Eventually Duncan got in, and found that the only zoo to successfully breed these huge, long-lived reptiles—one at London at the time was thought to have been brought back by Charles Darwin—was San Diego. Reading their papers and contacting their staff, he learned that the beak rot was caused by eating bananas, which stick to the lower part of the jaw. In the wild, such matter is brushed off by the long grass through which the tortoises walk, but in London they weren't, so the beak rots. Duncan took his findings to the senior keeper in charge of the reptiles, expecting to be able to implement the necessary changes, and possibly even be thanked for his efforts. In fact, the old man said, "I've been doing this job for twenty years. Who are you to tell me how to do my job?

Fuck off." Science, they say, advances funeral by funeral. Duncan isn't the type to wait around, so he left to become his own boss, importing marine fish from the tropics.

Now we both found ourselves running a zoo—or trying to—and while we knew we had to listen to and closely follow what we were told by our advisors, from keepers to curator to council, we also knew that there would be times when we would be able to innovate. Business managers know that often the best innovators are not insiders. Our trouble was that we weren't really business managers either. But at least we were outsiders.

We also knew that, for now, we all had to work together, and to use the Environmental Health officer Peter Wearden's phrase, "ticking the right boxes," was what counted most in the run-up to the inspection. Sometimes those boxes could be ticked, after a struggle, via a different chain of events from those prescribed or recommended, like with the wolf dispute, or the monkeys, but this always took time, and invariably, during the hiatus before resolution, our fragile credibility would be eroded. Until the box was actually ticked, when it became an invisible issue, and everything moved toward the next box. Time we did not have, and we had to get as many boxes ticked as possible before our inspection, now set firmly for 4 June. We had to enter into a box-ticking frenzy, otherwise the bankers and the lawyers would gleefully produce their own clipboards, offering much less room to maneuver, and with much less friendly boxes.

There was an exhilarating sense of teamwork—a truly flexible, skilled, and dedicated team working together to achieve a common aim. On paper, this was our business, and everyone was an employee contriving, in the long run, to produce profits for us. In actuality, I don't think anyone thought like this—least of all us. Day in, day out, it felt like we were all battling to save a beleaguered public resource, and most important, a collection of

beleaguered animals, safe for the future. And if we failed, the
consequences were unthinkable. Tourette Tony did an excellent
job, swearing his way through countless setbacks, dancing his
digger through ridiculously skillful and efficient maneuvers,
and working himself and his team as hard as was humanly possible. Anna and Steve were absolutely invaluable, Anna handling
the complicated paperwork, feeding back to us exactly which
boxes we needed to tick, and exactly how, while Steve deployed
himself as laborer, keeper, supervisor, roller driver—whatever he
needed to be. Hannah, Kelly, Paul, John, and Rob alternated between keeping and maintenance tasks, and a crew of temporary
laborers got stuck with unpleasant tasks like dredging slimy
moats, sweeping acres of wet leaves, and tensioning hundreds of
meters of new fence mesh, which bites into the hands, made
more painful by the chilly breeze. Owen and Sarah led their
troop of junior keepers from the front, working incredibly hard,
leading, training, and instilling appropriate modern practices,
though a little harshly it seemed to me at times—Owen told me
that to train a novice you had to "break them down and build
them up again, sometimes." This didn't chime with my preferred
(though admittedly made-up-as-I-went-along) management
technique, but then I wasn't from that culture. Inevitably, this ongoing process had its occasional rows and threatened walkouts,
but the overall atmosphere was of everyone knuckling down and
doing whatever was necessary. It was going as well as it could.
And then came the rain.

After the exceptionally sunny and buoyant May, we entered
the wettest June in the UK for a hundred years. The Southwest
suffered just over twice the average precipitation since records began in 1914, but it felt like it rained every single day. The gnaw-
ing doubts of whether we could accomplish the task in the
allotted time returned. Working in waterproofs, many tasks like

fencing and barrier replacements could still be achieved. But things like welding outside, concreting, chain-saw work, and often, using the digger, were out of the question.

The peacocks, so recently a symbol of hope, now looked bedraggled. One female sat on the grass verge outside the toilets for several weeks, and when I asked the keepers if she was okay, it turned out that she was roosting some eggs. In the rain. Within a few yards of where she sat was a perfectly viable bush, which would at least have provided some cover from the elements and, at least as important, foxes. But this dumb-assed bird—apparently the only one to succumb to the male's elaborate, evolutionarily expensive spring display—persisted in trying to rear her delicate brood fully exposed to the elements and predators. Eventually three eggs hatched, and she wisely moved her little ones around each night, but as they grew and she roamed further afield—she and her little trio of actually quite pretty chicks, desperately trying to keep up with their mum—we gradually lost track of them, and I can't honestly say whether any of them survived or not.

Even in the rain there was much to do, both inside and out, and I threw myself into work. By now, less than three months after Katherine's death, I could notice significant physiological changes in my response. Mainly, I didn't feel so leaden, as if the life had been sapped out of me with her passing—though my Stella Artois diet, much reduced but still a significant part of my routine to get to sleep after putting the kids to bed, was expanding my waistline so that, in reality, my physical leadenness was actually increasing. But the energy within was beginning to return. The many daily triggers were becoming more recognizable and more bearable, I was much less likely to be wrong-footed by something unexpected, and the amount of crying I needed to do gradually reduced. I would occasionally be overwhelmed by dipping into the enormity of what we had lost. A couple of brief but necessary trips to London, every part of which I seemed to have visited with Katherine, during this period were particularly horrible. But generally, I could feel it was getting better. And the children seemed to be thriving at the new school, and adapting with the malleable resilience of the very young.

Obviously they were still profoundly affected, and I made sure that I kept talking to them whenever they wanted me to. Increasingly, though, they seemed to be protecting me—and themselves—from my grief, which must have been alarming for them, but was impossible (and I thought, inadvisable) to hide in the early stages. They confided occasionally to friends and neighbors, and Amelia, who trickled their concerns back to me. Once they both came up with the idea of wearing one of Katherine's jumpers in bed, and as I rummaged through her drawers of neatly folded clothes, last visited during those all too memorable weeks of dressing and undressing her, I felt myself becoming increasingly upset. Milo, watching closely, smiled and wagged his finger at me, saying good-naturedly, "Uh, uh, uuh, Daddy. Don't turn on the tears." It cheered me up no end and I promised him that I wouldn't, and reassured him again that whenever he wanted to talk about Mummy I wouldn't cry. Which is where we are now.

Outside in the park, the inspection date loomed, and the rain often made it impossible to see farther than a few yards. We persevered, and even a few weeks before the inspection, the mood on the ground was lifting; the consensus seemed to be that we had "ticked enough boxes" to show willingness. It is almost unheard of for a zoo that has had its license withdrawn to haul itself back from the abyss, but the feeling was that we were probably going to do it—though we couldn't afford to slack off for an instant. Our short resumé looked good. We had the right people, the right intentions, and if not quite the right amount of money, at least we were spending it in the right way. One of the most important parts of our license requirement was the conservation measures we were going to implement. Steve and Anna have good contacts with an endangered species program in Sri Lanka, and Owen and Sarah's back catalog of successes was filtering through to us with promises of breeding programs for the future, which also scored us points. As did creatures like Ronnie, the officially "Vulnerable" tapir, and Sovereign, our prize stud-book jag. But increasingly, local conservation measures are seen as at least equally important. Fortunately, we were in a good position to implement many. On the edge of Dartmoor, itself a thriving habitat of many species that are declining nationally, we were perfectly placed to help endangered animals of the much less glamorous variety. Like dormice, horseshoe bats, vulnerable ground-nesting birds, newts, snails, and even certain mosses and lichens. One species I already knew a tiny bit about was a certain kind of fritillary butterfly thought to have one of its last toeholds in the country in Dartmoor, which I happened to have written about briefly for the *Guardian*. I called the Butterfly Conservation Society ("Butterfly Conservay-shun, how can we help you?" they cooed), who informed me that we could work to provide habitats on our land that could be suitable for butterflies. We already had a couple of acres of dedicated conservation woodland, but the requirements for specific plants may have been detrimental to what was already there. They would welcome a donation. Er, maybe one day.

Another thwarted effort was the Dartmoor pony, down to fewer than nine hundred breeding mares (making it even rarer than that conservation figurehead the giant panda), and subject of a concerted local campaign to protect them from ruthless landowners who sometimes shoot them or sell them for meat rather than pay the newly introduced £20 fee for a horse passport, now required under European law. The idea is to register animals that may pass into the human food chain so that any

veterinary drugs they have consumed can be monitored. The reality is that a Dartmoor pony can be sold for as little as a pint of
milk, and many hard-pressed farmers simply can't afford to comply with the passport law. Charities are looking for landowners
who can offer paddocks to small herds of ponies, who are periodically transported back to certain areas of the moor to graze
and manage it as only these tough little indigenous critters can.
My sister Melissa researched and promoted the scheme, having
once kept a Dartmoor pony—Aphrodite—who had a stubborn
but gentle temperament. I remember Aphrodite fondly, nonchalantly standing outside in the snow, with icicles clinking from her
whiskers, trying to reassure a namby-pamby semi-Thoroughbred
in its heated stable, wearing a thick horse coat, who had caught
a cold. This local project sounded perfect, and I brought up plans
to devote eight acres, which would support about eight to twelve
small ponies, to this admirable aim. But I hit a brick wall: it didn't
tick any boxes. Dartmoor ponies may be endangered, but the actual species, Horse (*Caballus*), can only be described as thriving.
Dartmoor ponies were artificially bred by humans a few centuries ago, probably to work in the local tin mines, and count as
a breed, rather than an endangered species. It's like trying to save
the Siamese cat, or the Staffordshire bull terrier. Of interest to local breeders perhaps, but zoologically insignificant. This seemed
to me a particularly irritating pill to swallow, but again, time was
not on our side, and we had to do what was necessary to get our
license, rather than what we thought we might like.

One local scheme, which I did manage to include as a central plank of our conservation strategy, was reinstating hedgerows.
There are an estimated couple of kilometers of hedgerow border-
ing and crisscrossing our thirty acres, most of it depleted and
sparse, providing little of the rich habitat for local wildlife it once
did. Some hedgerows (though not, it has to be said, ours) are

more than seven hundred years old. Properly maintained, hedgerows are giant elongated ecosystems in their own right, acting as corridors for wildlife to pass along, and protecting many wildflowers, plants, insects, birds, and mammals that experience difficulties when out in the open. We also had pockets of different kinds of hawthorn, which could be transplanted from other parts of the site, and this project, fortunately, was given an enthusiastic thumbs-up by the authorities. It also ticked my own personal box for a long-term, slow intervention, a gradual enhancement of the broader ecosystem of the park, unlikely to provide shocks, but very likely to provide long-term benefits and educational opportunities—and security, as thick hedgerows are a good barrier against intruders, as well as certain errant exotic animals. And—AND—where we took out hawthorn, it freed up space for other uses, like public viewing areas. It went into the plan, and we set about putting out feelers for those wise in the ways of the hedgerow to train us up. Fortunately, in this area of Devon, these old countryside practices still go on, and I looked forward to one day being able to lose myself in the ancient art of coppicing for a few hours a day before too long.

Meanwhile, over at the restaurant, the ringmaster Adam was gradually drawing everything together, though it took an experienced eye to discern through the chaos that some coherence was emerging. The kitchen was still "shambolic," as was the eating area and the shop—covered in sawdust and work tools—which somehow had to be transformed into clear public access or commercial space. But there were signs that it was changing for the better. The vile ceiling had been covered with crisp new plasterboard, then skimmed with plaster to an almost ethereal smoothness by three men in less than a week, which at four hundred square meters was pretty good going. Mind you, it had to be. It had to dry, be painted, and have the lovely, new, brushed-chrome flush spotlights (Katherine would have approved) installed.

There had been much talk of off-whites, even strong colors, being used on the walls, but Mum and I stuck to our guns: everything was going to be white. With the oak floor, oak counter and bar, and brushed-steel details, this vast room was going to give posh London restaurants a run for their money.

Remember that design meeting I was in when the wolf escaped? We didn't use those people for our leaflets in the end, as their mock-ups were much too fussy. (Instead a friend from London volunteered to finish off what Katherine had started, much more in her style; thanks, Paul.) But something good did come out of the meeting. When I outlined my ideas for the overall aesthetic for the restaurant, and ultimately the park, mentioning Terence Conran as a guiding principle, one of the designers came up with the excellent description "Conran meets *Out of Africa*." I jumped on it readily. (Pretentious? *Moi?*) However pompous this model may sound, if we could pull it off I was certain it would work in the market we were aiming for. Good design is becoming more mainstream, and modern buildings are springing up in zoos as fast as they are anywhere else. Bristol Zoo recently spent £1,000,000 on a new monkey house that looks like it could feature in a Swedish *Grand Designs* program. People who regularly eat at McDonald's won't actually be put off by understated good taste (well, "good taste" in my humble subjective opinion anyway), nor will they be put off by good food, as long as it is reasonably priced. Besides, my most optimistic interpretation of our business plan was that we (and the surrounding roads) could probably only support a maximum of 200,000 to 220,000 visitors a year, and one day we may have to raise prices to limit the numbers. Why not prepare for that market now? It was easy to get ahead of yourself (our most pressing aspiration, to just break even, with 60,000 visitors, was thought by many to be optimistic) in the upbeat atmosphere of the restaurant, particularly with Adam in "can do" mode, still juggling quotes and materials, and interviewing catering staff on a very tight timeline. Looking at the progress, and looking at Adam, I knew he was going to succeed. This was absolutely vital, as the restaurant was going to be the financial engine of the zoo—and, ideally, somewhere I could eat without having to worry about cleaning up for the next twenty-five years.

As another vital part of the business plan, we had to have at least one good kiosk, ideally two, or if the hugely successful nearby Paignton Zoo was anything to go by, one every fifty meters. Adam rejected a ready-made building next to the future petting zoo, a configuration of facilities through which I have been milked for tea, cake, and ice cream many times since becoming a parent. Owen pounced on the building to incubate birds' eggs on public display instead, while Adam made a strong case for focusing on a purpose-built kiosk at the top of the picnic area. Obviously this site needed a kiosk one day, but I was disappointed that he was eschewing an existing building, and I took some persuading that we should initially obtain what sounded like a quite expensive shed, instead of waiting and putting in a modern, curvy model that had just won the award for Best Leisure Facility Kiosk in Denmark (so many awards, so little time). But Adam was adamant: the outlay of £2,000 would repay itself in a single good summer's day by keeping people in the best part of the park, marveling at the proximity of the tigers on Tiger Mountain, being treated occasionally to the lions' roar and the wolves' howl, and buying tea, cake, ice cream, and, as we are in the Southwest, pasties like there was no tomorrow.

As an aside, I have learned two things about pasties, or meat pies, since I came here. One is that the thick outer rim of crust, which in an authentic pasty clogs up your mouth like a packet of cheese crackers, is not actually meant to be eaten, because it was designed to be the handle by which the meal was held in the grubby hands of miners on their lunch break. Sorry if you already knew this, but I enjoyed the discovery because it makes me feel less guilty about leaving that dehydrating arc of carbohydrate, or throwing it away to be eaten by ants. Organic, biodegradable handles and food packaging, generally, are things we should be thinking about now, but they were already being addressed as early as 1510. Which brings me to the second thing I've learned. The "Cornish pasty" was invented in Devon. Yeah, where I live. It was recently discovered that 1510 was the first recorded date when a pasty was mentioned, in the accounts of the council for the city of Plymouth. Which is in Devon. Across the Tamar river, "there be monsters," and this can be proved by the next mention of the pasty, in 1746, when this Devonian recipe was allegedly stolen by pirates and introduced to Cornwall. What kind of pirates were these? Outriders for some despotic, early Martha Stewart? The irrefutable fact remains, at the moment, that the pasty came from Devon. So get used to it, Cornwall. And yes, everybody already knows that pasties originally had two chambers, one savory and one of fruit filling, the world's first two-course convenience meal. Even I knew that.

The Great Pasty Debate apparently continues to rage acrimoniously between the two counties, though I must admit, in eighteen months here, I have never overheard a single word of it. And frankly, now, I'm getting a bit sick of pasties.

So Adam persuaded me that the new structure would be a good use of our rapidly depleting funds, and called me over the radio to watch it arrive. I still had my reservations, in the driving June rain. It still seemed an expensive option compared with refitting the existing building a hundred yards away, and, to me, a bit too square. The team that arrived to erect the prefabricated structure was resolutely professional, working efficiently through the rain on a small site we had paced out and leveled to the kiosk's requirements. Once again I had a small opportunity to get involved in some DIY construction, supplying the odd hammer blow here, lifting a panel or two there, and I relished it. But once the structure was up, the team swarmed around it, fitting it out with internal panels and hammering down the roofing felt, and there was nothing for me to do, apart from stand back in the picnic area and marvel at how good it looked. Square or not, it looked like it had always been here, like it definitely belonged, and it was easy to get excited about the possibility of queues of paying customers lining up outside it. Though not in this weather . . .

The kiosk was a very important part of the overall plan and, as the business side of the venture, absolutely had to work. The animals, obviously, came first, but without satisfied customers—and lots of them—they faced an uncertain future. The inspection was only days away, and though it would focus on animal welfare, some attention would also be paid to the facilities for the public. The number of toilets, the state of the paths, disabled access, adequate stand-off barriers to prevent people's limbs being sheared off by giant carnivores, that sort of thing. What the inspector would not do—could not do—is tell us whether it was going to work as a business. That was down to us, the weather, an element of luck, and whether the local reputation of the park was already too irretrievably tarnished in the public mind. And that was a bit scary.

Inspection Day dawned a rare sunny morning, which augured well, though the pre-exam nerves infected everyone. As I met the keepers before the inspector arrived, they were barely recognizable. Smartly dressed—and clean! Normally mud spattered and sweat drenched, this crew of hardened workers who would think nothing of throwing themselves into a mire in pursuit of an injured animal, shoveling barrowloads of excrement, or covering themselves with blood while stripping down a horse carcass, suddenly looked like normal people, like you might meet out on the street. I didn't even know that Steve had a smart jacket, but here he was, looking slightly ill at ease in it, chain-smoking roll-ups while we waited for the examiner to arrive. I was particularly nervous, which took me by surprise, because I had taken soundings from everyone involved and had been persuaded that we had "almost certainly" done enough to pass. It was that "almost" that suddenly came home to roost as we waited.

The government-appointed inspector arrived with Peter Wearden, who would actually issue the license, should that be the recommendation. Peter winked at me, which was slightly reassuring, but the matter was out of his hands. The inspector, Nick Jackson, ran his own small zoo, a second-generation family operation with an international reputation, in Wales. So, he knew how to run a good zoo. We just hoped that he could discern the seeds of one in what we had done. The walk-around—normally an unequivocal pleasure, showing people what we had got and what we aimed to do and watching them transform from wide-eyed skeptics to energized enthusiasts by the end of it—suddenly became deadly serious. Mr. Jackson was being paid to ask difficult questions, from a position of extreme insight, and nothing was off-limits. He went into every single animal house, exposed every single area where we were lacking, and asked the most difficult questions. Meanwhile, Peter, in his role as Health and Safety Officer for South Hams Council, had some criticisms of his own. "Robin's Nest," for instance, where Robin had retreated to carry out his enclosure design work and the construction of signs, was a loft that, no one had seemed to notice or think strange, ended with an abrupt drop, next to his desk, of twenty feet down to the concrete floor of the workshop below. Obviously, Robin was aware of this and knew to stay away from the edge, but equally obvious was the fact that it wasn't safe. "I want this addressed immediately," he barked uncharacteristically. "And I mean TODAY." Other obvious oversights were the lack of signs on the doors of the dangerous animal houses for when people were working in the enclosures. "If I was working out there, I'd like to know that there was a sign on the door telling the keepers not to release the cats, just in case of a breakdown of communication," said Mr. Jackson. Though our operation was small enough and tight enough for everyone to know what everyone else was doing, it was a fair point, and Duncan radioed to Robin, who, his dangerous nest already being worked on, immediately began implementing this recommendation. I didn't help; for want of something to say while we waited for the keys to arrive to the tiger house, I pointed out that there was blood on the padlock of the external door. The inspector looked sharply at me and smiled. "I hadn't noticed that," he said. "Poor working practices." And he made a note. Damn.

At about five o'clock the inquisition was over, and rarely have I felt so relieved. But the day wasn't over yet. We moved to the office, where everyone sat down and endured a full two-and-a-half-hour debriefing, going over every point raised and being given some indication of our score on it. It was almost as grueling as the inspection itself, and although it was useful feedback in that we had scored quite well, it still wasn't conclusive, as the final report would contain extra material. I was relieved that my padlock remark, though drawing attention to our deficits, had actually played quite well, and was singled out by the inspector as part of "a culture of openness," apparently quite lacking at previous inspections over the years. He had also asked for private interviews with keepers and other staff, away from their employers breathing down their necks, and had been impressed by what he had heard from them about their interpretation of what we

were doing and where we were going. So no need to sack any-
body there, then (just kidding). Unless, of course, the result
came back with "Application Declined," in which case everybody
would be looking for new jobs.

I remember the next day vividly. I was (stupidly) unexpectedly exhausted, sitting on a bench outside the house with the children, when Rob came up to me. "I can't work any longer with
Steve," he said. Rob was head keeper, Steve was the curator, and
their relationship was vital to the smooth running of the zoo. This
should have been a bombshell. I should have felt panicky, or at
least alarmed, but instead I felt, from very deep down, *Whatever*.
I felt that we owed a lot to Rob. He had held on to the park, keeping it out of the developer's hands by taking on the collection
under the Dangerous Wild Animals (DWA) legislation when the
license to display the collection held by his grandfather was withdrawn. I had spoken to him and exchanged many e-mails during
the negotiating period when I was in France. Rob was one of the
most important people involved in us getting the park. I didn't
want to lose Rob, partly because we owed him, and also because
he was multi-skilled, and had a depth of knowledge about the
park that would be impossible to replicate.

I waited. He suggested moving to working on the grounds instead, which, after brief consideration, I thought was a very good
idea. With thirty acres to tend, we needed a dedicated grounds person (though we couldn't really afford one), and Rob was a qualified tree surgeon who knew the park as well as anyone. He needed
a less-stressful job due to a change in his personal circumstances,
as he was now single-handedly looking after a daughter he hadn't
seen in four years. Moving to grounds would take him from under the direct control of Steve, with whom he had a stormy relationship that seemed to reach the breaking point roughly every
two weeks. Under Tony, with whom he had a less-uneasy relation-

ship, he could work outside, not worrying about other people's rotas or changes in procedures he had grown up with being implemented by the new regime. He also knew a bit about the many exotic plants that flourish all over the park, mostly grown from cuttings by the green-fingered Ellis. (I have brown fingers; any plant in my care automatically shrivels and dies, though Rob told us early on that one rare plant, a kind of creeper, had thwarted Ellis for forty years, but that as soon as we arrived it had started to sprout leaves. This was a strange, apocryphal tale that was nevertheless nice to hear.) It would be a simpler life for Rob, and I almost envied him.

Steve was also delighted, and suggested that he would spend more time out in the park with the staff, encompassing the head keeper role, leaving more of the administrative side of his job to his eminently capable wife, Anna. Everybody seemed to be pleased with this new configuration, and I felt a bit like a soccer manager who had come up with a new way of deploying players; instead of 4–4–2, we were going for a radical 1–1–8. Or something. I have to admit I'm a bit shaky on soccer, but that's roughly what it felt like. Probably.

So, oddly jaded but also rejuvenated, we all set about filling the time until we heard our fate. We had to assume we would pass the inspection and open soon, but when, exactly, we could not predict. This was a complicated issue, because publicity material needed to be printed with dates and opening times for distribution all around the county. When the printers, up against their last possible deadlines, pressured us for information, we simply didn't know. In the end we went for "Opening Summer 2007." We had better be.

Finally the day came when Peter Wearden summoned me to appear at the council offices in Totnes to hear the result. I drove with Steve and my mum (maybe Peter would be more lenient with an elderly lady present). The last time I had been there was to register Katherine's death three months before with Ella, when I had played with her afterward in the small maze in the courtyard. But I tried to put this out of my mind because, as the King of Swamp Castle says in *Monty Python and the Holy Grail*, about the wedding disrupted by the slaughter of many guests by the exuberant Lancelot, "Please! This is supposed to be a happy occasion." Peter smiled, I smiled, everybody smiled. It was looking good. He handed me the report, which was long but fortunately had a covering letter. "I recommend that Dartmoor Zoological Park be granted a license to trade as a zoo . . ." Wow. At last. We had done it. We thanked Peter and drove back elated, and presented the news to all the staff, some of whom shed tears. We set a definite date for our opening, two weeks away, on 7 July—07/07/07—which everybody agreed was somehow auspicious.

Most important, it was just before the school holidays, at the beginning of the busiest period, though it meant we would have to hit the ground running. It would have been nice to have a gentler opening in June, to get a bit of practice at actually dealing with the public before exposing our newly revamped infrastructure to the (ideally) swarming hordes of July. If those hordes found any holes in our plan they would burst through them, impelled by market forces, and puncture the whole damn balloon. But 07/07/07 was set in stone. We really were opening on that date, no matter what. If the restaurant wasn't ready, there would be sandwiches. If the kiosk wasn't wired up properly, we'd run an extension lead. If the play area was uninstalled, we had bouncy castles, lent to us by Adam's Bouncy Castles, a secret part of our customer services manager Adam's former life. *It was going to happen.*

But the money had run out. We had tried—in vain, as it

turns out—to keep track of our reserves. But by the time Joanne, our bookkeeper, had got a grip on the situation, it was to tell us that we had about £60,000 left, and about a month to go before opening. An endangered zoo eats money like a specially designed money-eating machine, and for the valiant army of Dartmoor Zoological Park, £60,000 was a pittance. An industrial shredder specially adapted for banknotes couldn't get through money any better. As well as hungry mouths to feed—lions, bears, tigers, monkeys, and otters, to name but a few—all those animals require expensive veterinary dental checks, fecal screening programs, routine vaccinations, microchipping, and a whole gamut of other services, which for a custodian of exotic animals, is the first priority.

But these are so unequivocally part of what the zoo is about that they present no dilemma. The Day of the Dentist was a memorable, and memorably expensive, inauguration of just what is needed to responsibly maintain so many exotic animals. Fudge the bear, as well as needing a second go at cutting her claws, which had grown semicircular and impeded her walk, looked like she had a toothache. At twenty-nine, she could be expected to live perhaps another seven or so years in captivity (though she would have been long dead in the savage wild where her kind are down to perhaps five examples in the Pyrenees, and are still being hunted for sport in Eastern Europe). Her claws were one issue, but she seemed subdued and slow moving, and the occasional glimpses into her mouth she offered revealed a horrifying set of broken gravestones, cracked and covered in brown grime, as well as what looked like an abscess. It was enough to slow anyone down, particularly a venerable old lady.

One of the pumas was also ailing, and dribbling, which had been consistently diagnosed as gingivitis and treated as such periodically over the last several years. The trouble was that gingivitis is usually an acute condition—very rarely chronic—but this puma rarely showed her teeth to the keepers, and was in fact recently revealed to be an entirely different puma from the one we thought we had. An X-ray taken a few months previously showed that she had a metal plate in her leg, which she was not supposed to have, and meant that she was someone else entirely. We had to find out who she was and what was wrong with her.

The third, and arguably most important, client was Sovereign, the Ninja-escapist jaguar and the most endangered animal of the three. He had somehow cracked both his upper canines, one of which was flat at the end. It had been suggested that both these teeth might need to be extracted, which bothered me, because Sovereign was still a young adult and these teeth were the tools of his trade. Obviously he didn't need them for hunting at the zoo—we could feed him mince, if he needed it—but I was concerned for his psychological well-being if these teeth were lost. He would feel the loss. And I was concerned that preoccupations with preventing future abscesses would not include this in the calculations. I wanted to be there when these decisions were made.

So the Day of the Dentist was set, and we prepared. How we prepared. Peter Kertesz is the UK's leading specialist in exotic animal dentistry, and is also, mainly, a Harley Street practitioner on humans. He happens to have taken an interest in animal dentition, and has become one of the world's leading experts. Nick Masters, from the IZVG, was going to handle the anaesthetic and carry out general health checks on each animal while it was under. Both of them were booked, and we had to be ready.

In the predawn darkness of 6 AM the team started to assemble at the park, and most of the normal routine procedures and feeding began. By 8 AM, Steve had endured his increasingly familiar dance with Sovereign, who had been darted successfully and transported to the park's shiny new vet facility. Sovereign made a spectacular first patient for the vet room, his beautiful markings contrasting with the sterile white environment and green-coated medics. On examination, both Sovereign's two chipped upper canine teeth exposed some of the pulp, so there was a real possibility he might lose them. But Peter was unfazed and simply trimmed them, using a terribly efficient little grinder which makes all the worst noises that you don't want to overhear during human dentistry. Having stabilized the external structure of the teeth, he set about performing root-canal work. For us, this involves a special pipe cleaner about two inches long, which is inserted into the hole in the center of the tooth where the dentine once was, and shuffled back and forth to clean all the residual tissue out of the cavity deep in the bone. Thank God for anaesthetic. For Sovereign, the pipe-cleaning probes needed to be at least five inches long to get deep enough into his enormous roots, but also to travel the extra inches of the length of the teeth themselves, for Peter to dig out all the pulp. Fortunately, for such a dangerous patient Sovereign was as good as gold. Nick Masters ensured that he was under a closely monitored general anaesthetic; there were tubes in his mouth, monitors on his heart, and machines that went *beep*. After some very in-depth reaming, and then a similarly comprehensive filling, Sovereign's root-canal work was complete, and he was returned to a bed of straw in his enclosure.

Then it was the turn of a female puma, who we thought was probably Holly, who had been dribbling saliva in an unusual way. We carried the prostrate cat on a stretcher that had been lent by another zoo for the occasion. It was a short haul, with a relatively small cat, and the drugs were internationally recommended, so I didn't feel too apprehensive about this. The transfer went well, and once she was on the table, Peter immediately saw that the problem was a couple of premolars on her lower jaw, which had noth-

ing above them to chew against. For the last several years she had
been biting against her gums, which were bleeding and causing the
dribbling, and now extraction was the only option. But this was
all routine to Peter, and forty-five minutes and two extractions
later, the procedure was completed, and Holly was on her way
back to her enclosure to recover in her bed of warm straw.

Everybody broke for a late lunch, and a refreshed team faced
what they hoped would be a simple task of clipping the overgrown claws of the park's oldest mammal, Fudge, the twenty-
nine-year-old European brown bear. Fudge was tricky to sedate.
Her weight was unknown (it turned out to be 147 kilos on the
scales in the vet room—she's a small bear), so it was difficult to
get the dose right. And she was tough. Eventually six people managed to transport a sleeping Fudge to the operating table, where
we manhandled her into position for Peter and Nick. Nick, as
anaesthetist, had priority initially, to stabilize her, and his array
of beeping machines ensured that she was safely under, with all
her vital signs monitored. As soon as this was established, Peter
took over with a flourish. Neither Nick nor Peter are tall men, but
both are fit and extremely precise in their movements—archetypal medical professionals—and it was a real privilege to watch
them work. They looked the part too, both choosing blue para-
military-style boiler suits with leg pockets, Peter's to carry the
rechargeable battery pack for the elaborate headlamp he wore
throughout, sometimes fitting it with extra optical devices, like a
sort of jeweler-surgeon. Which, I suppose, an exotic-animal dentist probably is. Peter is perhaps twenty years older than Nick,
and though in the glamorous role of specialist, he gracefully de-
ferred to the anesthetist whenever he needed access to check the
tubes going into Fudge's mouth or made recommendations
about how long he could take. He'd stand back, tools in the air
with all the time in the world, saying, "You do what you have to

do. I'm just the technician." But though Peter was charming, he also constantly supplied a monologue about what a superb job he was doing. "Look at that," he'd say, cutting around the gum and deftly extracting a minor rotting tooth, then stitching up the gum with one hand. "I'm probably the only person in the world who could do that. From diagnosis to extraction in under twenty minutes. Good job I'm here." There had been rumors that Peter would arrive with a new, attractive female assistant, and he did (he always does). Unfortunately, though extremely competent, she was not quite as fast as Peter demanded, and he gave her several ruthless dressing-downs. But of course, this was a serious business. The bear could only stay under for so long, and all the people involved had been working for many hours, with several more to go, during which no one could afford to make mistakes.

The more Peter looked, the more bad stuff he found. In the end Fudge had five extractions, the molars, and particularly her remaining upper canine, were not twenty-minute jobs. "Bears' teeth are built to last," said Peter as he struggled with Fudge's well-rooted dentition, which involved using a small stainless-steel hammer and chisel. It was all hands on deck as the dental nurse, Anna, Steve, Duncan, and I all held Fudge steady while Peter tugged and cajoled the teeth out and sewed up her bleeding gums. Sovereign I had met before under general anaesthetic, and his languid musculature had been no surprise. "Holly," the puma, was past her prime, and had seemed like just a very big domestic cat—though one you wouldn't want to mess with. But Fudge seemed unbelievably solid, perhaps like the wild boar that Leon had so wisely declined to pursue in France. She felt like she could go through anything, and Nick was impressed with the strength of her vital signs throughout. I was totally impressed with Fudge. She was really a beast. And during these procedures, it became clear why Fudge had been moving slowly for some time.

Peter uncovered and drained an abscess the size of a golf ball in her lower jaw, which if left untreated would sap the immune system and could be fatal. One of the earliest examples of a skeleton of early man was found by a lake in Africa and diagnosed as having died of a dental abscess that had eaten at his jaw and killed him, probably very painfully, in his prime. In the wild, Fudge would have never lived this long, as this abscess would probably have killed her.

Three and a half hours later, the operation was over, and Fudge was returned to her enclosure through a park shrouded in darkness once more, as when we had begun. It had been a long and fairly gruesome day, and though it was impossible not to reflect, at least for a moment, on the cost (£8,000 vet bill, plus vet room, staff, etc.), it felt great to have diverted some funds from the world in general and channeled them into this hugely worthwhile cause. Now at least, if we ever did have to disperse the animals, these three would be healthier and a more attractive proposition for rehoming. But it was more than that. The optimist in me found it enormously satisfying to be able to provide such highly skilled, expert care for these amazing animals here in our own facility on the site. There was no doubt that Nick and Peter were, quite literally, world-class professionals. And we had managed to deploy them to address long-term health problems in three animals in our care who hadn't previously been treated.

I looked on Peter's Web site and there he was, with a range of animals and in locations far more exotic than ours: the most impressive shot was an elephant on its back, with, I counted, twenty-nine people hauling it into position so that Peter could perform an extraction, probably of a tooth the size of a rugby ball. Compared to that, six people on standby for fourteen hours and a man with a large gun posted outside was small potatoes, and it was an honor that he asked if some of the pictures taken could go on his Web site with the others. But it had been exciting for us nonetheless.

All three animals made excellent recoveries, and far from seeming subdued by their day at the dentist's, all three animals seemed to have an extra spring in their step as their long-term painful conditions were finally addressed. The next day Sovereign eagerly stripped a huge piece of meat with his newly filled teeth, Holly the puma ate some diced chicken, and Fudge happily crunched through a bucket of apples, despite the many stitches in her gums.

Vets' bills make up just one column on the spreadsheet. In the bigger picture, it's just a necessary expense in the running of the business. The trouble was, there still was no business. Several potential lenders had pointed this out early on, and some had even cited it as a reason not to lend us money. *How unreasonable*, I'd thought at the time. But I was beginning to see their point.

Obviously, we had now passed our license inspection, and we could soon open to the public and begin trading. But unfortunately, the date for this to happen had kept slipping further down the calendar—April, then Easter, then June—until it had hit the very worrying month of July. Sixty-five percent of the year's trading in a seasonal attraction like this takes place in July and August. If any of July went missing from the figures, we would be in serious trouble. And we still weren't there yet. We had enough to pay the wages and essential creditors until October, then that was it. People had to come in July and August, and in significant numbers. If they didn't, we could close at the end of our first season. It was sobering, but we ploughed on, using things we already had in stock, recycling existing materials, and enthusiastically turning off lights at the end of the day, though this probably had little impact on the staggering £6,000 monthly electricity bill.

The license had come with a few conditions, mostly things we could address over the next twelve months, but one or two things—like the restaurant—needed to be brought up to standard before we opened. It was all in hand, though, and probably on about 1 July, Adam happily informed us that the bar was now fully functioning, able to serve wines, spirits, and draft cider and bitter, our very dry ale. And Stella Artois. As Adam's taillights disappeared down the drive that night, Duncan and I and Max, a cameraman with whom we had bonded particularly well, opened up the bar and began sampling this important commodity, for quality-control purposes, of course. The bar became a convenient place to meet at the end of the day to debrief each other and discuss story lines that needed following up with Max. Strictly business meetings, of course. Ten days later, the eighty-four-pint barrel was empty, Adam having sold about six pints to the paying public. "I can see that in order to make a profit on the Stella I'm going to have to charge about £12.50 a pint," he lamented, perhaps slightly tetchily. We sniggered like naughty schoolboys as he walked away—though I am six years older than Adam, and Duncan and Max are considerably more. Of course we realized that this was no way to run a business, though it seemed necessary at the time.

With one day to go before opening, the restaurant was actually ready, the shop was stocked with appealing fluffy toys and DZP-printed merchandise, the meat and vegetable rooms for the animals were gleaming, the new paths were surreally flat and groomed, and the picnic area was dotted with restored picnic tables in front of the new kiosk, whose power and water supply was almost complete in anticipation of the hordes who would, we hoped, soon be swarming around it. Even more striking were the staff, newly kitted out in their pristine uniforms, green for keepers, blue for maintenance, white for catering and retail. Each shirt was emblazoned with Katherine's logo of a tiger-striped DZP, the last thing she ever designed, destined now, apparently, to outlive her by many years.

The only thing that wasn't playing ball was the weather. Having passed through the wettest June on record, early July showed no inclination toward becoming summer either. The rain was relentless, and we even had prolonged periods of fog, making it impossible to see more than twenty yards. As Kelly succinctly put it on the eve of our big day, "We're opening tomorrow, and we're living in a fucking cloud." There was nothing to do but have one last tidy-up, one last walk-around, then turn off the lights and see what tomorrow was going to bring.

9

Opening Day

S o, the day of 7 July 2007 dawned, and we were going to open to the public at 10 AM. And, amazingly, for the first time in about six weeks, it was sunny. It was actually hot. The sky was cloudless, even the park itself was cloudless, for a change. Down in the car park a small crowd was collecting from half past nine onward, and a ribbon had been strung across the entrance, ready to be cut as the zoo was officially reopened for business for the first time in fifteen months.

Mum, Duncan, and several of the smartly dressed staff were already down at the bottom when I arrived, but we were far outnumbered by the expectant crowd of mums with buggies, family groups, and the odd OAP (old-age pensioner). The day before, the weather would have made this highly unlikely, but this sudden gap in the clouds was like the curtains unexpectedly opening on the cast of a play, long in rehearsals with the opening date constantly threatened with delay. Suddenly we were on. These were real customers, all genuinely wanting to visit a real zoo. Some would even be wanting to buy a toy, have a meal, and go to the toilet; so, for the next eight hours (for the first time in our lives), this was our job: to see that this randomly selected cross-section of the public got what they wanted, and left content with their experience.

Mum made a short speech thanking everyone for coming and the staff for all their hard work, then declared the park open and cut the ribbon. Watching her cut her first ceremonial ribbon in seventy-six years, I thought she might have been thinking a little about the house where she was born, which was not even a two-rooms-up, two-down in Sheffield, but a one-up, one-down plus a small attic on top, with tin baths in front of the fire in the living/dining/kitchen/bathroom. But in fact that was just me being sentimental, and Mum was thinking along much more practical lines of, "Thank God there's finally some money coming in" and "How can I get up to the top of the drive before all these people?"

As it happened we were carried up the drive at the head of the surge on a huge wave of positive energy and optimism. Apart from me worrying about the steep gullies on the side of the drive which, it had been helpfully pointed out to me many times over the last few months, could easily snap an ankle if someone went over one the wrong way (though in forty years they never had). Everyone in my immediate vicinity somehow made it up the drive safely, but soon they would be at the top, and the first complaints about the restaurant would start to come in, then about the kiosk, the pathways, the toilets, and the rubbish bins. And then, of course, there would be the Code Red. Animal-rights activists cutting some wire, or an excited keeper making a mistake, and suddenly Solomon is running across the picnic area with a baby in his mouth. The screaming crowd disperses never to return, and the sale of the zoo doesn't cover the claims because we only had £5 million public liability insurance.

Everywhere I looked, there was something that could go wrong. I constantly fiddled with my radio, checking that it could scan both frequencies simultaneously, so that I could pick up customer services catastrophes as well as animal department disasters. I wasn't actively expecting these things to happen in a pessimistic way, but I wouldn't have been in the least bit surprised at this stage if any of them did. The emergency mode had been going on for so long, it was hard to stand back and see this day for what it was. An enormous, unqualified success.

People were coming—pouring—up the drive, wandering around, enjoying the facilities. They were buying ice cream, cups of tea, lunch, and toys in the shop and smiling. Furthermore, they were saying nice things to us and the keepers. How well everything looked, what a refreshing change it was, how happy the animals seemed, how hard we must have worked. None of us were used to this. Up until now, most visitors from the outside world had been officials, bankers, inspectors, lawyers, or creditors of one sort or another, stressing the extreme seriousness of our position, the enormous amount of work ahead, and the disastrous consequences if anything at all went wrong. But here we were, having finally got it right and being praised, continually all day, by a smiling and even grateful public. Toward lunchtime I made my way up to the picnic area, and Solomon was nowhere to be seen, safely behind the wire, entertaining rather than eating his public. And the public were eating at the kiosk. Every picnic table was full; people were sitting on the grass, relaxing and sipping tea—tea they had bought from the kiosk—while small children in socks burned off energy on the bouncy castles. I couldn't resist a head count, and that first one revealed forty-two adults visible from the bottom corner, which, times £8 entrance fee, translated into £336. Right in front of me we had raised enough money to more than pay for that incredibly expensive power drill we'd had to buy three months before. Plus coffees and teas, plus all the other people milling on the site and in the restaurant. Maybe it was going to work after all.

Then I received my first complaint. "Why have you got these

bouncy castles here?" demanded a mildly irate mother. "I brought my child here to see the animals, but he won't come off. They're just a distraction." I didn't know quite what to say, so I tried out my new customer services mode, apologized, but pointed out that many people used the bouncy castles as a chance for a break so their children could go back to looking at the animals when they'd burned off a bit of excess energy. This platitude seemed to work. Though I took the complaint very seriously, as it was offered, and it made me question the core idea of play facilities momentarily, I was confident enough by now that every zoo and almost every leisure attraction has a play area of some sort, after all, and this was all we could afford at the moment. Usually it's seen as a form of public service. But there really is no pleasing some people, as I have discovered, though that was the only complaint of the day.

As the day wore on, nothing bad happened. The keepers were smiling almost in disbelief at being showered with compliments, praise, and positive feedback. It had been a long haul for them too, the old and the new, in very trying times and with a level of un-certainty about their future that most had not experienced before. What they had experienced before, however, was the public, and I was struck how at ease they all seemed in moving through the crowds, giving impromptu talks, then getting on with their rou-tines. It made sense, of course. None of them had worked in an empty zoo before they came here; crowds were normal.

The only zoo I had ever worked in, however, was this one, which had always been empty. Any member of the public on the site was our responsibility and had to be escorted at all times. In between being granted the license and opening, less than two weeks before, the local school had asked to visit. I had said yes, and though it was technically allowed as a private visit, it had not gone down well with Steve, Anna, and Peter Wearden. Under strict supervision it had been a tense time, shepherding twenty-six vulnerable youngsters and their six or so adult caretakers through the minefield of dangers that, I had been trained, the zoo presented. Now, suddenly, there were children everywhere, running and laughing, virtually unsupervised and oddly unharmed. I loved seeing them, recognizing the glee on their faces that said they were having a special day out. Here, in our zoo. It was hard to take in.

The restaurant was also a teeming success: cakes, coffee, tea, panini, hot meals prepared by Gordon, our new chef, all selling well, all being consumed happily, nonchalantly even, by a satisfied public who took for granted that this should be the case. If they had only seen the room where they were eating even a week before, no one would have thought this achievement possible.

Then something did hit me: Katherine. Throughout the day, amongst the stream of general well-wishers, several people had come and shaken my hand to offer their condolences about Katherine. News of her death had reached the local paper, which had sent a reporter a couple of weeks afterward to cover it. I hadn't minded, as the questions were suitably restrained, and the young reporter was suitably uncomfortable asking them. Until the photographer turned up. He was a talker, a spiel merchant, which probably served him well with uncertain old ladies whose cats had been rescued by the fire brigade or surly landowners with oversized marrows. It didn't irritate me much, until he asked for the photo of Katherine he had warned me in advance they wanted to reproduce. I didn't mind this either, and handed over the only photograph I had of her—one of my favorites, which, to me, could have adorned the cover of *Vogue*. I asked him to take care of it and post it back afterward, but he said there was no need to take it away, he'd just take a close-up digital picture of it with his vast Nikon, and that would be fine. Even better.

But when I handed it to him, he said, "Oh, great. She's

beautiful. Yeah, lovely," and by the time he had the photograph of Katherine in his viewfinder, something clicked in his brain and the spiel came on again, as if he were talking to a living person, in his tacky, squalid monologue. "That's it, lovely. Beautiful, looking good there"—*click, click*—"Yeah, that's it, my lovely, come on, one more"—*click, click, click*. I can't tell you everything that went through my mind; suffice to say that I realized that killing him would probably be counterproductive, so I wandered off.

This article and this picture was produced over a full page in the local paper quite prominently, page three I think, and had been widely read by the local population, it seemed. On opening day, perhaps fifty people came up to me to offer congratulations, and maybe seven of them offered their sympathy about Katherine; one or two really hit a nerve I hadn't known was there by saying, "I'm sure your wife would have been proud," or words like it. Obviously, with any comment from any member of the public, you are forced to trawl the validity of their observations, as with the complaint about the bouncy castles. And I had to conclude that perhaps Katherine would have been proud to some extent (though she'd have said something suitably sarcastic about it all). But I wasn't expecting to have to think about that on this day, until other people brought it up. I was expecting a Code Red, but not one from inside my head.

To be fair, I had had some warning, though not really in time. The day before the formal opening we had held a VIP reception, where local councillors and various people we were indebted to—or soon to become indebted to—were invited to experience the newly revamped facilities and eat and drink at our expense on one of those jollies I had so often experienced—virtually lived on, in lean times—as a journalist. This, again, was no problem and though a new experience to be on the other side of the fence, it was a delight to be hosting, until people started pulling me aside and saying that same thing: your wife would have been proud.

I was required to make a short speech, and to thank various people for their help, so I went to the office to prepare something, with the party audible a few rooms away. Unfortunately, there was the article with Katherine's picture, unearthed and left out by some well-meaning member of staff for me to take over to the house. It was too much, and too unexpected on this day. I felt like I had prepared for everything else, during which processes I had managed to put Katherine to the back of my mind most of the time during the day. But here she was, smiling at me, looking so gorgeous and carefree, little knowing that in a few years she would be dead, under the ground in Jersey, about a mile from where the photograph was taken, leaving her two little children motherless. Such an undeserved death. Would she have been proud? She'd certainly have been pleased to be there, just to have been alive for one thing, but she'd also have absolutely *made* the occasion, with her effortless, genuine charm. I couldn't come out of the room for at least an hour. When I finally emerged to make the speech, which was indeed very short, I forgot to mention by name one or two members of the staff, who promptly went into a sulk. I tried to apologize later, but the sulk continued, and though I didn't mind, my mum was verging on apoplectic. She finally sought out the sulkers and gave them a stiff dose of her plain northern speaking, which, take it from me, you don't want to be on the receiving end of. A couple of days later, the sulk was at an end.

But we had other things to think about, like the next day, and the next, stretching into the distance as far as we could see. It had occurred to me while guiding the dumper truck through some of the narrow gateways of the park, which had taken a few weeks to learn how to do efficiently, that I could be driving a dumper around this park for the next twenty-five years. I liked the idea. I'd once spent seven years as a contributing editor on a glossy magazine, and realized that more than half a decade of my life was measured by the yard or so of copies of this mag pressed together on my bookshelf. What was I doing in August 1996? Researching and writing the pieces published under my name in the September 1996 issue, and so on. I had many happy memories, I'd learned many skills, been sent all around the world and met many interesting and lovely people, but it still suddenly seemed like a bit of a treadmill, or a gilded prison. Okay, I'd been sent out on an icebreaker in northern Finland to meet a husky team and go dogsledding for three days; I'd done several free-fall parachute jumps from 14,000 feet (the horror, the horror); I'd been paid to go snowboarding at Lake Tahoe, California, for ten days; I'd swum with dolphins in the Florida Keys (those pesky dolphins were the ones who snapped me out of it). And driving a dumper truck full of manure in the rain may seem less glamorous and more agricultural, but it contained the seeds of something far more important, far more worthwhile. The depth of potential for internal expansion and development on this site in pursuit of such a worthwhile cause was limited only by the imagination. It didn't seem like a prison at all. As one good friend said to me, when we first started at the zoo, as I was enthusing to her on the phone, "It's like your whole life has been a preparation for this moment." And it does seem like that. It feels like a vocation.

Milo and Ella were also thoroughly enjoying the exposure to these sorts of experiences—what child wouldn't? At first they used to tell everyone they met that they lived in a zoo (usually met with total disbelief), and that Daddy climbed trees in the lions' den to feed them. Gradually they have developed a deeper understanding of the animals and their needs, cross-referencing their daily exposure with a boundless appetite for natural-history documentaries. They've watched so much of *Monkey World* on Sky television that they probably know more about chimpanzee group dynamics than I do. When we finally get our bonobos (or gorillas or orangs), I'll probably have to employ them as consultants. But it's the hours at a time spent out in the park actually watching the animals close up that is really giving them such a thorough grounding in how the world works, and their place in it. Ella hasn't decided yet, but Milo wants to be a zoo director when he grows up. This zoo director wouldn't necessarily recommend the position, though it does have enormous benefits. Most of the time is spent on more-or-less tedious matters of infrastructure worries, staff issues, and other concerns that come with running a business open to the public. But every now and then you are called on to spend quality time with, or make a decisive intervention about, the animals. Which is what it's all about. I can't imagine investing this much time or emotional energy in any other cause that repays it all so fully.

Mum, too, is delighted with her new and invigorating role as a zoo director. Though still caught up in the daily running of the place, she always makes time to walk around the park, coo to the animals, and enjoy them—particularly the big cats. Having stroked lions in Namibia instead of retiring to a life of memories in her late seventies, she is notching up other exotic-animal petting conquests—bear, tiger, jaguar, and puma (all anaesthetized)—which leave her fulfilled and make her the envy of her contemporaries. One of these days, she'll be out there as we planned, with her sketchbook, drawing from life her own tigers.

Without the animals, there is nothing I can envision that would have lured me from my life in France—and nothing that could have helped us all so much to cope with the terrible loss of Katherine. With the animals, there is a clear mission, which everyone here feels part of.

Epilogue

The day after opening, a Sunday, was also a scorcher, and more people came. Again we were flooded with visitors, awash with praise, and nothing went wrong. It was astonishing. It was a weekend, of course, but before the school holidays had begun this could only be considered a good turnout. Now all we needed was a summer full of such days, and the seamless plan would glide effortlessly into the future.

Unfortunately, after our wettest June, we then experienced the wettest July for a hundred years as well. But on the good days, it was unbelievably good. People flocked to the park, spending the whole day here, buying stuff, having a nice time. And learning about animals and conservation, and experiencing the natural world from closer up than most had ever seen it before. This was a massive, unexpected pleasure. I loved seeing the people swarm over the park, enjoying themselves, enthralled by the animals. It is uniquely infectious being amongst a crowd of people who are so clearly having such a good time, and knowing that you have in part been able to provide it. Seeing the animals I had become accustomed to—though not blasé about—through new eyes, particularly those of children, was enormously refreshing.

The animals liked having the public there too. A lot of visitors say that they like the intimacy of this zoo, where you can get much closer to the animals than is usual. This is not because the enclosures are small—many are far larger than those of bigger zoos. We just have fewer of them, and several are designed, like Tiger Mountain and the jaguar and bear enclosures, so that there is no wire between viewer and beast. This creates an intimate—and often spine-tingling, hairs-up-on-the-back-of-the-neck—experience, which seems to work two ways. On that opening weekend, the animals were out and about much more than before. The tigers and the wolves in particular were clearly showboating. Of course, having been born on site, they were used to crowds (though not so many in recent years), and seeing people milling around restored their normality. It was good to see them sniffing the air, taking it all in, and settling down somewhere conspicuous to watch us watching them.

August was less wet, almost like a proper summer month, and packed with busy days, many of them breaking records set the previous week. On August bank holiday we had nearly twice the number of visitors as on our opening day itself—according to Robin, who has been here for nearly twenty years—as busy as any day he had ever seen.

Other good news was the arrival of the lynx from France. We had been trusted by another zoo to look after a gorgeous, young Siberian lynx, on the stud book and ready to breed. We would need to build her an enclosure, but in the meantime she could go into quarantine in the enclosure Sovereign had vacated when he went back to his revamped home at the top of the park. (Sovereign's old pad had been passed by DEFRA as suitable for this purpose.)

The lynx was gorgeous, so much more sleek and lithe than the elderly lynx, Fin, we already had, for whom she was to be a companion when she finished her quarantine, though obviously she was a bit tense at the unfamiliarity of her surroundings. She was deposited successfully into the quarantine pen, which we were confident she could not escape from; if Sovereign couldn't get out, no one could. And I hardly saw her for the next six months, partly because she was a bit shy, but also because it was a nuisance to negotiate the gates and footbaths necessary to maintain the quarantine.

The rest of the summer passed in a blur, up early, bed late, a blizzard of meetings and decisions in between, but all moving in the right direction. One slightly sad adjustment for me was that, shortly after opening day, the camera crew, having got what they needed for their four-part series, packed up and left. As a journalist I had got on well with the crew, and the core group—Francis the producer, Joyce, Max, Charlie, and Trevor—had been embedded with us for so long that they seemed like part of the staff, only less prone to bickering. Over the months they had watched us develop, and we had watched them—particularly Trevor, who had arrived on his first day in a gleaming rental car and unpacked a brand-new pair of walking boots from the back, still wrapped in tissue paper in their box. He didn't look like he'd last long, but Trevor was quietly steely, and by the end he was usually spattered with mud, and his boots were unrecognizable, worn in and virtually worn out on a single job. At the start I had related to the crew at least as much as the staff, because they were from a world I knew. But by the end, hearing them talk longingly of Paddington Station, where they arrived after their week's shift in the countryside yearning for overpriced cappuccinos and Soho eateries, I realized that I had changed. I didn't yearn for these things, and the few times I had been required to go to London, I couldn't wait to get out, and back to the clear air and big trees of the park. But I missed their banter. Trevor had a particular phrase when he was pleased with a sequence he'd shot: "That's TV gold," he'd announce, grinning and putting down his camera if something had gone well, like when an animal had strolled into the shot.

However, after the summer, the numbers dropped off sharply. So sharply, in fact, that several people got nervous that the business was going to fail, and one or two even resigned to look for safer jobs. I was glad to see them go. With their kind of loyalty, the business would surely work better without them, but it increased the workload and the recruitment process was inevitably time consuming. I am happy to say that we now have a full complement of dedicated, harmonious keepers and maintenance and catering staff who all seem to get along seamlessly, though in my new role as Someone Who Sacks People, perhaps I'd be the last to know if they didn't.

Soon, the mild autumn and the marketing of the new education officer produced regular snaking, gabbling, grinning convoys of school parties, holding hands in pairs, making a sound like a mobile babbling brook, watched over by fraught, young (so young!) teachers. These boosted our income, increased our profile locally, and provided the educational service we're here for.

It had been a stormingly successful summer, in terms of gate numbers on sunny days, spend per head, customer satisfaction, and feedback. But I knew the bank wouldn't see it like this. And they didn't. As far as they were concerned, July hadn't produced as much money as we had said it would, and they refused to extend our credit ("It was raining, guys, but more people came on the other days." "That Does Not Compute . . .") for the winter if we needed it, even though they had promised that they would if the basic business model seemed to be working. Which it clearly was. But once again, we were on our own. And once again, it was looking bad. The late start to the season had cost us dearly, as had the rain, and the reserves we needed to pay wages and running costs for the winter were not as big as we'd hoped. Even closing for a few months, as many attractions do, would make little difference, as we needed core staff to keep going, and the bills would keep coming. We sensed distant lawyers reaching for box files and dispassionately perusing repossession clauses.

And then the TV series started.

Ben's Zoo went out on BBC2 from late November to early December, from 8 to 9 PM, and was watched by an average of 2.5 million people a week. Things started to change. During the first program, Adam monitored the Web site and reported a thousand hits during the transmission, many of them much-needed animal adoption inquiries. The next weekend, fortunately mild, the trickle started, and rose to a torrent over the next few weeks. By the time the Christmas holidays had begun, we were inundated. And everyone had nice things to say. Mainly locals, many of whom had been to the park before and drifted away during the years of decline, congratulating us on the improvements. It was a lovely feeling, like summer all over again. Keepers were being recognized and given presents of chocolates and flowers by an adoring public, and I found it impossible to move about the park without being congratulated every few yards by a gaggle of well-wishers. Though it meant having the same conversation about fifty times a day, I didn't mind in the slightest, and I was genuinely, enormously grateful to everyone who came. The crushing handshakes became a problem, though, as all the men around here seem to have huge, strong hands unlike my "women's" hands, made delicate by fifteen years of typing for a living. One old man in particular, a little guy on crutches, actually gave me a sprain. I asked him, while massaging my hand, what he had done for a living, expecting him to say crushing rocks with his bare hands in a circus. "Graphic designer," he replied, which wasn't good for my ego.

Inevitably, after such public exposure, there were people who wanted to sympathize about Katherine. And again, it was usually the men who moved me most. From women, who are usually better at communicating emotions, you expect sympathy and soothing words. But for men it is much harder (I could bore you for pages on why this is so, so write in at your peril). One woman hailed me from a distance to say, "Ben, I know what you're going through. I lost my husband nine years ago and I still haven't got over it," which I thought was a bit insensitive. But one man in particular stands out. He stood out at the time. At least six foot five, built like a rugby player, and with the inevitably crushing handshake, he looked into my eyes, his own filling with tears, and simply said, "Well done." Enough said, he strode off, message delivered. That's male communication for you.

Speaking of male communication, my dad was also a man of relatively few words. Not that he was taciturn—he just didn't believe in filling the air with unnecessary waffle, and he had the gift of *précis*, even in speech, so that his utterances were precise and measured, and usually laced with a desert-dry wit, which often took a while to sink in. None of this would have been possible without my dad, whose lifetime of diligence, hard work, and devotion to his family happened to give us this remarkable opportunity to save this run-down zoo after his death. Of course, he would never have approved, and would probably be rendered speechless if he could see us now. But the rest of us could afford, thanks to him, to be a bit more reckless. Mum, my sister Melissa, and brothers Duncan and Vincent, all without hesitation put in everything they possibly could to make this harebrained back-of-the-envelope plan work. And it has. Boxing Day was our busiest day on record, and the winter has been nearly as busy as the summer, so that despite missing a third of the season, we have just—*just*—managed to get through the winter without more support from the bank.

My dad was also called Ben, but just Ben, whereas my family knows me as Benjamin. It irked a bit that the TV series was called *Ben's Zoo*, largely because this was in no way the effort of a single person. But in a way it's apt. It is Ben's zoo, but a different Ben from the fatuous front man, me. It's Ben Harry Mee's (1928–2005) zoo.

To say it's been life changing is an understatement. But watching the stream of people pouring through every day, leaving energized and enthusiastic, having learned something about the natural world, and being in a position to expand this amazing facility, recruiting animals increasingly from the IUCN Red List to protect for the future, is a rare privilege indeed. It's been hard work, but it doesn't feel like work. It feels like a vocation. Thanks, Dad.